Dear Senator Smith

Dear Senator Smith

Small-Town Maine Writes to
Senator Margaret Chase Smith
about the Vietnam War, 1967–1971

Edited by Eric R. Crouse

LEXINGTON BOOKS

A division of
ROWMAN & LITTLEFIELD PUBLISHERS, INC.
Lanham • Boulder • New York • Toronto • Plymouth, UK

LEXINGTON BOOKS

A division of Rowman & Littlefield Publishers, Inc.
A wholly owned subsidiary of The Rowman & Littlefield Publishing Group, Inc.
4501 Forbes Boulevard, Suite 200
Lanham, MD 20706

Estover Road
Plymouth PL6 7PY
United Kingdom

British Library Cataloguing in Publication Information Available

Library of Congress Cataloging-in-Publication Data
The hardback editon of this book was previously cataloged by the
Library of Congress as follows;

Crouse, Eric Robert, 1960–
    Dear Senator Smith : small-town Maine writes to Senator Margaret Chase Smith
about the Vietnam War, 1967-1971 / edited by Eric R. Crouse.
        p. cm.
    pt. 1: The Johnson years, 1967–68. A growing war ; A worried nation ; Rising
opposition — pt. 2. The Nixon years, 1969–71. Nothing new under the Sun ;
Cambodia fireflash ; Winding down road.
    Includes bibliographical references and index.
    1. Vietnam War, 1961–1975—Public opinion. 2. Public opinion—Maine. 3. Smith,
Margaret Chase, 1897–1995—Correspondence. 4. United States—Politics and
Government—1945–1989—Public opinion. I. Title.
    DS559.62.U6C76 2008
    959.704'31—dc22   2007035038

ISBN-13: 978-0-7391-2484-0 (cloth : alk. paper)
ISBN-10: 0-7391-2484-6 (cloth : alk. paper)
ISBN-13: 978-0-7391-2485-7 (pbk. : alk. paper)
ISBN-10: 0-7391-2485-4 (pbk. : alk. paper)

Printed in the United States of America

∞^{TM} The paper used in this publication meets the minimum requirements of
American National Standard for Information Sciences—Permanence of Paper
for Printed Library Materials, ANSI/NISO Z39.48-1992.

Contents

Acknowledgments

$\mathcal{S}$ome of my earliest childhood memories are of family summer vacations at Province Lake where my aunt and uncle from Boston owned a cottage near the border of New Hampshire and Maine. In the sixties, my family experienced fun times traveling throughout the Maine countryside, visiting small towns and relaxing, swimming, and boating on the lake with Aunt Sue and Uncle Jack. In recent years, as I collected and read the letters sent to Senator Margaret Chase Smith on American involvement in Southeast Asia, I reflected on my childhood innocence in New England when people around me debated the war. As I pursued my interest of Cold War America, I found that there is not much scholarship on the war opinions of ordinary people, particularly those living in the hinterland of major urban centers. I believe that a close look of Vietnam War correspondence from Americans living in small communities and rural areas sheds important light on political ideas and public opinion in small-town America. Senator Smith's profile as a popular female politician, born in small-town Maine, raised in a working-class family, and without a college education, offers an excellent vehicle to uncover the voices of ordinary people divided over America's foreign policy and involvement and strategy in Vietnam against a peasant communist foe.

Every member of the staff of the Margaret Chase Smith Library in Skowhegan has been exceptionally welcoming and helpful. In particular, collections specialist Angie Stockwell and director Dr. Gregory Gallant offered outstanding support in many ways. I greatly value their assistance. I also benefited as a recipient of the Ada E. Leeke Research Fellowship for more than four years.

Additional financial support came in the form of the Tyndale Faculty Research Fund, and financial assistance from Tyndale President Brian Stiller.

viii   *Acknowledgments*

I am grateful for the support of Dr. Daniel Scott, Dean of Tyndale University College, and Dr. Earl Davey, Provost. My thanks to other Tyndale individuals, including Rachel Boadway and Joy McEwen who assisted me with the word processing of the letters and Brad Longard for his work on the index. I am also thankful for the unceasing encouragement from my fellow Tyndale faculty members.

I owe a debt of gratitude to anonymous readers who offered excellent suggestions and to the scholars from whose impressive work on the Vietnam War years I drew on for my editorial introductions and notes.

It is always a pleasure to spend time in Maine and I must acknowledge my appreciation for the many people who shared their stories of Senator Smith.

Finally, I would like to acknowledge and give thanks for the love and support of my parents Lebaron and Paula Crouse, brother Edwin, sisters Susan and Diana, and my wife Ann-Marie and daughters Emily and Elizabeth.

Introduction

$\mathcal{T}$he Vietnam War evoked much debate among politicians, policymakers, intellectuals, professors, activists, journalists, and others whose views had a wide hearing.[1] However, far less is known of the home-front views of ordinary Americans living in small towns distant from major cities and their powerful political, business, academic, and media operations. As a result of a media that logically focused its attention on the provocative images and inflammatory words that were part of large antiwar protest gatherings in major cities and the counter rhetoric of the government and well-known war supporters, it is no surprise that the voices of small-town Americans have received little attention. Yet those living in small towns and rural areas did convey their views of the war in letters sent to politicians.

Senator Margaret Chase Smith was the sole female senator from 1967 to 1972 and letters sent to her hint of a relationship that may have been warmer than was generally the case with male politicians, particularly those Washington politicians groomed by private schools and a charmed inner circle of professional connections.[2] For all of her political accomplishments, Smith did not fit in the category of "the best and the brightest."[3] Lacking a college education mainly because of her modest economic background, she shared common ground with many ordinary Americans living in rural locations, villages, and towns. Having a people's touch, she appeared to encourage a high level of honest, heartfelt commentary from Americans, even when they disagreed with her. Letters sent to Smith from small towns of Maine shed light on the far-reaching tensions and polarized environment that exploded on the scene during Lyndon Johnson's government and continued into Richard Nixon's administration. There were letters that suggest conservative, religious, and traditional sensibilities, but there were also many with a radical tone.

1

Smith was a product of small-town New England, born in the little community of Skowhegan, Maine, in 1897. From an early age she embraced the Yankee characteristics of straightforwardness, hard work, self-discipline, moderation, and integrity. Smith had French-Canadian Roman Catholic roots on her mother's side and puritan roots on her father's side. Biographer Patricia L. Schmidt notes Smith's moral center and "Yankee Protestantism" that directed her to identify right and wrong within herself and not be swayed by the passions of political banter. In the eyes of recent biographer Janann Sherman, Smith was a "simple, rural, and New England conservative" who trusted her Yankee values for courage, moral authority, and order.[4] In her later years, she relied heavily on her Yankee regional identity when she faced the disorderly, emotional, and extremist forces rising from national politics.

Raised in a poor working-class family, Smith had an early introduction to thrifty living and wage labor. A hard worker with ambition, she dreamed of attending college after high school, but instead pursued the more realistic path of employment. From a teenager to an adult, her employment ranged from dishwasher, textile mill employee, five-and-dime store clerk, office worker, schoolteacher, telephone switchboard operator, and reporter and business manager of a weekly newspaper. In 1930, at the age of thity-two, she married Republican politician Clyde Harold Smith, an older man by twenty-one years. The personable Clyde Smith had impressive success in business and politics. Beginning in 1915, he was first selectman of Skowhegan (comparable to mayor) for more than fifteen years. His gifts of distinguished oratory, good judgement, and compassion for working people took him further; he served terms in the Maine House and the Maine Senate before going to Washington as a member of Congress in 1937 until his death in 1940. Without any college education, Margaret Chase Smith began life as a politician when she assumed the work of her deceased husband. After a successful string of electoral victories as United States Representative for the Second Congressional District of Maine, she became a member of the Senate in January 1949, thus becoming the first woman in American history to be elected in both the House of Representatives and the Senate.[5]

In 1950, Smith, the only woman among ninety-five males in the Senate, was the first elected official to take any effective public action against fellow Republican Senator Joe McCarthy and his distasteful methods to root out communism in American life.[6] A political gamble, her "Declaration of Conscience" generated nationwide attention with some newspapers printing the entire text accompanied by "florid prose."[7] The high praise found in editorials continued in letters sent to Smith from ordinary Americans. Making reference to Abraham Lincoln's Gettysburg address, Sidney R. Sharpe of North Anson, Maine, declared that given the simplicity of Smith's words and the force of the great truths uttered she should expect to learn that she "made one of the most eloquent speeches in history."[8] Rinardo Giovanella of Kezar Falls, Maine, wrote: "This may be premature, but I do hope that you may become President of the U.S. in the very near future."[9]

That others disagreed with Smith is no surprise given the support that a mass of conservative American people gave McCarthy. Responding to her attack, one Californian wrote, in a telegram, that she was "a schoolmarm who used too much language." McCarthy had no choice but to ram his way into the fight against communism since the government was only espousing "double-talk." Making a reference to the masculinity of liberal politicians, this critic had little patience for "old-maidish senators from the New England states, as they never were two-fisted."[10] In the end, more pundits viewed her opposition to McCarthy as representative of a more appropriate anticommunist Americanism devoid of selfish political opportunism. She had her own strong endorsement from ordinary Americans, particularly her Maine constituents, who saw her as a non-elitist politician with a common sense understanding of national security and individual freedoms. While Smith disapproved of McCarthy's method, she remained a stalwart foe of communism; she had presented bills, in 1953, to outlaw the Communist Party in the United States.[11] Her bills puzzled some liberals, but many others took her anticommunist action in stride during this period when liberals such as Senators Hubert Humphrey and Wayne Morse were introducing similar legislation.[12]

Smith survived a McCarthy backlash including her demotion seven months later from the Permanent Investigations Subcommittee, replaced by the newly elected Junior Senator Richard Nixon. In the eyes of Smith, this relegation engineered by McCarthy was an act of revenge that violated Senate custom and procedure.[13] Although she also faced hostile reaction from McCarthyites within the Republican Party who were suspect of her loyalty, she made sure her anticommunist credentials were above reproach throughout her remaining years in politics. She won at the polls in 1954, 1960, and 1966. In 1964 she became the first woman of a major political party to run for president. She had no realistic chance of winning the Republican nomination and the party selected Barry Goldwater, who lost badly to President Lyndon Johnson in November. Smith continued to serve her constituents before losing her Senate seat in 1972 at the age of seventy-four. Serving in Washington for thirty-two years, she could be proud of her remarkable political career.

In Smith's day, a female politician seemed a contradiction-in-terms for many Americans, but in her unique way Smith was not adverse to seeking and claiming power. In an age when the public perceived women as above and beyond "politics as usual," Smith masterly maintained her credibility in the eyes of many voters, who championed her individualism and self-confidence. Her political success was no easy feat when the expectation was for women to remain within the domestic sphere and keep the home in order and take care of the family. Her story is one of a small-town girl making her way successfully in the corridors of political power. Much of her success was a result of her firm support for defense and national security issues. When the Soviets labeled her an "Amazon warmonger," she embraced this epithet proudly.[14] Smith did well in the Cold War America of the 1950s and into the 1960s, but after 1965 American anticommunist idealism and moralism went awry in the jungles and rice fields of Southeast Asia. When President Lyndon Johnson escalated American involvement in Vietnam, Smith held a powerful position in America's foreign policy hierarchy. As the minority leader on the Armed Services Committee and a loyal supporter of Johnson's defense program, her brand of Cold War assertiveness on the issue of American involvement in Southeast Asia garnered respect. Still, a significant number of Americans sought to persuade her to take a more liberal path in the confusing and pessimistic climate of the late 1960s and early 1970s.

Concerning the interaction of women and American foreign policy, there are scholars who argue that because war glamorizes male roles, females lose social power. The best possibility for women, who have a more mothering, caring, and peaceful nature than men, was to promote peace in order to avoid further subjugation. Other scholars downplay the idea of nurturant motherhood, dismiss any real differences between men and women, and praise female aggression. In his study of women and American foreign policy, Rhodi Jeffreys-Jones sees Smith as a "peace-seeking stateswoman," though in a number of ways she upheld a masculine Cold War stereotype. For example, in the spring of 1970, when there was a revitalization of antiwar protest due to Nixon's Cambodia "incursion" and the killing of four Kent State University students by the National Guard, a growing number of people perceived her as being too warlike.[15]

It may have been a balancing act on Smith's part in order to gain the necessary power to promote her own agenda in a political environment that favored manliness, but the sense of ambiguity of whether Smith favored peace or war meant that she likely offered something for both antiwar protesters and administration supporters. There are clear indications of antiwar correspondents focusing on the potential action of her stateswoman qualities and influence, in contrast to more hawkish correspondents finding reassurance in her assertive Cold Warrior manner. Each group appeared to believe they had a reasonable chance to persuade her to their way of thinking. Many Americans perceived her as an approachable politician with no shortage of integrity, and, more important, her individualism gave letter-writers hope that their words could influence foreign policy.

Measuring the impact of the letters on changing her mind and influencing foreign policy is another matter. Because there are methodological barriers for comprehending the role that public opinion plays in foreign policy-making, scholars argue that the evidence for the public's impact on foreign policy is "often impressionistic."[16] There are two items to consider here. First, many small-town writers likely had an exaggerated notion of the possibility of influencing Smith. For example, college students reacted in shock when they learned in May 1970 that although letters to Smith were running 6 to 1 against Nixon's policy of widening the war with the "incursion" into Cambodia, she continued to support Nixon. As reported in the *New York Times*, "for those who had been told to write to their congresswoman rather than demonstrate, her response was hardly encouraging."[17] Second, unaware that the influence of Smith and others outside the small circle of the president and the White House was negligible, many writers overestimated her ability to help shape foreign policy decisions. The war experience in both the Johnson and Nixon years reveals the frequent powerlessness of Congress, notably when major decisions went into operation without public knowledge.

If one cannot accurately assess the impact of public opinion on foreign policy, one can at least uncover the varied concerns weighing on the conscience of ordinary people. Michael Foley's valuable collection of letters about the Vietnam War sent to Dr. Benjamin Spock confirms the importance of hearing the voices of ordinary Americans. It is essential to search beyond professional activists and political gadflies in order to better understand the complex relationship of the American people and war.[18] Although most were mistaken, ordinary Americans who sent letters to Smith believed their words could make a difference. Letters demonstrated commitment on the part of the writers; the letter-writing process for most represented a considerable investment in time and energy, far greater than sending e-mails in the later computer age. The whole letter-writing course of action confirmed dedication and passion, and letters to Senator Smith reveal much about the dynamics and emotions of small-town thinking as the war unfolded.

All in all, Smith was critical of aspects of the Vietnam conflict and did not trust Secretary of Defense Robert McNamara, but ultimately she maintained that the war was morally defensible.[19] Having a good relationship with President Johnson since 1945 when they served together on the House Naval Affairs Committee, Smith identified and respected his Texas hill country pragmatism over the urbanity and intellectualism of other powerful figures in Washington. Speaking in Maine in December 1965, she stated: "I support

President Johnson's policy in Viet Nam and will continue to do so."[20] While she had disliked the "old" Nixon, she supported President Nixon's policy even in the face of wide opposition, as was the case in early May 1970 when college students confronted her at Colby College.[21]

Whether agreeing with her position or not, many of her Maine constituents and other Americans recognized and applauded her integrity, independent thinking, and sense of fair play that she had demonstrated throughout her political career. In one example, a female constituent stated: "I have chosen to write you, because I consider you a person of great integrity; and, one who is interested in serving the people whom you represent." Another wrote, "I appreciate that you are the kind of person to whom I feel free to write my thoughts." Often there was evidence of a sense of familiarity and, thus, one lady shared: "I can't seem to write out Maggie, and just Margaret doesn't seem enough. . . . We're so proud of you" while another correspondent from Eastport, Maine, wrote: "Let me also say the criticisms I have to make are in no way personal either, as I feel confident, though I may not have always agreed with your decisions, in my opinion you have always acted in the way you felt best for our country. We in Maine, irregardless of party affiliations love and respect you." An educator from Bath, Maine, offered a similar assessment: "Many of us in Maine greatly admire the tremendous work you have done not only for our state, but for the nation. You reflect an honesty which is gratifying to see in a public servant. I personally feel that you exemplify the qualities of statesmanship that we so desperately need. I don't always agree with you, but I never question your sincerity."[22] Smith heard from many who appeared comfortable sharing their Vietnam War concerns and ideas with a no-nonsense and reassuring female politician. They poured their emotions out to her and her care was obvious in that she responded to her mail, with characteristically impressive discipline.[23] Her typed letters varied in length from a short paragraph to several pages, but most remarkable was the typical swiftness of her replies to every letter sent.

This book consists of letters of ordinary folk who lived in smaller communities with a population less than 10,000.[24] All the letters are from Maine people and yet this collection does represent small-town New England sensibilities as a whole. Press reports expressed the commonality of New Englanders. For example, the *Portland Press Herald* wrote that Senator George D. Aiken of Vermont and Smith "shared qualities of common sense, wit, frugality, and iron principle." Aiken, the editorial proclaimed, "could have been a Mainer."[25] In size, geography, and history, the small communities of Maine had similar counterparts in other coastal villages, inland rural communities, or small thriving historical towns throughout New England. Whether it was the shoreline communities of Westbrook, Connecticut (3,820), Narragansett,

Rhode Island (7,138), and Chatham, Massachusetts (4,654), or the interior communities of White River Junction, Vermont (2,379), and Effingham, New Hampshire (360), there was considerable likeness of small-town New En-gland values and characteristics.

Until 1820, the District of Maine was part of Massachusetts and in the decades that followed Maine did not lose the idea of citizen engagement in politics that had roots in the "New England town meeting." In the tier of northern New England states in particular, a "moralistic political culture" dominated the landscape that set small-town New Englanders apart from large urban dwellers and Americans living in other regions. These New Englanders shared the idea that all citizens had a stake in the well being of the community and, thus, there was a moral obligation that ordinary folk participate in civic life.[26] Given the New England identification with civic engagement, it is not surprising that Smith received letters from over 110 small towns and rural communities on the Vietnam War issue alone.

The state of Maine consisted of many isolated small towns, with only three cities with a population over 25,000. A number of letter-writers did live in communities near larger centers, but the largest of these was Portland, with a modest population of 65,116.[27] Other cities near the homes of people who sent letters to Smith were significantly smaller than Portland. The influence of large metropolitan centers was not a major issue in Maine communities that upheld small-town values. The isolation of some communities was striking. For example, letter writers from Limestone, Rangeley, or Calais, to name just a few, were one to three hours of driving time from a major city in that period.

Smith did receive letters from Americans coast to coast. While having a collection of Vietnam letters from all parts of the nation has merit, a regional approach has one advantage in providing a better sense of the representation of people's views on the war. It is more difficult to make concluding statements from a compilation of two hundred or so unscientifically selected letters from across the nation. What are the standards for selecting letters of an antiwar or pro-administration theme from a particular city in the Deep South, a certain town in the Midwest, or a community in any other region? The correspondence at the Margaret Chase Smith Library consists of approximately eight hundred letters and telegrams filed under "Vietnam War." There is no knowledge of the exact total number of Vietnam letters that Senator Smith received over the years and the criterion for those retained by the library is unknown. Whether by accident or by conscious decision years ago, only a small number of letters for the years 1965, 1966, and 1972 are part of the library collection.[28] In order to provide greater consistency, this collection of letters does not include correspondence from these years. The letters in this book do not represent an unsystematic selection. Virtually every "Vietnam War" letter written by an individual or couple (but no form or group letters) regardless of position or theme is included providing it met three clear conditions: a minimum length of 100 words that covered Vietnam material, a complete mailing address, and origin in communities with a population less than 10,000. The few letters not included that met these three conditions contained too much personal information about the writer, their family, or close associates. In total, the balance of Johnson and Nixon letters is remarkably close, 101 letters for the Johnson years and 91 for the Nixon years.

Maine people living in small towns had their own understanding of the war that was no less important than others receiving greater media attention in larger cities. But who were these people living in communities with a population under 10,000? How does one define or characterize a small town? Earlier in the twentieth century, small towns came under attack by a number of writers, the best known being Sinclair Lewis. In his novel, *Main Street*, published in 1920, Lewis offered a scathing assessment of small-town American society.[29] A more recent study of small-towns states that they have "virtually disappeared from the cultural radar."[30] In comparison to rural and small communities, the urban experience of New York, Chicago, Los Angeles, Boston, and numerous other big cities was more cosmopolitan, modern, and secular. One case in point is the religiosity among Boston draft resisters and supporters during the Vietnam War. Michael Foley's study of draft resistance indicates that almost half of his sample of resisters and supporters were either agnostic (25 percent) or atheist (23 percent). The occupation of the fathers of this group was almost 60 percent professional and the percentage of farmers was 1.7 and semi-skilled workers 4.3.[31] Of course, Boston draft resisters were hardly representative of the city's view of American involvement in Southeast Asia, but the point is that certain organizations and characteristics common in large cities were virtually nonexistent in most small towns and communities.

In the second half of the twentieth century, the construction of interstate highways lessened the importance of main streets and caused a "cultural education deficit" in understanding American history and geography.[32] But simplified notions of small-town life are wide of the mark. What is interesting is the variety and often sophistication of the Vietnam letters in this collection, demonstrating that the letter-writers shared little with the conformist, repressive, and unwholesome Main Street that Sinclair Lewis created in his novel and what popular culture often assumes to be the case.[33] There are carefully crafted letters that indicate conservative, religious, and traditional sensibilities often associated with small communities, but there are also passionate letters that have similar arguments to those voiced by better-known antiwar activists, including those of a more radical nature. If many young radicals left their small towns for large cities, the intimacy of small towns still encouraged the sharing of contentious ideas that promoted opposition to the war.[34] Any debate or protest probably was not threatening to the community because absent were the type and size of confrontation that occurred in the large cities between the government and organized radical groups. Moreover, scholars point out that with Maine politics a "moderate tendency" was more the rule than the exception. An equally important Maine characteristic is its independent streak; extreme ideological views were rare, but Maine citizens could be contrary in their political engagement.[35]

In small towns, there were cantankerous types for and against the war who debated heatedly, but they were less likely to be strangers to each other or of a different economic class. The letters suggest that most correspondents were ordinary working people with a high school education (there were many typed letters and others were on personal letterhead, though often of a plain style). Even the typed letters that were of poor quality hint of a satisfactory education.

The Vietnam War was mainly a working-class war and one might expect that more families in small-town Maine came closer to this class alignment than affluent professionals living in the suburbs of large cities.[36] The per capita personal income of Mainers for the years 1945 to 1967 averaged 84 percent of the nation's average and many people faced economic hardship. Having a small, scattered population over a large territory (relative to other New England states), Maine experienced a lagging economy that resulted in much of its working force receiving low wages.[37] Chronic underfunding meant that nationally Maine was close to the bottom in statistics relating to education. For example, in 1957, Maine ranked thirty-ninth in the nation for the number of young people completing at least four years of college, and thus many of the adults of the Vietnam War years had fewer opportunities to pursue career choices that required higher education. It was especially bad in the small rural towns. The one statistic that Maine did not rank near the bottom nationally was the number of draftees rejected "for mental and educational deficiencies!"[38] The number of inductees from the small communities and towns of Maine who had lawyers, doctors, or politicians to assist them with deferments likely represented a small number compared to the number living in the wealthier neighborhoods of cities and suburbs who evaded the draft.

There were letters from young people, but most authors provided evidence of maturity (some were ex-soldiers), marriage, or having children or grandchildren. Only a few letters came from businessmen, lawyers, physicians, and other identifiable professionals living in small centers. Professors writing from private colleges such as Bates College (Lewiston), Bowdoin

College (Brunswick), and Colby College (Waterville) did not make the collection because of their location in cities larger than 10,000. Overall, the selection of letters allows for a confident conclusion that these people represented the common folk of small-town Maine.

These letters are not from high-profile activists, politicians, or other "stars," but it is important to note that even in a region that encourages civic engagement in politics most "ordinary people" would never consider writing a letter to a politician. In any study of public opinion, it is impossible to have a perfect match between letter writers and societal views. Set apart from the norm, a significant number of those who wrote to Smith were likely to have a particular leaning or special interest toward things political. The unknown political views of countless small-town people are frozen in time and not recorded because in many cases people were either less political than the average letter writer or were far too busy with employment, families, church life, sports, clubs, or cultural activities. Scores of people simply had little taste for letter writing. Of course, many of these busy people and others did share similar views of the war as those writing letters to politicians.

Another important point relates to the norms of human nature in that people are more likely to voice protest than praise. Smith saw this clearly in the configuration of her mail. In a response to a constituent, she acknowledged that correspondence for withdrawal from Southeast Asia dominated, but she stated that this was not necessarily an accurate reading because "the mail pattern over the years has been clearly mail from protester rather than mail supporting a particular policy." To make her point, she gave the following example: "my mail was heavily against [Harold] Carswell [for Supreme Court] before the Senate vote—but my mail was heavily critical of me after the vote and against me for voting as I did. Thus, before and after the Carswell vote it was anti—first anti-Carswell and then anti-Smith for being anti-Carswell."[39] In the final tally, the letters in this book are representative of small-town Maine with some necessary qualifications that any study concerning public opinion must face.

The following letters are arranged in six chapters, three in part I, the Johnson Years, and three in part II, the Nixon Years. Each chapter has between three and five sections that correlate with a specific theme or focus. There are introductions before part I, part II, and the chapter sections, and brief editor's notes throughout, but center stage are the letters and the messages of those rarely heard in a larger national forum.

Of this Smith collection, the majority of the writers lived in communities smaller than five thousand people in a time when small-town America was shrinking and suburbanization of cities across the nation was growing and reshaping community life. If they lived in centers that were becoming increasingly overlooked, many people themselves kept abreast of the burning war issues of the day that reached beyond the boundaries of metropolitan life. Some letters identify specific reports from television, newspapers, magazines, and books. During the war, 51 million Americans in an evening watched war coverage on ABC, CBS, and NBC, and another 38 million readers referred to the weekly news magazines *Newsweek, Time,* and *U.S. News & World Report,* the former the most liberal and the latter the most conservative.[40]

Those who wrote to Senator Smith saw her as an approachable and respected figure and many shared their emotional ideas for and against American involvement in Southeast Asia. The letters covered numerous themes such as the threat of communism, the counterculture movement, the morality of the war, and whether dissent was patriotic. Not all letters, however, stated a clear case of support or opposition for the war. Some voiced their concerns or inquiries to Smith on specific issues that seem inconsequential compared to larger questions of what America stood for or whether the war was a noble cause. But even the mundane is revealing. By going beyond the circle of political and antiwar elites, this collection allows each letter to build a better picture of how ordinary letter-writing Americans upheld or protested Cold War ideology, offered new paradigms, or generally experienced the new challenges that correlated with the battles that were being lost more than won both in Southeast Asia and on the home front.

NOTES

1. In *Dictators, Democracy, and American Public Culture: Envisioning the Totalitarian Enemy, 1920s–1950s* (Chapel Hill: The University of North Carolina Press, 2003), Benjamin L. Apers applies the term "cultural producers" to include "professors, policymakers, speechwriters, presidents, filmmakers, novelists, and business leaders" whose impact on society was hegemonic (8). The quantity of literature on the Vietnam War is gigantic, but a good starting point that offers a variety of perspectives on policymakers, well-known activists, or other "elites" include the following: Charles DeBenedetti and Charles Chatfield, assisting author, *An American Ordeal: The Antiwar Movement of the Vietnam War* (Syracuse: Syracuse University Press, 1990); Larry Berman, *No Peace, No Honor: Nixon, Kissinger, and Betrayal in Vietnam* (New York: The Free Press, 2001); Gerard J. DeGroot, *A Noble Cause? America and the Vietnam War* (Essex: Longman, 2000); Michael S. Foley, *Confronting the War Machine: Draft Resistance During the Vietnam War* (Chapel Hill: The University of North Carolina Press, 2003); Adam Garfinkle, *Telltale Hearts: The Origins and Impact of the Vietnam Antiwar Movements* (New York: St. Martin's Press, 1995); David Halberstam, *The Best and the Brightest* (New York: Fawcett

Crest, 1972); Kenneth J. Heineman, *Campus Wars: The Peace Movement at American State Universities in the Vietnam Era* (New York: New York University Press, 1993); George C. Herring, *America's Longest War: The United States and Vietnam, 1950–1975* Second Edition (New York: Alfred A. Knopf, 1986); Jeffrey Kimball, *Nixon's Vietnam War* (Lawrence: University Press of Kansas, 1998); David W. Levy, *The Debate Over Vietnam*, Second Edition (Baltimore: The John Hopkins University Press, 1995); Robert Mann, *A Grand Delusion: America's Descent into Vietnam* (New York: Basic Books, 2001); Melvin Small, *Johnson, Nixon, and the Doves* (New Brunswick, New Jersey: Rutgers University Press, 1988); Small, *Covering Dissent: The Media and the Anti-Vietnam War Movement* (New Brunswick, New Jersey: Rutgers University Press, 1994); Tom Wells, *The War Within: America's Battle over Vietnam* (Berkeley: University of California Press, 1994); Randall B. Woods, ed., *Vietnam and the American Political Tradition* (Cambridge: Cambridge University Press, 2003). For an analysis of key figures in the pre-1966 period, see Frederik Logevall, *Choosing War: The Lost Chance for Peace and the Escalation of War in Vietnam* (Berkeley: University of California Press, 1999) and David Kaiser, *American Tragedy: Kennedy, Johnson, and the Origins of the Vietnam War* (Cambridge: Harvard University Press, 2000). Two notable books of the many personal accounts written are Robert S. McNamara, *In Retrospect: The Tragedy and Lessons of Vietnam* (New York: Vintage Books, 1995) and Daniel Ellsberg, *Secrets: A Memoir of Vietnam and the Pentagon Papers* (New York: Viking, 2002). A study of liberal religious figures opposing the war is Mitchell K. Hall, *Because of Their Faith: CALCAV and Religious Opposition to the Vietnam War* (New York: Columbia University Press, 1990).

2. One example of warmth toward Smith, albeit subtle, are two letters sent by the same person to her and Senator Edmund Muskie; the writer uses a slightly softer tone in the Smith letter: "I *wish you* would send this where you think it might do more good. *With kind regards, I am Sincerely. . . .*" The writer's letter to Muskie ends: "I have written Margaret Chase Smith and *ask* that you send this letter to her when you get time to do so. *Very truly yours. . . .*" [italics mine]

3. Halberstam, *The Best and the Brightest.*

4. Patricia L. Schmidt, *Margaret Chase Smith: Beyond Convention* (Orono, Maine: University of Maine Press, 1996), xxi; Janann Sherman, *No Place for a Woman: A Life of Senator Margaret Chase Smith* (New Brunswick, New Jersey: Rutgers University Press, 2001), 5.

5. In addition to Sherman, *No Place for a Woman* and Schmidt, *Margaret Chase Smith* there is Patricia Ward Wallace, *Politics of Conscience: A Biography of Margaret Chase Smith* (Westport, CT: Praeger Publishers, 1995).

6. Studies that survey American anticommunism throughout the twentieth century include: Ted Morgan, *Reds: McCarthyism in Twentieth-Century America* (New York: Random House, 2003); Joel Kovel, *Red Hunting in the Promised Land: Anticommunism and the Making of America* (London: Cassell, 1997); Richard Gid Powers, *Not Without Honor: The History of American Anticommunism* (New York: The Free Press, 1995); and M.J. Heale, *American Anticommunism: Combating the Enemy Within, 1830–1970* (Baltimore: The John Hopkins University Press, 1990).

7. Sherman, *No Place for a Woman*, 112.

8. Sidney R. Sharpe to MCS, 6 June 1950, Declaration of Conscience Speech, Maine Reactions, Margaret Chase Smith Library (MCSL).

9. Rinardo Giovanella to MCS, 4 June 1950, Declaration of Conscience Speech, Maine Reactions, MCSL.

10. W.M.J. to MCS, 5 June 1950, Declaration of Conscience Speech, Out of State Reaction, MCSL. Helpful studies on gendered discourse include Robert D. Dean, "Masculinity as Ideology: John F. Kennedy and the Domestic Politics of Foreign Policy," *Diplomatic History*, Vol. 22, No. 1 (Winter 1998): 29–62 and K.A. Cuordileone, "'Politics in an Age of Anxiety'": Cold War Political Culture and the Crisis of American Masculinity, 1949–1960," *The Journal of American History*, Vol 87, No 2 (September 2000): 515–545.

11. Sherman, *No Place for a Woman*, 130–32.

12. See Mary S. McAuliffe, "Liberals and the Communist Control Act of 1954," *The Journal of American History*, Vol. 63, No. 2 (September 1976): 351–67.

13. Margaret Chase Smith, *Declaration of Conscience*, ed. William C. Lewis, Jr. (Garden City, New York: Doubleday & Company, Inc. 1972), 21.

14. Sherman, *No Place for a Woman*, 145.

15. Rhodri Jeffreys-Jones, *Changing Differences: Women and the Shaping of American Foreign Policy, 1917–1994* (New Brunswick, New Jersey: Rutgers University Press, 1997), 5–6, 106, 127.

16. Melvin Small, "Public Opinion" in *Explaining the History of American Foreign Relations*, Michael J. Hogan and Thomas Patterson, eds. (Cambridge: Cambridge University Press, 1991), 165–76. Richard Sobel, *The Impact of Public Opinion on U.S. Foreign Policy Since Vietnam: Constraining the Colossus* (New York: Oxford University Press, 2001), x.

17. Schmidt, *Margaret Chase Smith*, 311.

18. Michael S. Foley, ed. *Dear Dr. Spock: Letters about the Vietnam War to America's Favorite Baby Doctor* (New York: New York University Press, 2005). The television, film, and literature material on the experiences of American troops in Southeast Asia is vast. Another impressive collection of letters is Bernard Edelman, ed. *Dear America: Letters Home From Vietnam* (New York: Pocket Books, 1986).

19. Jeffreys-Jones, *Changing Differences*, 125.

20. Schmidt, *Margaret Chase Smith*, 304–5.

21. *Ibid*, 308–9.

22. See letters # 97, #40, #76 (Johnson years) and #23 and #68 (Nixon years). In part because of her profile as arguably the most powerful female politician in Washington, many Americans from the largest cites of New York, Chicago, and Los Angeles and from centers in every corner of the nation also wrote to her about American involvement in Vietnam.

23. Sherman, *No Place Like a Woman*, 2.

24. Population figures are from: U.S. Bureau of the Census, Census of Population: 1970, Vol. 1, CHARACTERISTICS OF THE POPULATION (U.S. Government Printing Office, Washington, D.C., 1973). One exception is the university town of Orono (population 9,989). It was not included in the sample because its population likely exceeded 10,000 due to student numbers.

25. One letter from a Mainer is sent from Falmouth, MA (see #85, Nixon years). On Senator Aiken, see Press Reports, Aiken-Smith Correspondence, MCSL.

26. Matthew C. Moen, Kenneth T. Palmer, and Richard J. Powell, *Changing Members: The Maine Legislature in the Era of Term Limits* (Lanham, Maryland: Lexington Books, 2005), 14–16.

27. According to the 1970 Census the populations were: Portland 65,116, Lewiston 41,779, Bangor 33,168 and Auburn 24,151.

28. For this figure, I am thankful for the assistance of Angie Stockwell of the Margaret Chase Smith Library. Since January 1973 the letters have been re-filed in a different manner at least once. There are also letters that have some Vietnam War content, but are filed in other folders because of possessing a more dominating theme than the war itself.

29. Sinclair Lewis, *Main Street* (New York: First Caroll & Graf Publishers, 1996).

30. Richard O. Davies, *Main Street Blues: The Decline of Small-Town America* (Columbus: Ohio State University Press, 1998), 7.

31. Foley, *Confronting the War Machine*, 351–52, 355–56. The sample size for religious affiliation was 183. In his larger study, Foley corrects a number of misunderstandings, notably the distinction between draft resistance and draft evasion.

32. Chester H. Liebs, *Main Street to Miracle Mile: American Roadside Architecture* (Boston: Little Brown, 1985), viii.

33. H.L. Mencken was another who ridiculed small-town America as narrow-minded. See Amy D. Greenberg, "Babbit Who? The Decline of Small-Town America," *Reviews in American History*, 27, 2 (1999), 268. In countless biographies, novels and Hollywood films, a common message, subtle or not, is that urban life is far more culturally superior then the small-town "backwater" experience.

34. David J. Russo, *American Towns: An Interpretive History* (Chicago: Ivan R. Dee, 2001).

35. Moen et al., *Changing Members*, 17. For example, Mainers voted a political independent for governor twice in recent decades.

36. Christian G. Appy, *Working-Class War: American Combat Soldiers and Vietnam* (Chapel Hill: The University of North Carolina Press, 1993.)

37. Richard H. Condon, "Maine Out of the Mainstream, 1945–1965" in *Maine: The Pine Tree State from Prehistory to the Present*, Richard W. Judd, Edwin A. Churchill, and Joel W. Eastman, eds. (Orono: University of Maine Press, 1995), 531, 540.

38. *Ibid*, 542–44.

39. MCS to A.T., 27 May 1970, Vietnam War Correspondence File, MCSL.

40. James Landers, *The Weekly War: Newsmagazines and Vietnam* (Columbia: University of Missouri Press, 2004), 2, 199–224.

A Note on Letter Methodology

𝒯he letters are originals left untouched, typing and writing errors included. While there are no changes to grammar, spelling, underscoring, or italicization of the letters, there are some minor deletions to protect the privacy of the writers and other individuals mentioned. Initials replace full names and there are no street addresses given. Smith's return letters were helpful in determining, for a few unclear cases (initials or neutral names), whether the writer was a male or female. In some letters, non–Vietnam War material is removed. For consistency, all paragraphs are indented without spaces, the author's initials and gender are at the bottom left, and there is further standardization in that the date and place of residence for each letter is at the top right.

Part I

THE JOHNSON YEARS, 1967–1968

TIME LINE

November 22, 1963	Assassination of President John F. Kennedy
August 1–4, 1964	USS *Maddox* allegedly attacked twice in the Gulf of Tonkin
August 7, 1964	The U.S. Congress approves the Gulf of Tonkin Resolution
November 3, 1964	President Lyndon Johnson defeats Barry Goldwater in election
February 13, 1965	President Johnson authorizes Operation Rolling Thunder bombing campaign
March 8, 1965	First U.S. ground troops (Marines) land in South Vietnam
December 31, 1965	About 184,000 American troops to Vietnam
November 8, 1966	Senator Smith elected for a fourth term
March 25, 1967	The Rev. Martin Luther King marches against the war in Chicago
April 15, 1967	Hundreds of thousands protest the war at the United Nations, N.Y.
October 21, 1967	Large antiwar demonstrations in Washington, D.C.
December 31, 1967	About 485,000 American troops in Vietnam
January 31, 1968	Tet Offensive throughout South Vietnam
March 16, 1968	My Lai Massacre of unarmed Vietnamese civilians
March 31, 1968	President Johnson announces his withdrawal from presidential race
August 26–29, 1968	Antiwar protests at the Democratic National Convention

$\mathcal{S}$enator Margaret Chase Smith supported American involvement in Southeast Asia during the years covered in this collection of letters, but she questioned the wisdom of the United States ever getting involved in the war in the first place. In early 1967, she reflected on the 1950s and President Dwight Eisenhower's opposition to any American involvement in a ground war in Asia and how there was no anticipation that the first military advisors placed in the Republic of Vietnam (South Vietnam) would lead to the beginning of heavy combat operations years later. The number of advisors in South Vietnam was near 900 when Eisenhower left office and it increased to almost 16,300 at the end President John F. Kennedy's administration.

The assassination of Kennedy and succession of Lyndon Johnson saw no change in American policy of supporting South Vietnam's struggle against the communist Democratic Republic of Vietnam (North Vietnam). American servicemen continued to instruct and train the Army of the Republic of Vietnam (South Vietnamese army). In 1964, there was a rise of military operations by the North Vietnamese Army and the guerrilla arm of the communist National Liberation Front (Viet Cong) that had officially organized four years earlier. Also, greater political instability in South Vietnam and a number of coups resulted in the frequent rise and fall of governments. When North Vietnamese PT boats attacked the destroyer *Maddox* in the Gulf of Tonkin in early August 1964, President Johnson took the opportunity to secure Congress approval of the Gulf of Tonkin Resolution that gave the president a blank check "to take all necessary measures to repel any armed attack against the forces of the United States and to prevent further aggression." Only Democrat Senators Wayne Morse (Oregon) and Ernest Gruening (Alaska) opposed the resolution. Having secured overwhelming support, Johnson responded immediately with retaliatory air strikes against North Vietnamese bases on August 4. As it turns out, there was confusion on whether the North Vietnamese had actually carried out a second attack against the *Maddox* and another destroyer *C. Turner Joy*, three days after the initial confrontation of August 1. With more information becoming public the following year, people began to doubt the authenticity of the second attack and a growing number of senators and representatives concluded that the White House had purposely mislead them in order to pursue more aggressive action against the communists.

Escalation of American military involvement occurred quickly in 1965. In February, Johnson ordered a raid on the North Vietnamese Army north of the Demilitarized Zone and a bombing campaign against North Vietnam called Operation Rolling Thunder. The following month the U.S. 1st Marine Division also entered the conflict. No more in South Vietnam as an "advisory" role, the American military began an expanded offensive action and troop levels in

Vietnam rose from 59,900 at the end of June to more than 184,000 in December. At the end of the year, public opinion polls showed overwhelming endorsement for U.S. involvement. The plan to keep U.S. troops in the war until the communists agreed to American peace terms had the support of 82 percent of the American people. In 1966, bombing raids increased and by the end of the year there were 385,000 American troops in South Vietnam. Entering 1967, more Americans questioned the wisdom and justification of this growing war.

General William Westmoreland, the United States Commander in South Vietnam, required more soldiers to defeat communist forces and by May 1967 there were 436,000 American troops in South Vietnam. Receiving economic and military support from China and the USSR, North Vietnamese leaders understood that a protracted war favored the communists and their successful guerrilla operations. Ho Chi Minh expected that in time the Americans would lose their will to continue the fight. At home, an increasing number of Americans were becoming more frustrated as 1967 progressed without any conclusive evidence of overall military success. The antiwar movement was showing strength beyond the college campuses of the nation. The Rev. Martin Luther King, Jr., and other civil rights leaders expressed their opposition to the war. By early 1968, there were approximately 500,000 American troops in South Vietnam when the North Vietnamese Army and Viet Cong carried out a series of attacks known as the Tet Offensive. The coordinated assaults on many provincial capitals and major cities throughout South Vietnam were a psychological blow to the American government and people. Fierce fighting followed for weeks before the communists met a crushing defeat. The Tet Offensive, however, shook the United States, and on March 31 President Johnson informed the American people, on television, of his decision not to run for re-election. The remaining year witnessed episodes of sadness and turmoil on the streets of America.

Letters sent to Senator Smith in 1967 and 1968 capture the erosion of popular support for the war. The selection of the following 101 letters is not due to any manipulation to substantiate an antiwar or pro-administration position; included is almost every "Vietnam War" letter, at the Margaret Chase Smith Library, sent from an individual or couple, living in a community smaller than 10,000, who devoted at least one hundred words to a Vietnam War issue. A successful politician since 1940, Smith worked in the elite circles of Washington political life, but a persisting image was her small-town and modest beginnings and independent streak that set her apart from many other politicians. Small-town people from Maine who wanted the government to hear their voices believed that Smith was the ideal conduit for their concerns about the Vietnam War.

A Growing War

I. ANTI-WAR

*A*s the intensity of the war grew in 1967 more people were speaking out against the government as shown by the following letters that cover the January to April months. The first letter is an emotional appeal to stop "the killing of our sons." The remaining letters voice the same theme and speak of the destructiveness and tragic nature of the government's Vietnam policy. One writer finds it troubling that Americans were dying without a declaration of war approved by Congress. The final letter is uncommonly critical of Senator Smith, suggesting that she cares more about her party than the good of the nation.

1. "wrong, wrong, wrong"

Cape Elizabeth, Maine
January 15, 1967

Dear Senator Smith:

Since I am unable to travel to Washington to join the women led by Jeannette Rankin protesting our involvement in Vietnam to our legislators, I wish to express my views in a letter.

I feel that our government should have heeded the advice of our military and state department. Their analysis stated that Vietnam was not strategic to American interests.

The war has escalated to the point where my taxes and the cost of living are unbearable. I see no need and I am unwilling to sacrifice my comfort to a government which would have been non-existent except through our intervention. I see no need to pay taxes to support a country who is unwilling to draft their 18 year olds while we have no compunction in sending ours halfway across the world. I see no need to pay taxes to support a people who view our efforts as examples of American imperialistic business interests. (Reported on the Huntley-Brinkley news program, and by a roundtable discussion of war correspondents on educational television.) I see no need to pay taxes to support President Thieu who stated this morning that peace negotiations should be done by the South Vietnamese, not the Americans who happen to be doing most of the fighting and footing the bill. I see no need to' pay taxes to support a war which the rest of the countries decry. Their support is minimal. And what they do give is offset a hundredfold by war profiteering. (Senator Fulbright in the Senate, Oct. 31.) I see no need to pay taxes in a vain attempt to establish democratic procedures and reform to a corrupt government. (New York Times, editorial, Dec. 19, 1967 on land distribution. Week of January 8th, growing Thieu and Ky disagreements on reforms. Januarty 13, delay of Thieu in reforming army.)

No indeed, Senator Smith. This war is wrong, wrong, wrong, and has been a terrible mistake. Let us not compound our folly by continuing to send our boys to be killed. Let us call a halt to the increase in taxes. Let us face up to our mistakes and veer sharply from the path of irrationality to rational maturity by ceasing the bombing of North Vietnam and going to the conference table with all combatants, willing to compromise and negotiate for an end to the killing of our sons.
Sincerely yours,
J. C. (female)

[Editor's Note: In 1917, Jeannette Rankin (1880–1973) took her seat as the first female to be elected to the United States House of Representatives, three years before the nineteenth amendment secured the vote for women. The Montana-born pacifist opposed American entry in both world wars and during the Vietnam War she campaigned against the war with thousands of American women organized as the Jeannette Rankin Brigade. Although Senator J. William Fulbright (1905–1995) was supportive of President Johnson's Gulf of Tonkin Resolution (1964), he became a vocal war critic and attacked Johnson's Vietnam policy. Nguyen Van Thieu (1923–2001) was the president of the Republic of Vietnam and Nguyen Cao Ky (1930–) was the vice president.]

2. "horrible barbarism"

Phillips, Maine
February 20, 1967

Dear Senator Smith,

I am writing to tell you that I, for one, am increasingly appalled by President Johnson's policy in Viet Nam. "Saving the world for Democracy" has worn pretty thin during our century. And I feel that the horrible barbarism of American mass-firepower daily thrown upon the civilians of that wretched country cannot be justified by any practical politics. Certainly not by a nation which hints that it might possible subscribe to Christian principles.

As a school-boy, I learned in the Constitution that: "Congress shall have (or "has") the power to declare war." How so are we at war in Viet Nam when you and your colleagues have not declared one? Am I to accept President Johnson's explanation that "there is no war"?—but merely a 350,000 man multi-billion dollar "police action"? May I approach that semantical debate with a paraphrase on Shakespeare: "A war by any other name is just as deadly". If the Congress feels that war is essential to American survival, then please call it to a vote. I for one could follow with much more confidence the decision of over five-hundred law-makers than I do the judgment of a singular president and his non-elected advisors. At least it would be more nearly a decision "by the people". The nation's spiritual needs and moral rights are not being served by our being brought into undeclared wars by the buck-passing gimmick of "no, we do—yes, we don't" Congressional resolutions.

Further, I implore you—don't let President Johnson drag us into the coming Chinese civil war, supporting the "good" Communists, so-called, against the "bad" Communists—or unleashing Chiang Kai Shek against them both. Let the suffering Chinese people work out their own destiny, as fraught with mistakes, chicanery, plot, counter-plot, and disillusionment as it may be. We Americans are not the Devinely chosen guardians of the world. And though we may have the greatest technology, we have no monopoly on the world's brains. However I abhor terror-imposed Communism, I'd rather risk one or several of the world's peoples suffering under a Communism imposed by their own "zealots" over a national lethargy for a decade or score of years—then to rise against it on their own initiative than to enforce Democracy on them at the tip of American Bayonets—and see America hated by them for a century or more.

There is not substitute for Christian generosity. Let our foreign policy be: "Help our neighbors when we can be truly useful to their well-being. When we cannot, leave them alone as they learn to walk by stumbling."
Yours truly,
M. S. (male)

[Editor's note: Anti-communist Chaing Kai Shek (1887–1975) was the president of the Republic of China in Taiwan after the Communists took power in China in 1949. As part of her world tour to investigate international communism, Senator Smith visited Chaing Kai Shek in early 1955 and supported his talk of bold action against mainland Red China. Smith also met Madame Chaing whom she corresponded with for many years.]

3. "a civil war"

January 26, 1967
Eliot, Maine

Senator Smith:

As one of your constituents and a conscientious American citizen, I urge you to review your position on American involvement in Vietnam. I strongly urge you to consider the positions of Senators Fulbright and Morse, John K. Galbraith, Arthur M. Schlesinger Jr., Walter Lippman, Pope Paul, and countless others who, in my humble but earnest opinion, have the knowledge, insight and courage to see this thing for what it is.

I have no substantial evidence to disagree with U Thant's contention that Vietnam is not within the realm of United States' vital interests, that the bombing of the North is irrelevant since the conflict is essentially a civil war, and that a cessation of the bombing must be initiated immediately in order to achieve peace—if that's what we really want. Non-recognition of the Viet Cong as the specific "enemy" borders on farce. In the interests of peace and the honor of our country I implore you, Senator Smith, to consider the above.

Sincerely,
J. P. (male)

[Editor's note: Senator Wayne Lyman Morse (1900–1974) was a consistent war critic. Economist John K. Galbraith (1908–2006), historian Arthur M. Schlesinger Jr. (1917–2007), journalist Walter Lippman (1889–1974), and Pope Paul VI (1897–1978) favored negotiation to end the conflict in Vietnam. U Thant (1909–1974) served as Secretary-General of the United Nations.]

4. "munition makers"

Gardiner, Maine
January 14, 1967

Dear Senator Smith,

I have just finished listening to "Meet the Press" discuss our economic situation, with Mr. Heller plugging for a tax increase. It leaves me more unconvinced than ever. Why is it possible to pass a tax increase bill, when it is <u>impossible</u> to plug the countless tax loopholes that there are in the present laws?

<u>Why</u> are immensely wealthy people permitted to pay little and sometimes no tax on their fortunes and tax exempt securities are allowed to exist as a way to dodge taxes?

. . . <u>When</u> is the Pentagon going to realize that it would cost less money to buy off the Viet Cong than it does to kill them? $100, 000 per Viet Cong to kill, according to one NBC reporter on their year end summary. And how can we know whether the North Vietnamese offer is legitimate or not if we don't give them a chance to sit down. <u>How</u> can we ever justify ruining the countryside of South Vietnam, with 2,000,000 people in concentration camps, in defense of one segment of the population? Even if we should win the war militarily and there seems to be doubts that we can do that, it seems to me it will be a variation of the old saw "The operation was successful but the patient died."

Do you know Piet Hein's classic from "Grooks" which Pauline Frederick quoted the other night on NBC's <u>Losing Face</u>

> The noble art of losing face
> May one day save the human race
> And turn into eternal merit
> What weaker minds would call disgrace.

I've been going to send it to LBJ for a long time but I'm sure he heard it the other night on NBC.

I have never talked to <u>one</u> person in Maine, New York, Connecticut or New Jersey who thought we had any business in Vietnam in the first place. Of course our munitions makers are making a killing out of the war and I suspect all polls are taken among them. I couldn't possibly think the <u>people</u> are behind this.

Kindest regards and thank you for being a good listener!

Sincerely yours,

M. P. (female)

[Editor's note: Walter Heller (1915–1987) served as Chairman of the Council of Economic Advisors in the early 1960s. Better known for supporting tax cut legislation in 1964, Heller's "plugging for a tax increase" was due to his apprehension about inflation. The costs of the war and government programs were rising and the above letter writer was angry that tax loopholes meant that tax increases were going to adversely affect ordinary Americans much more than the wealthy. A pioneering broadcast newswoman, Pauline Frederick (1908–1990) covered the United Nations for NBC.]

5. "get out immediately"

Northeast Harbor, Maine
February 23, 1967

Dear Mrs. Smith:

You must be getting a great deal of mail from your constituents which is adverse criticism of the Vietnam War. I hope you will add this to your list of letters which say to get out immediately at almost any cost.

Apparently we are stalemated, with North Vietnam refusing to go to the peace table until we stop bombing, and with us refusing to stop bombing until we get some definite peace feelers from North Vietnam. To me, the initiative must be ours. If it's a question of losing face, by all means let's lose some—announce to the world that we are suspending all warlike operations there, not just the bombing, and bring our men back down into a quiescent and waiting position, doing absolutely nothing. Or we could land the whole mess in the laps of the U.N., start folding up, and come home.

I know all this sounds naive, and that there are undoubtedly all manner of diplomatic, military, and otherwise strategic reasons why we should not do this; but I am sure that we will gain the respect of the world if we do so. The trouble with powerful, strong individuals is that they won't admit to mistakes; the same is true on a national basis.

We did make a great mistake in going in there. It was not, by any means, the decision of the majority of the people in this country. This war is morally wrong, and we all know it. Our stock all over the world has gone down because of our participation in it. We cannot conclude this thing gradually. What will really impress the rest of the many countries watching us is for us to admit that this is not a civilized answer, hand it over for arbitration, get out, and get out now.

I really am not a rabid, opinionated person. Up until now, I have never expressed an opinion although I have steadily and gradually been formulating one.

Sincerely yours,
E. F. (female)

6. "tragic situation"

Southwest Harbor, Maine
March 7, 1967

Dear Sen. Smith,

First, let me express appreciation of the deep concern with which you are facing our tragic situation in Vietnam. As a citizen of Maine I feel grateful that I am represented by you.

Secty. MacNamara urged upon the church pastors and laymen recently in Washington that the president and our legislators "need" expressions of opinion from their people. So—

I find myself increasingly persuaded of a point of view I have held since the beginning of our commitment in Vietnam. What is our <u>real</u> political aim?

Is it not to develop a non-communist state? We say we favor "free elections." Suppose those elections produce a communist government: Would we not in that case look for a means of overthrowing such a government? (We have done so in other countries.)—Even after we may have won the war, can we achieve our objective of a non-communist government?

Why not halt the bombing as North Vietnam asks (it can always be started again, alas)—welcome internationally supervised elections, abide by the result (even communist), "save our face"? Robert Kennedy suggests that "a nation which commands half the wealth and power of the globe need not be fearful of the result."

Sincerely yours,

M. F. (female)

[Editor's note: Senator Robert Kennedy (1925–1968) initially supported the war effort, but by 1967 he questioned the Johnson administration's handling of the conflict.]

7. *"ill-advised war"*

Round Pond, Maine
March 24, 1967

Dear Senator Smith:—

If I may, I should like to quote from Bruce Catton's GLORY ROAD. He had just been speaking of the heavy bombardment of Fredericksburg prior to that disastrous battle and he said, "General Hunt had wrecked Fredericksburg, but he had not driven out the Mississippians. Huddling under cover, they had had a hard time of it, but they had not had more than they could take, and as soon as the gunfire ceased they were ready to fight again. They were teaching Hunt THE LESSON WHICH ARTILLERISTS HAVE TO LEARN ANEW EACH GENERATION—THAT BOMBARDMENT WHICH WILL DESTROY BUILDINGS WILL NOT NECESSARILY KEEP BRAVE DEFENDERS FROM FIGHTING ON AMIDST THE WRECKAGE" (my caps for emphasis)

That statement is as true today as it was a century ago. Bombardment from airplanes is a form of artillery attack—with heavier explosive charges, perhaps, and usually with less accuracy. The law applying to

artillery applies also to airplane bombing. IT WILL NOT CAUSE A DE-
TERMINED ENEMY TO QUIT. Furthermore the economic law of di-
minishing return also applies. The bulk of our people did not understand
this. I am afraid that our military men and our political leaders did not understand this either.

Had they understood that no cheap, easy victory through bombing was
possible, it seems likely that we would never have gotten into this ill-advised
war. But we are in it, and if we win it it will be with the blood of many, many
American boys. Airplanes and helicopters cost a lot of money but American
blood is more expensive. We can not withdraw now no matter how foolish we
were to get into this mess, but we can change our policy and conduct a holding action from now on. We can avoid escalation. We can make it clear that
we mean, when we talk about negotiation, that we do not mean that our terms
must be accepted without abatement. The South Viet Nam Republic is not
our puppet. Therefor we should not let ourselves be put in the position in
which this becomes OUR war. There is a difference between lending a helping hand and assuming "the white man's burden". I think we have gotten beyond that point.

There is another point too. IS WORLD COMMUNISM SUCH A
DANGER TO US THAT WE MUST FIGHT IT WHEREVER IT AP-
PEARS ANYWHERE IN THE EARTH? I do not think so. I am frank to
say that I believe that we should get off our high horse, abandon our self-
righteous attitude and our silly notion that "one-world" is just around the corner if we only act as policeman and Lady Bountiful for a little while. Let's
show a little humility and offer a little "give-and-take". I firmly believe that
the world would be better if we were to do so.

All this has been written because I am, as a hard-shell Republican, disturbed at the posture Dirksen and Ford are taking. I always thought that our
party was the party of common sense and prudence and moderation, and I do
not like the trend it seems to be taking. We do not have to play Tweedle-dee
to the Democrats Tweedle-dum.

Did you, by any chance read the article WHAT WE SHOULD DO
NEXT IN ASIA, by Reischauer in LOOK for April 4th.? I think it's well
worth reading. Sorry to have run on so long. With best wishes
Cordially yours,
F. D. (male)

[Editor's note: Minority leader in the House and future vice-president and
president, Gerald Ford (1913–2006) and Senator Everett Dirksen (1896–1969)
promoted hawkish war views. Dirksen, whose parents were German immi-
grants, described communists as "a cold, relentless, and inhuman enemy."]

8. "ugly and sad war"

Winslow, Maine
March 25, 1967

Dear Mrs. Smith,

I, like many other mothers, am deeply concerned about our position in Viet Nam, and the standstill in the war.

I am writing to you to ask if anything can be done to influence the present administration policy in Viet Nam that can bring this war to a quick and satisfactory conclusion.

It does seem criminal that our fine young men are dying at the rate they are in, what seems at the moment, a futile attempt to be a part of any victorious end to this terrible conflict.

The citizens, at best, feel helpless, confused, <u>bewildered</u> and frightened about the reports we have concerning Viet Nam and our position there.

Can any pressure be brought to end this ugly and sad war? I will be happy and glad to be a part of any venture which would be influential in any way.

Very sincerely,
S. D. (female)

9. "intolerable waste"

Oakland, Maine
April 4, 1967

Dear Senator Smith:

We seem to be determined to see the Vietnamese people go the way of the American Indian! <u>I find our continuation of the war in Vietnam an intolerable waste of money and human resources.</u>

President Johnson could open peace negotiations (and I don't mean Viet Cong surrender which seems to be inherent in our terms of negotiation so far) within a few weeks if:

1) We stop the bombing in the north
2) We reduce operations in the south, and
3) We recognize the real opponents, the Viet Cong. (Remember, the infiltration of northern troops to the south has been increased and strengthened <u>by our presence.</u>

It would mean we would have to <u>recognize all political elements in the life of the country</u>—even if we didn't approve of some of them.

We are the most powerful nation in the world. Our power could be used in positive ways of helping fight the real world enemies: injustice, poverty, disease, national pride, the abuse of powers, and the hatred and war that are their creatures and creators. We must become the world leaders as we are capable of becoming.

I plead with you to exert your influence in helping this war come to an end.

Yours truly,

N. M. (female)

Later, same day

P.S. Today's newspaper (Waterville Sentinel) contains a front-page story: "Sen. Smith Suggests U.N. control of South Vietnam". This is certainly a positive step. Thank you; may I encourage you to continue following this line!

10. "lonely fight"

South China, Maine
April 6, 1967

Dear Senators [Smith and Edmund Muskie]:

Our strong wishes, as your constituents:

Urge Pres. Johnson immediately respond to U That's (and Kosygan's) overtures to negotiation via a bombing pause. A direct, personal "big three" meeting may not be senseless. If this doesn't work, for Heaven's sake, let's go all-out to WIN the war instead of continuing to try to fill the Asian "bottomless pit" with our boys' blood. If we are afraid to "go for broke" to win, we had no business getting into it at all.

Then, let's concentrate on making our beloved U.S. the example of the decent, sensible, happy, productive people we should be doing instead of trying to force our way of life on other people with dollars or guns—("military advisors" who get killed "advising" the unwilling recipient!)

. . . It's a sad state of affairs if we, the American voters, are so economically blind that we think our government can "carry" us instead of realizing that we, the people, are the government. We support it, financially included, and we can't earn enough to support the world, nor should we try to breed enough sons to "contain Communism"—or whatever it is we're trying to do.

. . . The country of which we have always been so proud is the object of criticism from other countries; our dignitaries are scorned, sneered at—and we are receiving no appreciable help, even from countries wherein we are spreading around hard-earned American dollars. For how long will the American people be expected to continue this lonely fight? And how many more of our young boys will have to be torn from their homes to perhaps die—to sacrifice life—death is so permanent—they'll get no second chance to live. . . .

Perhaps Mr. Kruschev's promise to "bury us" will manifest itself this way: The strength of our country, our young men, will be critically decreased—as will our economy—and our morale. We will then be vulnerable to attack from any quarter. Who will our friends be, I wonder? I hope every ally has our conscience.

We continue to have faith in your integrity and your ability to represent us. It isn't easy. Nothing worthwhile ever was. We appreciate your efforts.

Yours sincerely,
Mr. and Mrs. A. A.   *All Out to win*

[Editor's note: In 1968, Democrat Senator Edmund S. Muskie (1914–1996) of Maine received the nomination for vice president. Aleksei Nikolayevich Kosygin (1904–1980) was Soviet premier who met with President Johnson the following month (June), urging him to stop bombing North Vietnam. Stating that communism would triumph, Nikita Khrushchev (1894–1971), first secretary of the Communist Party, made the "bury you" comment to Western diplomats in late 1956.]

11. *"bothered me"*

Ogunquit, Maine
April 13, 1967

Dear Senator Smith—

There is something that has bothered me for sometime.

Our Constitution says that only Congress has the power to declare war. We are in one if more than 500, 000 of our boys are involved and means anything. Who was war declared against? and by whom.

I don't remember seeing it, so can your office furnish me with a copy of the joint or separate resolutions that seem to have transferred this power to an individual and will this set a prescient for the future?

I would like to read it and if you cannot furnish it, can I get it from the Government printing office without buying a whole issue of the Congressional Record.

Possibly you have some thoughts on this situation.

Very truly,
M. D. (male)   *Sarcastic critic of war or grants*
                        that it must be declared by Congress not POTUS

[Editor's note: This apparent sarcastic letter makes the point that Johnson bypassed Congress and used the Gulf of Tonkin Resolution as validation for the escalation of American troops in South Vietnam.]

12. "oppose the war"

Freeport, Maine
April 14, 1967

Dear Senator Smith,

   In reply to my letter urging you to oppose the war in Vietnam, you answered me on April 11th as follows: "Have you asked Senator Muskie, whom you so avidly support, to do the same thing that you ask of me, whom you so avidly oppose and criticize?"

   To which question my first reaction is: don't you think we should keep politics out of an issue so momentous as war? In my book, anyone who will help end this horrible and senseless war, be he (or she) a Republican or a Democrat, deserves well of his country and well of mankind. With equal fervor I have praised Senators Fullbright (D.Ark.) and Hatfield (R.Oreg.) for taking a stand against it.

   But to answer your question directly: yes, I have frequently and avidly urged Senator Muskie to oppose the war in Vietnam. . . .

   You see, I agree with Senator Fullbright that "Criticism (of the government) is more than a right; it is an act of patriotism." And for me, Mrs. Smith, patriotism comes before party.

Sincerely,
D. G. (male)

Critic of war who believes its more imports
than Dem v Rep

[Editor's note: Republican Senator Mark O. Hatfield (1922–) of Oregon opposed the Vietnam War.]

II. WAR STRATEGY

Most Americans were unhappy with the lack of progress in Vietnam, but only a modest number in 1967 accepted the idea of immediate American withdrawal at any cost. Letters to Senator Smith presented various strategies to force the North Vietnamese to the peace table. The first letter, long and detailed, suggests using "sonic booms" as a psychological weapon in the skies over North Vietnam rather than bombs. This writer and others appeared to be comfortable in testing their wide-ranging ideas with the approachable Smith. Extreme frustration over the "restrained" approach of the American government was evident in the letters that demanded no restrictions on the bombing of key strategic sites in North Vietnam, particularly Hanoi.

13. "sonic booms"

Eddington, Maine
January 17, 1967

Dear Senator Smith:

A belated congratulations on your re-election and your recent election as Chairman of the Republican Conference Committee.

My purpose in writing to you is to suggest to you as a United States Senator and more particularly as a member of the Senate Armed Forces Committee an idea, and a relatively simple one in execution in my opinion, that might possibly shorten the present armed conflict in Vietnam, or at the very least, would exert pressure on the Viet Cong and Hanoi to consider negotiations in one form or another. . . .

Now to my suggestion: It is to take a supersonic fighter wing, (minimum of two squadrons and preferably three), or F-4C's and arm them only for defense against enemy fighters. Then utilize these fighters, preferably singly, to conduct super-sonic runs across Hanoi, Haiphong and other worthwhile concentration of personnel at all altitudes, at any and all times of day, from all directions and under all weather conditions. They would not be permitted to fire armament except to defend themselves against enemy aircraft and they would not be permitted to carry bombs.

The Air Force in extensive tests of sonic booms has concluded that such booms do not cause structural damage. The overpressure caused by such booms will cause glass breakage.

But the Air Force has not published, to my knowledge, the tests it ran in Oklahoma recently as respects the psychological impact of sonic booms. I know here in Maine where the booms are negligible, six or so a month, the people complain continually and remember it for long afterwards. They argue long and vociferously that booms cause damage to their homes, including structural damage, which the Air Force denies.

There is nothing in any international convention that I am aware of which would forbid such an operation. I am certain that international engineers would verify and support the conclusions of the Air Force that no structural damage can occur. On the medical side, excluding psychiatrists and psychologists for the moment, I am equally certain that international medical people would concur that such booms cannot cause physical trauma or other physical injury to personnel subjected to them. On the other hand, I would suspect that the mind doctors might have strong opinions that such booms occurring over a long, continuous period of time would have a definite, psychological, damaging effect on personnel subject to them. But this same damaging effect can result from isolated instances of napalm, 1000 pound bombs, etc.

If my suggestion has any merit, I would like to offer in conclusion, a few basic requirements that I consider the absolute minimum to implement it:

1. The selection of an F-4C Wing of three squadrons that has consistently demonstrated its ability to operate in the field, day or night, under any and all weather conditions, its ability to supply and maintain its aircraft in a combat ready status, with a minimum of aborts.

2. Three widely, well protected air bases within striking distance of Hanoi and Haiphong. Place the Wing Headquarters with its Combat Operations Center on the base nearest the center of the other two bases.

3. A separate classified communications net which would give instant communications between all units and the Combat Operations Center at all times, this net to include all types of communications and to be supported directly by its own Communications and Electronics Squadrons.

4. A detailed conference with the USAF Thunderbirds and; if Canada would authorize, with the Golden Hawks of the RCAF, to work out procedures of multiple aircraft approaching the same geographical location at high speeds from different directions. The whole theory of the operation would be to submit Hanoi, Haiphong, etc., to a continuous barrage of sonic booms, day and night. Some would be single and others multiple.

5. And such strikes must not establish a pattern. To do so would permit the enemy to adjust its anti-aircraft in such a way that our losses could become unacceptable. (They might even turn back the clock and use barrage balloons.) To counteract this, I would assign this special unit a computer complex and a highly specialized intelligence force. The computers to be used to set up detailed, exact strike patterns that have no ascertainable predictability. And the intelligence unit, including agents in Hanoi and Haiphong, to determine exactly what is going on and to have the means to report it or anything else of importance (i.e. barrage balloons) immediately.

6. I would beef up this Wing's weather section so that it would have the best possible weather information, particularly as respects the target areas and going to and from them.

7. Finally, although I would keep this Wing's strikes secret even from our own other units, I would brief other units generally that certain special operations are being carried out by F-4C's and to stay away from them unless requested to provide assistance. On the other hand, this special unit should know at all times exactly what other operations are being carried out so that it can make its plans accordingly.

It goes without saying that if this suggestion were brought, such a unit would need a period of time for special training. This possibly could be accomplished against a remote Pacific island which had been properly instrumented to record the results, possibly using animals and/or even human volunteers to test its effectiveness.

Senator Smith, I offer this suggestion with all sincerity. I am not of the firm belief that it is feasible and that it is absolutely humane, and that there cannot be any international complaint against carrying it out. I also firmly believe that, if properly supported, it would work and it would shorten considerably the present armed conflict.

If you have any questions on this proposal, I would be most happy to answer them and elaborate further. If this idea is bought, and the Good Lord is willing. . . .

With best regards and continued success in your important endeavors, I remain,
Sincerely,   *Favoring Psychological Warfare*
C. G. (male)
P.S. If this had merits, I hope and pray that it is <u>not</u> staff studied to death.

14. "half-way job"

Union, Maine
January 17, 1967

Dear Mrs. Smith:

I had the privilege of dining with one of our men who has been in Vietnam for nearly two years and was home on a thirty day leave. He informed me that our men are just as unsafe in Saigon now as they were a year ago.?

Why should we not bomb the North Vietnam air fields? We are sacrificing our finest men and airplanes and not doing enough to protect them. Ther is too much politics as Paul Harvey said on radio this noon and General Maxwell Taylor has made such complaints. We ought to send some of these soft heads over there.

I have been reading a book on the Green Berets and there are instances of political interference with our forces over there. It states that if they were not deprived of some of their reinforcements by the politicians they would have saved many of our men and much material.

The Viet Cong were allowed to seek refuge in Cambodia and infiltrated the South Vietnam forces. We need to get this war over and not drag it out indefinately. We are doing a half way job.

I wish you would send this where you think it might do more good.

With kind regards, I am
Sincerely,
B. N. (male)   *Advocating Bombing*

[Editor's note: Former chairman of the Joint Chiefs of Staff and ambassador to South Vietnam, General Maxwell D. Taylor (1901–1987) was an advisor to Johnson from 1965 to 1968.]

15. *"bomb Hanoi off the maps*

Ellsworth, Maine
February 13, 1967

Dear Senator Smith,
    . . . Another thing which irks me is that we are waiting for North Viet Nam to make all the peace moves. They want us to stop bombing them but are still double crossing us at every opportunity so I would like to see someone in our government have the nerve to issue an ultimatum: "If you won't come to the peace table within—say 30 days we bomb Hanoi off the maps" as its generally known they are building their defense industries in the middle of the residential districts.
    As you know by now I have a very low opinion of our trying to fight a war and please everyone. You fight a war to win not go to a certain line and stop as in Korea. If McArthur had been allowed to fight instead of stop like Truman wanted there now wouldn't be any trouble in Viet Nam, and as far as I can see our Defense Dept is doing the same exactly in Viet Nam.
    They should listen to Curtis LeMay instead of Dean Rusk, Johnson, & McNamara. After all we pay for the Generals & Admirals' etc education to fight so why ignore their advice when it is needed.
    I wrote Sen. Everett Dirksen on the above line and he gently slapped me on the wrist by telling me the Gov. men know best! That's a laugh! Its a pity someone in the Government hasn't read Barrons Financial Weekly Feb. 6th story on the Congo "Law of the Jungle".
Yours truly,
H. P. (male)

[Editor's note: Former Chief of Staff of the United States Air Force, General Curtis LeMay (1906–1990) endorsed a hawkish approach to the point that his critics characterized him as a warmonger who was too trigger-happy with bombs. While some question whether he actually said it, LeMay's statement that the United States should "bomb them [North Vietnam communists] back into the Stone Age" captures the tone of the inflammatory rhetoric surrounding the war (biographer Thomas Coffey claims that LeMay failed to catch the quote placed in LeMay's memoirs by writer MacKinlay Kantor). Dean Rusk (1909–1994) was secretary of state in the Kennedy and Johnson administrations. Robert McNamara (1916–) was secretary of defense from 1961 to 1968.]

16. *"unwarranted timidity"*

North Lubec, Maine
February 28, 1967

My dear Senator Smith:

It is my pleasure to write my thanks and congratulations to you for your seven points concerning the conduct of the war in Vietnam. The feeling of deep frustration that we Americans feel over what seems to us to be an unwarranted timidity in high places and a fear of communism when the communist nations have repeatedly shown respect only for a firm stand and a show of force. You have expressed our feelings most pointedly and, we hope, with the authority of your high position and with some chance of effect.

General Sherman said that the most humane manner prosecute a war was to bring it to the earliest possible conclusion with every means at our disposal. That still holds true as it did in the Civil War. You have indicated the same opinion, which we share.

We have seen the great mistake made in WW I when we made only a token gesture in support of a democratic government in Russia. We saw the mistake made in ordering General Eisenhower not to allow his troops to capture and hold Berlin and the territory to the west. The mistake made in not allowing our men to liberate all of Korea and the dangerous aftermath which still exists. We appear to be on the same road once more when we limit our strength and so prolong the war and increase American casualties in Vietnam.

I am enclosing a clipping from the Bangor Daily News which you may not have seen, because it points up part of the same problem as it exists on the home front. We cannot understand why riots are permitted even to the point where the physical safety of the Vice President of the United States is threatened. We wonder why, without any danger to free speech, such affairs cannot be held within civilized bounds. It disturbs us when the C.I.A. can be publicly pilloried for doing its duty against a well financed and organized effort to mislead our young people.

Those of us who live on the Canadian border are appalled at the subtile but vicious anti-American campaign which we hear and see over the Canadian Broadcasting Corporation programs from stations across the entire country. Our President is insulted. Our history, our flag, our national anthem are burlesqued in a very offensive manner. Many prominent Americans are invited to appear on their programs (evn including a U.S. Senator) only to be hissed and booed and greeted with yells of, "Yankee go home". This may not be an official policy of the Canadian Government but some responsibility rests with their officials for their C.B.C. is a government owned and operated station. I am sure that if all Americans could hear what we along the border hear there would be few visitors from this country to their Expo 67. I wish their were some courteous way for the President to stay away from an area where he may be insulted and threatened.

Perhaps the Canadians take their cue from such articles as the one in "Ramparts" which has so seriously affected the work of the C.I.A.

I only wanted to thank you for your courage and for expressing our feelings so much better than we could have done.

Faithfully yours,   *Wants to use full strength to end war;*
R. H. (male)   *also upset with anti-American sentiments by the CBC*

[Editor's note: Offering an alternative to American programming, the publicly owned Canadian Broadcasting Corporation seeks to protect Canadian cultural sovereignty. The CBC's tilt to the political left, in part, explains the level of anti-Americanism in its programming that the above writer experienced. The relationship between President Johnson and Prime Minister Lester Pearson (1963–1968) was poor after Johnson brashly berated and physically seized Pearson by the lapel of his coat at Camp David, April 3, 1965, in response to an anti-bombing speech delivered by Pearson at Temple University in Philadelphia. In an October 1967 letter to the president of the University of New Brunswick, Smith took issue with Canadian college students participating in antiwar protests in Washington: "I uphold the right of dissent. But I question the discretion of foreigners going into another country to give support to demonstrations or movements against the government of a nation that has always been a friendly supporter."]

17. *"contradictory announcements"*

Medway, Maine
March 22, 1967

Dear Senator Smith:

Before I say anything I admit to considerable ignorance of the details of the matter due to the fact that I have not had the opportunity to read the newspaper as thoroughly as I should have. I would like to communicate to you my approval and support in your questioning the contradictory announcements made by the Secretary of Defence about the effectiveness of the air war in Vietnam. I remember being very confused by his saying one week that the air war was not effective and then saying at another time that is was definitely needed. It seems to me that the effectiveness of the aerial bombardment is one of the mysteries of modern warfare. It always seems to be less than initially thought by the side that uses it. (Apparently German industry reached its peak production in World War II only a few months before surrender, and this in the face of the massive bombardments that were being mounted on Germany by that time.) Then the authorities begin to speak of the effectiveness of aerial bombardment in terms of morale and psychology. I question whether they are on firm ground when they shift their emphasis from directly ascertainable military effectiveness to something as nebulous as war psychology.

I don't like the thought of our killing and wounding South Vietnamese civilians for the sake of "imponderables" which are only understood by those who apparently can not communicate them in such a way to the public as to make for a firm and unambiguous support by men of reason. If the raids are effective, then there is a justification for them. A justification—perhaps not complete but at least one firm justification. But if the reason for the raids boils down to the psychology of a small group of people who are afraid they have made some errors of judgement and wish to be relieved of their doubts by dramatic effects, then there is no real justification for them. A difficult matter, of course, and one in which I am quite ignorant but still rather concerned. We have come to help the people of South Vietnam. I trust we won't end by loving them literally to death.

Yours sincerely,
T. M. (male)

Advocating aerial bombardment & saying if the only reason were not is for morale & psych reasons that's ridiculous

[Editor's note: During the war years and since, military leaders, politicians, and scholars have intensely debated the topic of military strategy and why America failed to reach its military objectives with far superior firepower in Vietnam. The effectiveness of strategic bombing was one component of this larger discussion. The Rolling Thunder bombing campaign had caused significant damage in North Vietnam, but the overall and long-term impact of the air attacks was minor because the communists' ability to recuperate quickly was "of a high order."]

18. *"humiliating begging"*

Bar Harbor, Maine
March 23, 1967

My Dear Senator,

As a republican resident of Maine . . . fairly well acquainted with the Far East, may I state to you my views shared by most of my friends, regarding the conduct of the "undeclared" war in Vietnam. It is obvious that since we did not deliberately enter the war, but rather slipped into it "we were just advisors etc", this full grown conflict cannot stir up the enthusiasm and patriotic support of conflicts like World Wars I & II. Out best young men do their duty—grimly. Others are rebellious. There is bound to be increasing resentment and anger at the fast augmenting loss of lives and the maiming of our youth.—The loss of treasure is nothing compared to this—All the more, as there is no end in sight and no real effort to seek an end—The humiliating begging a scornful enemy to come to the peace table shows a woeful ignorance of the Oriental mind and will leas us nowhere. If a president like Theodore Roosevelt had been in charge, he would not have been intimidated by hostile world opinion—always hostile whatever we do; but, secure in his conviction that it was a righteous act, he would have used the full might and strength of our nation . . . . The hostile clamor would have ceased with out victory. Russia and China are too well aware of their own interest to risk a war of annihilation with us.

—Wont you urge the President to try the one thing he has not yet: the use of our full power, lifting restrictions which lower the morale of our fighting me, encourage the enemy and lead only to despair—Ultimately, he will have to do it—Public clamor and indignation will force him to—why wait for that?

Yours Sincerely,
J. S. (male)

Advocating the use of full strength

19. *"everyone helping, or move out"*

Rangeley, Maine
March 27, 1967

Dear Senator,

As you know, I don't like this Viet-Nam war, as time goes on I like it less.

As a combat infantryman (wounded) in world war II my heart goes out for these poor boys. In that war we had the whole country in back of us, Congress, workers, everyone, and everyone served.

In this war, last week over 200 men died. I see thousands of young men (this winter skiing, in the summer water skiing, etc, while I look around and I find the poor families, there boys have gone. This is no democracy. If this war is important for our survival it is important too everyone or no one.

Lets get this war over with, with everyone helping, or move out.

Yours truly,
L.W. (male)

American lives are lost everyone needs to pitch in on and on the war effort

[Editor's note: In his message of unification to win the war, this writer introduces the important theme of class and the over-representation of low income young men fighting in Vietnam. The issue of young males from wealthier families avoiding the draft resulted in long-lasting emotional scars. For example, James Fallows's "What Did You Do in the Class War, Daddy?" published in *The Washington Monthly*, October 1975, offers an astute and personal account of the shameful treatment of working-class boys who fought in Vietnam. Fallow writes of the contempt that the college "high-brow" had for these boys. More letters relating directly to the draft system are found in chapter 2, part IV.]

20. *"top priorty"*

Chisholm, Maine
April 3, 1967

Dear Senator Smith,

I would like to tell you some of my thoughts and feelings about the war in Viet Nam. I will admit readily that I do not have all the knowledge on this subject that I would like to have. However, I really think that as long as we have American men risking and loosing their lives in Viet Nam the war should have top priorty. Tonight I heard a mother who has lost her son in the war tell of his writing for oil for his rifle. I have heard men who have returned mention shortages of other items of the same importance. I think that we are morally obligated to furnish these men with everything that they need to fight this war. If it is necessary to cut back domestic spending to do this I feel that this is in order.

Respectfully,
M. T. (female)

Complaining about lack of Supplies for the men to fight the War.

[Editor's note: Having played a critical role investigating ammunition shortages during the Korean War while on the Preparedness Subcommittee of the Armed Services Committee, Smith was sensitive to the issue of inadequate war supplies. In February 1967, as the ranking Republican on the Senate Armed Services Committee, Smith presented a seven-point indictment of the Johnson-McNamara defense record, including "reported bomb shortages and shortages of other necessary material and supplies." Smith had a long-time friendship with Lyndon Johnson and she maintained that America's national security required loyalty to the Commander-in-Chief, but she did not muzzle her criticism of the administration, particulary the "faulty judgement "of McNamara.]

21. "strange fashion"

Peaks Island, Maine
April 13, 1967

Dear Senator Smith:

As a mother of a high school boy who may soon be in uniform, I was appalled at this article. Why are American boys risking their lives to capture the enemy when we are going to give them a pat on the head, a good meal, tell them to be kind to us, and then set them free to fight against our boys again.

Must our soldiers fight the same man over and over again?????

I am looking forward to the write up on your views on Vietnam in this coming Sunday's Portland Telegram. I hope you will check into this and see why we are fighting this war in such a strange fashion.

Very truly yours,

R. S. (female)

[Editor's note: This letter is responding to a news report that many captured Viet Cong soldiers were too easily given freedom. Printed in the *Evening Express* (Portland), April 12, 1967, the article entitled "Only 4 P.C. of Captured Cong Sent to POW Camps" claimed that most captured communists were "detained, questioned and released."]

22. "not victory"

Berwick, Maine
March 7, 1967

Hon. Margaret Chase Smith

Here are a few questions, which in my opinion certainly deserve to be answered.

Why fight this war using as our chief military commodity the only thing our enemy has a superiority in—manpower?

Why does Congress allow our men to be sent into battle without a declaration of war?

Why does Secretary of State Rusk say that we will "accept help from any quarter" in Vietnam while refusing the offer of 600, 000 men from Formosa?

Why do we continue to engage in disarmament conferences and actual disarmament activity while engaged in the third largest war in our nation's history?

Why do half-way around the world to "fight Communism" while it festers unopposed only 90 miles from home?

Why do we rush to assist in sanctions against Rhodesia (bothering no one) while we do not even whisper against those who supply the Viet Cong?

Why does this administration desire increased trade with other Communist nations who supply the Hanoi regime and boast of solidarity with them?

Why do we make a big fuss over blowing up some oil depots one month, and sign agreements to trade "petroleum products" with the Eastern European suppliers of those depots the next month?

Why does the only seaport, Haiphong, which daily receives huge quantities of supplies from shipping which comes from both sides of the Iron Curtain, remain open and completely free from military action.

Why does our press, radio and TV suggest only negotiation or continuance of the present policy as alternatives, when victory appears to be the only honourable way to settle the conflict?

Why does the administration affirm that our goal is "not victory" while telling us in the State of the Union message to expect "more cost, more loss, more agony"?

I would also like to voice a very strong protest concerning the "Consular Treaty" which it appears the Senate is about ready to vote for.
Yours for God and Country,
R. B. (male)

III. RELIGION AND MORALS

In a number of letters, correspondents referred to moral issues or used Christian rhetoric to make their point. One letter boldly spoke of national leaders being reborn in Christ. Raised in a family that had Protestant and Catholic roots, Senator Smith counted herself as a Methodist. She rarely attended church, but she embraced the amalgamation of religious ideas and national identity favored by Main Street America. Three of the four authors of the letters on the issue of alcohol drinking were women. All four may have expected that they had the sympathetic ear of Smith, who did not consume alcohol.

23. "The words of Jesus Christ"

Dexter, Maine
February 1, 1967
Dear Mrs. Smith;

I do not very often write to those who represent me in Washington or Augusta. . . .

I feel that I must express myself and my opinion. I have chosen you because of your high rank on the Armed Services Committee. I know that you are not naive to be taken in by the parading, picketing, protesting ministers; to think that they represent or act for all of us in the State of Maine.

The information that I received about this conference was that they would go there to see what is being done and learn about the situation in Viet Nam and the present conflict. As soon as they arrive they begin their protests and begin making demands, which I feel they have no business to make. Evidently they did not go with an open mind to learn, but as a selected group organized to protest and persuade.

I am opposed to war. I sent some months in the service during World War II. I have two teen-age sons, and do not feel that mankind will learn in the next few years how to live together in peace; so I believe they too will have to take their turn in service of their country. I would rather be dead than red.

We have an ugly task to do in Viet Nam. I would like to see something done to allow the military leaders to carry the war to a successful conclusion as soon as possible. China is disorganized right now. Let's do all we can right now to win, and bring peace for the people of South Viet Nam and anyone in the surrounding countries who want to go there and live in peace. I do not want peace at any price as some of the demonstrating clergy are saying today.

The words of Jesus Christ have been true and fulfilled and will continue to be: "Ye shall hear of wars and rumors of wars" Matthew 24:6. If not in Viet Nam, then in some other part of the world.

Continue the good work that you are doing in Washington. I have not written in the past, because you only write to protest the actions of someone. We do not take the time today to praise or thank someone for doing what is good and right.

Sincerely,

P. M. (male)

Kind of a misquote

24. *"repentance and faith in Christ"*

Fairfield, Maine
March 10, 1967

Dear Mrs. Smith,

It seems folks seldom write to their Congressmen except to complain about what is wrong and we seem to be no exception. I think you probably agree with us on some of the subjects we mention on the following pages, but perhaps not on all of them. We probably are not sufficiently well-informed on some of these subjects to pass judgment on them, but, anyway, we have expressed our thoughts on a number of topics.

We are still most thankful for a Senator like yourself who dares to speak out and stand up for what you believe to be right.

Excuse mistakes. I don't practice typing enough and never did study it.
Sincerely,
Mr. And Mrs. R. M.

In regard to the war in Vietnam, it would seem that we should fight to win (demolish Hanoi) or get out of there. We don't need any more Korean stalemates. I suppose there is the danger of drawing Red China into the war, but if we wait till she has more nuclear weapons and the attacks us, it would be worse than getting involved with her now, would it not?

Negotiations with Russia or any Communists are useless, in our opinion. They are anti-God and have no honesty or scruples. Since when did they ever keep an agreement unless it was to their own advantage?

. . . We feel that McNamara is reducing our defenses dangerously and is ready to appease Russia and make armament reduction agreements with her. He is selling us out to Communism. Maybe this sounds drastic, but time will tell if this is true or not. It is, also a disgrace the way our military men are being "shushed" up. They should be allowed to speak their mind publicly. This war should not be run by civilians alone. By the way, the American people are losing faith in their government, a serious matter, when we see the dishonesty that is rampant in high places and we know that information is withheld from the public that they should have. We are thankful for those who are sincerely striving to do the right thing and to serve their constituents well as you are, but there are far too few of these it would seem.

. . . The Supreme Court is fast becoming a dictatorship. They should never be allowed to overrule Congress and the majority of the people. They allowed one mere woman to influence them in the Lord's prayer (or use of similar one) to be used in the schools. They did not consult Congress of the people. Now they say that Communists can teach our impressionable children and influence them, as they surely will, to be Communists or rebels. What would happen to American teachers if the situation were reversed in Russia? Now, I understand that this same lady or her ilk, who does not want God to be acknowledged in the school, want to tax the churches. By the way, I do not favor teaching religious doctrine in schools to influence children to favor a certain church, but surely the saying of grace at meals is harmless and a good thing.

Our church is a comparatively small one and many very good churches are small. Taxation would be a heavy burden for them. Any surplus church money is supposed to be used to win men to the lord. By the way, I am praying that all our national leaders, Congressmen, etc., who have not done so, will get back to the Bible and be reborn spiritually through repentance and faith in Christ. Personally I feel this is the only answer to personal, national or international peace. I have found this the way to peace in my own experience and the Bible says that this is the only way that leads to peace. History has proved that, when nations forget God and go their own way morally and spiritually, they go down to destruction and history will repeat itself if this nation does not wake up.

The return of Christ to this earth, which He has promised, will alone bring lasting peace (the millennium). According to signs given in the Bible, this return is not too far away. This country needs to get on its knees as Billy Graham is crying, like John, the Baptist, the "voice in the wilderness", saying, "Repent and believe the Gospel."

. . . Thank you so much for your patient listening to our views and keep up the good work you are doing.

Advocating that only true peace will come through Jesus

25. *"I protest, in Jesus' name"*

Eliot, Maine
March 13, 1967

Dear Mrs. Smith,

The report on the February Issue of the Maine "Civic League Record", that the army is shipping large amounts of liquor into Vietnam; also that APO privileges to missionaries, and in part to soldiers, is being cut off, is alarming and very bad, indeed. To all of which, I protest, in Jesus' name!

Knowing your principles with reference to intoxicants, I am sure that you also protest.

To me, it is unthinkable that missionaries and soldiers should be unnecessarily deprived of the privilege of receiving mail home.

Thank you very much, God bless you, in Jesus' name!

It is assuring and helpful to us to know that we have a Senator like you who is serving us in Washington.

Yours truly,
E. D. (male)

26. *"liquor can flow"*

Whitefield, Maine
March 11, 1967

Dear Senator Smith,

Many years ago . . . I had occasion to write to you several times and marveled at your speedy, friendly response.

We admire your ability and trust your integrity.

As the mother of [a soldier], serving in Vietnam in the army, I must protest the outrageous morale "drooper" caused when the letters we mothers, wives, sweethearts send our men are being "bumped" from reaching them in order that liquor can flow much too liberally, lulling our lads, but hardly inspiring them. [My son] said that although I write daily, a while back—I'd say all through February, few of these letters reached him. One day, he reported <u>36</u> bags of mail came in. Also in February a number of the boys were receiving December date-lined mail.

We also <u>understand that spiritual advisors</u> have been "bumped" in favor of <u>liquor shipments.</u> Kindly consult Civic League Record—Feb. 1967 for source of this report.

My son does not drink or smoke, nor does his stepfather, our any of our combined 13 children. We are not "odd-sticks" but fail to find any advantage in allowing any such medium to <u>control us</u>.

. . . We happen to be Conservative, Constitutional Republicans who highly admire you, Government. Reagan, yes even Barry G.—who lacked tact but whose advice, had it been taken, would have been the bud of the Vietnam nightmare.

I don't want our sons to die in vain. I can "jaw" about these things, but you, my dear, can act. Thank you.
Yours truly,
M. G. (female)

[Editor's note: In 1967, Ronald Reagan (1911–2004) was governor of California. Known for his hawkish views, Barry Goldwater (1909–1998) won the Republican nomination for president in 1964, but he was no match for Johnson in the presidential election.]

27. *"liquor of any kind"*

Skowhegan, Maine
April 1, 1967

My dear Senator Margaret,

I want to thank you for answering my letter to you, and I received the letter today from the Armed Service. The only fault is that they send over liquor of any kind, knowing what it will do to our boys when they drink. It is not only there but in our own company of young folks at home in our High School and colleges.

It is such a comfort to write to you. For we know you do not drink, if they all had a clear head as you do a good many things would be better.

Will be in my own home soon. May God bless you, give you health and strength for the work you do.

Most Sincerely,

A. B. (female)

28. *"shipments of liquor"*

Ellsworth Falls, Maine
April 19, 1967

Dear Mrs. Smith:

It has been brought to my attention that A.P.O. privileges to missionaries have been cut off in Vietnam so that shipments of liquor could be made. The report states that in some instances mail service to the fighting men has been cut off and preference given to the liquor shipments.

How terrible it is to think that the men fighting there cannot get their mail. I have just lost a nephew in Vietnam; and how heartbreaking it is to think that perhaps he did not get mail that could have brought a bit of cheer to him—just a lad of 19 and so far away from home.

Will you please see what you can do to have this mail service restored to the missionaries and servicemen? Thank you.

Very truly yours,

R. W. (female)

• 2 •

A Worried Nation

I. SMITH'S APRIL ARTICLE

$\mathcal{A}$s the ranking Republican on the Senate Armed Services Committee and a senior member of the Appropriations Defense Subcommittee, Senator Smith considered it her duty to make her voice heard on the issue of the war. She wrote a number of lengthy articles for Maine newspapers, including "Why I Worry About The War In Vietnam" (Maine Sunday *Telegram*, 16 April 1967). In this article her main points included: the initial American entry in Vietnam was questionable, but surrender was unthinkable; the Johnson administration policies of war were contradictory; and the war was emotionally dividing the nation. Critical of Robert McNamara's conflicting statements, she wrote: "I am worried about the degree of our national resolve when I see and hear the Secretary of Defense state on one hand that bombing in the north is 'designed to show them the price they pay for their continued efforts to subvert the south' but say on the other hand that he did not believe that unlimited bombing of North Vietnam 'would have affected the level of infiltration in 1966 in any significant way.'" One of her major worries was the rise of "extreme leftists" who were quick to use the label "warmonger" on those who favored a determined stand in Vietnam. The response to Smith's hawkish statements varied.

29. *"Thank you"*

Round Pond, Maine
April 16, 1967

Dear Senator Smith:—

    Thank you for your article, "Why I Worry About The War In Vietnam", in today's PORTLAND SUNDAY TELEGRAM. How long I have waited for some plain straightforward talk on this subject! While I do not agree with you in every particular I must say that I think you have done our country a great service.

There are some matters that trouble me. In the early days of our participation we were lead to believe that we were acting only in response to treaty obligations and were defending a weak people against aggression. Most of the people believed that then. Some fine, well-meaning, altruistic persons still think that is what we are fighting for. But there are others, and they are many, who have no special regard for the troubles of the South Vietnamese. To them the fight is to stop Communism. They believe in the so-called "domino theory". "If we do not stop them over there we will have to fight them over here." they say. I can not believe that. It just does not make good sense.

Communism is a very inefficient system. Both Russian and China are basically agricultural countries, yet they can not even feed themselves. Canada is shipping large amounts of wheat to China every year. We are dong the same for Russia and other Communist nations. More than that, After the Soviet Union had been in operation more than twenty-five years we had to help them out with industrial goods during the war. The system is simply not good enough to produce efficiently and take care of the needs of their people as our system takes care of ours. Why should we fear such a flabby-muscled giant? Moreover, every backward country they take over adds to their inability to provide for their people a good life. There was a time when everyone believed in ghosts and witches. Let's bury these ghosts and witches now.

If our enemy is North Vietnam, China and Communists in general, why do our men in the field, the reporters and others continually speak of the enemy as, "the VC"? Is it because there is doubt that Secretary Rusk always calls them, " the other side"? If our main opponent is the VC, are we not interfering in the internal affairs of another nation? Is it proper for us to take sides in a civil war in another country? Our Country was born as the result of an internal revolution. Are we being true to our heritage when we take on the job of putting down a revolution in another country far away from us—fighting against a group of people who never harmed us in any way? Since we have gotten ourselves into this ill-advised war we can not very well withdraw, but we can stop escallating; we can stop making this war our war: we can stop talking as if negotiations were something to be conducted between ourselves and North Vietnam alone; we can bend practically all our efforts to prevent infiltration of men and arms, leaving all other fighting to the South Vietnamese; we can make the maximum effort to prevent inflation in that unhappy country from any acts of ours; we can keep to a minimum those actions

[left margin, handwritten, vertical:] Why Communism is inefficient

[left margin, handwritten, vertical:] Questioning the right of the US to invade Vietnam

of soldiers in a strange land which always results in making the foreign army an object of hatred, we cam lean over backward to avoid destroying crops and soil and villages; we can so act that posterity can never say of us," where they make a desert, they call it peace". If we do all these things, perhaps we can feel that our honored dead shall not have died in vain.

I love my country too much to enjoy seeing it take a road which seems to me to be wrong.

Cordially yours,

F. D. (male)

P.S. I am enclosing a cartoon cut from the PORTLAND PRESS HERALD. It was quite shocking to me to see how I look to those who favor this war.

[Editor's note: The enclosed cartoon shows three middle-age male hippies with very long hair, beards, and funky clothes walking side by side in front of the White House, as a respectable-looking male with suit, hat, and glasses looks on with a worried look. One man is carrying a guitar and another a sign "LOVE NOT WAR." The cartoon caption reads, "Lord knows we've tried everything else!"]

30. "common sense middle"

Bethel, Maine
April 22, 1967

Honored Madam:

Your article carried by the Portland Sunday Telegram April 16, 1967 was a bit of clear reasoning in a world of muddled thinking.

The views you presented carry a lot of <u>common sense</u>, something rare in our national and congressional thinking.

Pardon these few lines of commendation, but I could not refrain from dropping a line of appreciation because your views expressed in the article happen to coincide with mine in so many ways.

Please keep on having that middle line. The extreme right and left did not make this nation great, but by the grace of God, the common sense middle roaders did.

As much as in you lies baring pressure to bear on the suppliers of our enemies. Interdiction of flow of supplies to North Vietnam must become a watchword.

Most respectfully yours,

W. S. (male)

P.S. Rest assured that our government and its Maine representatives are included in our prayers.

31. "a lot of sense"

South China, Maine
April 15, 1967

<u>Hastily written—</u>
<u>Nevertheless sincere</u>
U.S. Senate—Margaret Chase Smith
Attn. Mrs. Smith

Read your article with interest. Also thanks for your reply to my letter.

What you write makes a lot of sense but something worries <u>me</u>—You admit a <u>big</u> question re. whether we should be militarily committed in Vietnam. I believe its a collosal mistake on Kennedys and Johnson's part.

YOU SAY TO PULL OUT IS UNTHINKABLE. PERHAPS—<u>BUT</u> IF OUR BEING THERE <u>IS</u> <u>WRONG</u> SHOULD 200 BOYS OF OURS DIE EACH WEEK (+ THEIRS—+ CIVILIANS) BECAUSE OUR LEADERS HAVE THE GUTS TO LET PEOPLE CONTINUE DIEING BUT NOT TO ADMIT AN ERROR?

The red [marker ink] was for emphasis and not meant to symbolize blood but ironically this symbolism (which I hear so much about from my teenage girl) does seem appropriate here. Their blood for our—mistake.

Mrs. Smith—I love our country—our way of life—and I'd volunteer <u>again</u> tomorrow if <u>we were</u> <u>threatened</u> <u>but</u> I don't feel that we <u>are</u> going to accomplish a d— thing! If Ky is the image of what we're trying to perpetuate then I believe we are fools.

Pres. Mr. Johnson <u>is</u> in a <u>very</u> bad position. Perhaps Pres. Mr. Kennedy was more at fault but I say its time for an "agonizing reappraisal" and <u>IF</u> <u>WE'RE</u> <u>WRONG</u> <u>WE'D</u> <u>BETTER</u> <u>GET</u> <u>OUT</u> AND GAIN THE WORLD'S RESPECT IF WE TELL THEM TO LEAVE <u>US</u> ALONE AND IF WE STOP TRYING TO REHABILITATE THE WORLD. ISOLATIONISM? Perhaps if <u>we</u> set an <u>example</u> <u>at home</u> of <u>good</u> living they'll come to us!!!!

A.C. (male)

Keep up the fine work. Just keep in mind that <u>peace</u> <u>not</u> foreign entanglements is what the people want. Get this across before we have the whole world hunting our American Hawks.

Argoing to pull out of the Vietnam war

32. "I fully agree"

Dexter, Maine
April 16, 1967

Dear Mrs. Smith;

Have just been reading, with much pleasure, and appreciation, your fine article, "Why I Worry About The War In Vietnam", in the Portland Sunday Telegram.

I fully agree with every statement, every worry, and every prediction you have so ably expressed, and devoutly wish more of our people in high places in Gov't could and would come forward and fearlessly and confidently express to us their true views and personal concerns over the grave situation in which we are involved today.

I am just the most ordinary kind of ordinary Republican citizen, along in years, and retired, but I share your worries about the situation which you have so ably expressed, and sincerely hope more people will do the same.
R. L. (male)

33. *"I read it with interest"*

Newcastle, Maine
April 17, 1967

Dear Senator Smith:

Yesterday's Portland Press Herald printed in full your recent "Declaration of Conscience". I read it with interest and think I should tell you that I, for one, thoroughly agree with you. "We should never have gone over there except as advisors". But now we are there and probably should finish the job and not retire until our aims are accomplished. However it is tragic and how we all hope the end may come soon, and our boys come home.

Then I am sure, our President would have a real problem here, of his own makin—to find jobs for them! Seems his statistics of unemployment would be greatly increased. If this continues we will all be in financial condition where the Government will have to support us—maybe that is what he wants.
Sincerely,
C. T. (female)

34. *"I thoroughly agree"*

Cape Elizabeth, Maine
April 17, 1967

Dear Senator Smith:

I think this is the first time that I have written to a senator to express an opinion on matters pertaining to government, a fact of which I am not particularly proud.

The reason for this letter is your article in todays Portland Sunday Telegram that I have just finished reading. I am not going to say I enjoyed it as the subject matter is not such to give any one any pleasure. It is as you said something for us all to worry about and many of us do worry. I thoroughly agree with you and thank you for saying, much better than most of us could, what is on our minds.

We have just returned from five weeks in Florida where we met and talked with people from all over the country as far west as Iowa and Dakotas. If their opinions are indicative of anything it would seem that many people, like ourselves are much concerned with the "antics" of this administration, not only in Viet Nam but also at home especially their fiscal policies.

I am definitely not qualified to say what we should do in Viet Nam or if we should be there but I do think that now that we are there we should do all that is necessary to win this war and get an honorable peace settlement as quickly as possible.

I am also greatly concerned with the fiscal policies of this administration. Taxes are already a burden to most of us and getting worse every year and no end in sight. Any individual who spends beyond his income is asking for plenty of trouble and I believe the same is true of government. I fear that there will eventually be a sad day of reckoning some time in the future.

I am thankful that we have a few, too few I fear, like yourself in Washington who are more concerned with the welfare of our country than in getting votes.

Sincerely,

C. M. (male)

Criticism of general American politics and the current Administration

35. *"excellent article"*

East Millinocket, Maine
April 17, 1967

Dear Margaret Chase Smith:

I am not now or never have I been what one would call a compulsive letter writer.

In last Sunday's Portland Sunday Telegram there was printed your excellent article.

I went to bed on Saturday evening after watching several news cast very much disturbed or better said worried over what is happening to the moral and spiritual fibre of our country.

After church Sunday, I came across your article and read every word of it while my good wife was getting the Sunday dinner on the table.

I too am worried. I am worried for the very same reasons you are worried. I agree with every single word and the thoughts contained therein as your article was printed.

I agree with the right of the minority to express itself. God forbid when that right is no longer an integral part of our American way of life. This basic principle is one with which I have no argument. I do disagree with the procedure which is being employed to express it. I cry inside when I see the

American flag burned. This is something which I never thought I would ever see happen in my country. And the entire country able to witness it.

We are at war and it behooves every American to do nothing that will prolong it or add to the cost in human life. And unfortunately there are too many in the high places of our government who have upon their souls if not their conscience the blood of those who have made the supreme sacrifice.

I feel better for having read your article and you permitting me to share my thoughts with you.

Sincerely yours,

W. H. (male)

War tearing apart American unity.

36. "expression of opinion"

Topsham, Maine
April 25, 1967

Dear Senator:

Your page in a recent Portland Sunday Telegram stimulated this expression of opinion.

I have been wretched for many months. I care no more about my present or my future, sick with a conscience that cries out day and night to know what I could and should have done to prevent the awful sin of the United States.

If, as published in LOOK magazine, the Viet nam war has killed about 250,000 Vietnamese kiddies, and wounded by every horrible means another 1,000,000, aside from adult civilian casualties, how can history call this anything but calculated extermination?

I read recently a scientific prediction that in the near future, large nations will institute wars of extermination on small unwanted ones that are overpopulated. Should the present tense have been used?

Presuming the North communist by choice after the unholy French aggression, do they not, in the majority, have a sovereign right to choose their form of government?

Can they look at our history of cruelty to minorities and embrace democracy?

What or our unbridled crime, filth, official and court corruption? Are we fit to set standards for another nation?

Can Congress be excused for appropriating money for this purpose?

I know the brand history will put on this nation for the outrage.

I am concerned, and I believe 90% of Americans with my guilt.

I do not know a person who approves our foreign policy.

It is useless to write letters. Legislators will follow their conscience if they have any, or equivocate for personal gain.

It is useless to vote. Choosing the lesser of two evils gets monotonous and frustrating.

I sympathize with any suffering creature. Primarily I am concerned with the young Americans, some horribly tortured, needlessly killed, or even only deprived uselessly of their right to a normal life, for a philosophy thrust upon them.
Sincerely yours,
A. S. (male)

Critic of US foreign policy in Vietnam.

[Editor's note: Mention of the "unholy French aggression" is a reference to the 1946 return of the French to Indochina [Vietnam], seeking to resume its old-style empire that began in the 1880s, when France annexed Indochina. Defeated in 1954 by the guerrilla movement led by Ho Chi Minh, the French and their local allies had suffered almost 100,000 dead during the seven-year bloody conflict. The number of Vietnamese dead was over 300,000. Seeking to stop Ho Chi Minh and the growth of communism, the United States provided the French with more than $2.6 billion in military aid from 1950 to 1954.]

37. "'our' Senator"

Unity, Maine
April 27, 1967

Dear Senator Smith,

Your declaration of conscience in the Portland Sunday Telegram, April 16, was very welcome. I feel that the people need more evidence (even more than there is) of deep concern on the part of Congress about the war. The spectacle of Congressmen quibbling at such a time about the seating of one Congressman (I repeat: at such a time) and of Senators fussing over the expenditures of one Senator is not reassuring. By this I do not mean any criticism of you personally; I merely want to express one man's concern about our plight. We do look for leadership, and some of us look to you.

I worry about the same things that you do, but I feel that no tax burden is too great if it will help to save the lives of our young men or even the life of one of them, and that nothing that the war as it is presently being fought can do to our society can touch in importance what it is doing to our young men. I think that I speak with some objectivity as my brothers and I are all past forty and my children are both little girls.

The young men of my own generation fought in the Second World War, but we knew whom we were fighting and what for. We also felt that we had the support of the entire nation, that ending the war took precedence over everything else, and that the nation as a whole was straining toward that end. The young men today can have no such feeling.

Thus my pleas:

Please do all that is humanly possible to end the war. I know that you must be doing so without anyone's asking. I admire your integrity. I was a senior at Bowdoin in 1950 when you made your now-famous speech against Senator McCarthy's methods, and I wish I could tell you of the admiration that it elicited from all thinking students, of the pride that those of us who were from Maine felt in "our" Senator, and of the renewal of patriotism in all of us. I have always voted for you at every opportunity, including the last Presidential primary.

Please do all that you can to focus the attention of Congress upon the one task that dwarfs all others in ending the war. If Congressmen are afraid of offending voters, it seems to me that they will surely do so if they discuss anything <u>but</u> the war in Vietnam.

Please do all that you can to let our young men know that this <u>is</u> the paramount concern of Congress.

And my questions:

Is it impossible to defend South Vietnam without attacking North Vietnam?

Why have we by-passed the United Nations in this matter? Your paragraph on this subject was excellent. Can't you give us and the Administration more of the same?

Respectfully yours,

D. M. (male)

[Editor's note: Although the writer does not provide specific information, he might be referring to the Adam Clayton Powell controversy when he wrote of his frustration that Congress spent an inadequate time on the war while "quibbling" about the "seating of one Congressman." In the previous month, the House voted to exclude Representative Powell following allegations of corruption and misappropriated funds. Powell was a prominent African-American leader and this episode sheds some light on the stuggles within Congress over the issues of race, war, and social upheaval of the late 1960s.]

38. "I agree"

Skowhegan, Maine
April 30, 1967

Dear Senator Smith—

My sister has just sent me a copy of your article on Vietnam in the Portland Sunday Telegram of April 16, which asks that readers write to the paper about it, which I have done, about as follows; I agree with it in every way.

I think it is disgraceful for people safe at home in this country to protest the conduct of war when our fine young men are giving their time and their lives to carry out this far away war that no intelligent American wants to be mixed up in. The method of protest is disgraceful with protest marches, burning of draft cards, etc, when we ought to back our troops with all we've got.

I wish we could start an anti-protest movement among the right-thinking people and show our boys in the service that the great majority or we are with them.

I like your strong stand in this matter and wish I could help somehow.

I am also concerned about the National Debt, which keeps increasing. When is that going to reach the limit?

I am also concerned about corruption in Congress. How much more is going to be revealed?

I am very happily situated here at Redington and I like Skowhegan, and I believe God "holds the whole world in His hand," but I am concerned about how it is all going to turn out.

Best wishes,   *Ashamed of people protesting the war*
L. M. (female)

39. *"personal comments"*

North Windham, Maine
April 20, 1967

Dear Senator Smith:

Unfortunately I did not get to read your article on your thoughts on the Viet Nam war which I understand appeared in last Sunday's Portland Sunday Telegram. But I understand that in it you ask for personal comments from your constituents. So here are mine, written right off the "top of my head".

First off, I have the impression from some of your previous comments that you are an "owl" rather than either a "hawk" or a "dove." If so, I would say I think I would also fall in that category.

I deeply regret that we ever became involved in S.E. Asia but it is now a "fait accompli" and the burning question, of course, is how to extricate ourselves without abandoning the South Vietnamese to almost certain annihilation from the North—according to all that we read in the news media.

There is no use in bemoaning the "mess" we are in now, except it should caution us to very carefully avoid again getting ourselves into another like situation in the future. One way we might do this is to stop giving aid, especially military aid to potential aggressors—also to carefully screen what we so liberally call "foreign aid" economically. I think our foreign aid should pretty well be restricted to food to the needy and mechanical assistance to help overpopulated countries improve their methods of food production.

As far as how to meet the present war situation, strategically, I am just a layman; never have served in the armed forces in my nearly sixty years so cannot come up with any worthwhile solution. I do deplore our growing casualty lists, ours and our allies, together with the great number of civilians who are trapped in this cruel war. But I see no other recourse now but to gradually apply the pressure on North Vietnam until they decide the war is very costly to them and not worth the human sacrifice.

I am also quite concerned just how we are to operate when and if the problem reaches a conference table. Here's the place where we can lose the war and make our sacrifices all in vain. I don't think we did so well after the Korean armistice in dealing with these strange Asian people. Their philosophy is greatly different than ours—"East is East and West is West, but never shall the twain meet." I think that is quite apropos today.

I did not intend to "ramble on" to this extent, but I think I have presented a fair example of my present thoughts on this subject. . . .

Thank you for "bearing with me". If you can find time I would appreciate your comments on the above question at your convenience.

Very truly yours,

H. D. (male)

II. ANTI-WAR

For or against the war, Americans found the war increasingly worrisome. Beginning in April 1967, the ground war in South Vietnam became fiercer with the rise of major battles between the U.S. Marines and the North Vietnamese Army. The following letters to Senator Smith covering the months of April, May, and June reveal the degree of heightened emotion that the war was generating. Many of the letters were lengthy and exhibited impressive analysis of key events and leaders. The first letter makes reference to the "credibility gap" and the declining trust that many Americans had for their leaders. In one short letter, a woman does not blame the North Vietnamese for the death of her brother, a Marine killed near Da Nang, South Vietnam.

40. "disasterous path"

Christmas Cove, Maine
April 30, 1967

Dear Senator Smith:

As one of your constituents, I wish to advise you that I believe President Johnson is leading our country down a disastrous path with his Vietnam policy.

I have always voted for a Republican for President with the exception of the last election when I voted for Mr. Johnson—partially, because I agreed with his statements to the effect that he opposed sending American boys nine or ten thousand miles away from home to do what Asian boys ought to be doing for themselves.

With the waves of indignation in this country and in practically every country in this world opposing our President's position (as opposed to our country's position—in my estimation, this is President Johnson's war) I believe the Senate, which is supposed to give "advice and consent" to the President, should formally debate President Johnson's actions.

I do not believe that the Senate intended, by its vote of confidence after the Bay of Tonkin incident, that the President should be given the power to proceed as he has. Therefore, I believe the Senate must accept full blame for the President's actions unless it advises the President to the contrary.

I watched, over television, General Westmoreland's presentation before the Congress. I have read Ambassador Lodge's remarks as well as those of the President and others in his cabinet to the effect that lack of support for the President's position is tantamount to support for the enemy, the implication being that anyone who does not support the President's thinking is traitorous. I believe the President is wrong in pursuing such tactics. The United States is a democracy, and the strength in a democracy lies in the right and obligation of people to speak their minds.

There is no doubt but that General Westmoreland and his troops are loyal, fine people who are doing their duty as commanded to do so by their Commander-in-Chief.

But, I believe the basic point is being lost in a maze. The majority of people with whom I have discussed this subject believe that our mission, goal or policy in Vietnam is wrong. Of course, it is fitting for the Congress to support our troops in combat, but should they be in combat in Vietnam?

I love my country, but I am ashamed of President Johnson's Vietnam policy. Furthermore, I do not think it is our country's policy nor the Senate's policy.

With the misunderstandings and the credibility gap which exist in our country today, and growing worse every day, I believe it is high time that the Senate formally debates the Vietnam War. As it now stands, I think the President is making the Senators appear as a group of sheep. You are fine, forceful and intelligent people, and you should show the President, in formal manner, your current collective position. If you believe we have made a mistake, and I believe the majority of our people and the World so think, then advise the President that if he does not withdraw our troops you will cease to vote the money to sustain them there. If you believe we made a mistake, let us admit it. You have, I am sure, admired many fine people for having done so.

Such action builds character in a country as well as in a person. If the majority of the Senate supports the President, then I believe Congress should vote on the question of declaring war against North Vietnam.

I appreciate that you are the kind of person to whom I feel free to write my thoughts.

Sincerely yours,

J. H. (male)

Arguing policy in Viet nam is wrong.

[Editor's note: Appointed by President Kennedy, Henry Cabot Lodge, Jr., (1902–1985) was United States ambassador to South Vietnam, 1963–1964 and 1965–1967.]

41. *"disatrous course"*

Topsham, Maine
May 2, 1967

Dear Senator Smith,

I do not believe that in all good conscience you can support the recent steps toward further escalation of the Vietnam conflict, and I am writing to encourage you to join the many highly respected and deeply concerned people who are speaking out against our present disastrous course.

There is a very grave need for you to examine your own deepest convictions and have the courage to add your voice to those of such notables as Dr. Eugene Carson Blake, Senators Fulbright, McGovern, Hatfield and others.

I ask that you give this urgent matter your most prayerful, honest thought and then take appropriate action.

Yours most sincerely,

P. B. (female)

Release/christn appeals

[Editor's note: Dr. Eugene Carson Blake (1906–1985), an American Presbyterian clergyman, was general secretary of the World Council of Churches, 1966–1972. Democrat Senator George S. McGovern (1922–) was a vocal opponent of the war.]

42. *"a mistake"*

South Brooksville, Maine
May 9, 1967

My dear Senator Smith;

It is with growing concern that I see our esculation of the war in Vietnam.

I realize well your very difficult situation as Chairman of the Arms Services Committee to make wide and general appraisal of this mess we have in Vietnam. Your wisdom would somehow have to be divided within yourself. I can realize the unbelievably difficult situation that you particularly are in.

However I read that you do not believe we should be there in the first place but we are and must do the job to the best of our ability.

I think we are a nation big enough to admit a mistake and in admitting that mistake reverse our course. With each esculation of bombing or demand for manpower we make our position more difficult to change.

The cause of communism is enhansed by each esculation. The communist nations can well afford token support to this war while watching the U.S.A. weaken its economy, corrupt its own people and destroy the entire world's belief in democracy.

Or course we can esculate into the stage of nuclear war and at a recent gathering at Dow Airforce Base in Bangor I heard a speaker give the impression that we are prepared and eagerly waiting that day. If this would bring the wars end it would be because the other side would refuse retaliation. This small, pathetic country Vietnam would be completely destroyed along with the world's faith in democracy and America.

H. L. (female)   *Arguing Vietnam War will weaken Faith in America and Democracy.*

43. "not been honest"

Medway, Maine
May 9, 1967

Dear Senator Smith:

According to the article in today's <u>Bangor</u> <u>Daily</u> <u>News</u> by John M. Hightower (AP) the administration decided to resume bombing in the vicinity of Hanoi on December 13–14, 1966 while peace preliminary talks were being conducted in Warsaw. I do not think that the reasons given,—the many previous abortive offers and terror strikes in Saigon,—would justify bombing near the city at such a delicate time. I can not see how such a decision reflects a genuine desire to "keep the doors open" for negotiations. This fact and the denial by Washington officials that such a bombing would give the enemy sufficient cause to break off talks both seem to cast the US peace effort in a suspicious light, just as do the events in the following month, January 1967, in connection with Norman Cousins and the <u>Saturday</u> <u>Review's</u> revelation of a peace offer from Hanoi to Washington at that time.

I wish I were wrong in my suspicions. I want to see my country in the best light but I can not get rid of the haunting suspicion that we have not been honest with ourselves in evaluating the issue of Vietnam.

Yours sincerely,

T. M. (male)

44. "not negative military thinking"

Orrington, Maine
May 17, 1967

Dear Senator Smith:

In regards to the war in Viet Nam—I am still against the Unites States participation in this conflict.

Senator Church has written a declaration of the feeling of many of us. We dissent but it has to be understood that we stand behind our country whatever the occasion might be.

Martin Luther King is against this war or any war because his basic philosophy is against violence.

Dr. Spock is a logical dissenter. As a pediatrician he has written articles about his concern of the toy industry exploiting military toys. My seven year old son has always played with military toys. One day I told him he would be a soldier when he grew up. "But I don't want to" he said. "You will have to" I had to tell him. He does not play with those toys anymore. He wants to be a policeman when he grows up. Recently, I told him, Dr. Spock was working to stop war so little boys did not have to grow up and be soldiers and he was relieved.

There are legal ways conflicts could be solved:

1. The United Nations.
2. Actual communication with the enemy via television
3. We (the government) have pertinent knowledge concerning the enemy unavailable before in the history of the world.
4. The United States is an intelligent, humanitarian country.

In my study (limited) of our foreign relations we have not always done the right thing. I do not think we are doing the right thing now.

1. There is a negative attitude. Secretary Rusk repeats the same thing over and over. Secretary McNamara is inconsistent.
2. Ky is an admirer of Hitler. He comes from North Vietnam. He is our "puppet". If I were a citizen of Vietnam I would not trust him.
3. There is so much money being spent and no return. Each Vietnese citizen could be given $1000 and perhaps they would confirm their good intentions faster than they are now. We should have won over south Viet Nam long ago.

President Johnson is the hardest working President we have had in the United States. I admire him more all the time. He would like to solve this war but he tries politically to please the majority.

It seems to me that a panel or board with people like Senator Fulbright and Senator Mansfield and political scientists from around the United States could form some legal means to end this war.

1. Deal with Ho Chi Menh via satellite face to face.
2. Make an agreement for a base in Viet Nam as we have in Cuba.

3. Do not mention China of Russia. Blandly act as thought we had no idea they existed. This, in spite of the news this past week. Unless something is done soon, it is not going to be Viet Nam any way but a world war. These incidents of ship nudging and riots are not accidental.
4. Stress Viet Nam as a nation.
5. Make an agreement for that rare mineral we really want.
6. Make up an excuse for ending the war. The world will be glad that we have initiated such a move. We do no have to save Face or have petty Pride. We are the greatest nation today.
7. What we need is positive legal thinking not negative military think-ing.

Yours truly,
E. C. (female)

Vocal critic of the war, proposes alternative methods. Says she'll stop letter. Contra

[Editor's note: Democrat Senators Frank F. Church (1924–1984) and Michael J. Mansfield (1903–2001), clergyman and civil rights leader Dr. Martin Luther King, Jr. (1929–1968), and physician and author Dr. Benjamin M. Spock (1903–1998) were important critics of the war.]

Critics of the War

45. *"fleeced blind"*

Pittsfield, Maine
May 17, 1967

Dear Mrs. Smith;

This letter will in all probability never reach you personally; however my thoughts and feelings are so effected that I simple must express them to someone, be it only one of your secretary.

During this evening's news broadcast of C.B.S. News by Walter Cronkite I witnessed a film taken of three of our pilots that were shot down and held captives of the North Vietnamies. It caused me to hang my head in shame as it rightfully should any responsible Gov't official. I have a few questions in my mind that I simply can not find an answer for. Just why is it that we the people of these United States allow our elected gov't official to become so entangled in far off foreign countries? Just who do we think we are, the protector of the world? All reports are that we are being fleeced blind by these very people that our gov't officials have for some reason chose our finest sons to fight and die for.

I spent five of the critical years of my life in the services of these United States during W.W. II. Eighteen months overseas and for what may I ask? If I learned one thing during it all was that we were being used by the English, French and of all people the Russians. We are trying to by friends in this world which we can never hope to do. We are a big joke. Why these countries need us only so long as we'll pay the bills and spill our blood for them.

Now, twenty two years latter, I find myself struggling to pay bills, raise and educate [my children]; and what is in store for them may I ask? The future is very black yes indeed, as long as our gov't officials continue to get us involved in foreign entanglements. Now that we are involved they don't know what to do about it, thats the sad part. I can only come up with this conclusion we the people have been sold down the river, and by who may I ask? The rich get richer and the poor get poorer and all the time these gov't officials tell us we are so rich, so powerful a nation. How many billion are we in debt? How are our gold reserves at the present time? How many years will it be before we will need a wheelbarrow to carry the dollars in to buy the weekly supply of groceries. Just who are these gov't official kidding. As for power, if you by chance saw the film that I mentioned of these poor fellows you will I am sure realize how powerless we are.

Just who are these gov't officials who can demand so much from the people they are elected to serve. Yes as a country we are being fleeced and as a people we are being fleeced by our gov't. This is the only possible conclusion I can reach.

Very truly yours,   *Advocating for a US isolationist foreign policy*

R. M. (male)

[Editor's note: Respected by many Americans, Walter L. Cronkite (1916–) was the anchor and editor of the "CBS Evening News."]

46. *"insane war"*

Machias, Maine
May 18, 1967

My Dear Senator Smith:

Tonight, on television I saw three of our American boys who had been and were being tortured by the Viet Cong. In your position, you know of hundreds of similar atrocities.

Will you please try in every way possible to make it known to your colleagues that the American people have taken just about all they can.

I agree with you that our soldiers should not have been there in the first place.

World opinion is almost all against us; we have no sympathizers or allies. Anarchy is prevalent throughout the nation.

The first order of business is to end the war in Vietnam as quickly as possible—honorably or dishonorably. You and your colleagues have infinitely more knowledge about the situation than the ordinary citizen. You have only two choices, and only those in positions such as yours can know which is the better of the two. Begin withdrawal as soon as possible, in the best way possible. By the best way, I mean the way that will mean the least suffering and death for our men. I would not sacrifice even one man for world opinion. The other alternative is to unleash the most swift and mighty means at our command to end this war militarily. Any other way means more death and horrible torture for our men. The time has come to think of our men—not of world opinion. If swift and mighty military action is the answer, every hour that we wait our enemies are growing stronger and better prepared to fight us.

It is the most insane war in history; we are supplying Russia and other nations with money and materials which they are turning over to our enemy; and our leaders are afraid of offending them! Where are our guts? The fighting men have them, but not those calling the shots!

It is common talk—I hear it everywhere—That President Johnson will see to it that the war stops in time to make him look like a hero in time for the next election. Must our greatest treasure—the life blood of our youth be used for promoting a political party?

I am a heartsick, tired, angry American; and there are thousands of us. There will be anarchy worse than our political leaders realize if this war doesn't come to an end soon. President Johnson and the Democratic Party cannot afford to wait to play the part of heroes at the next election. They need to act now to end this war.

Up to the point where no American boy had given his life, most of us went along with it, but when we come to the point where we find that more than 8,000 men have given their lives and accomplished little or nothing it is time to call a halt.

Respectfully yours,

D. L. (female)

E. L. (male)

Advocating withdrawl from the war and seems only concerned with American interest

47. *"American cease-fire"*

Limestone, Maine
May 19, 1967

My Dear Mrs. Smith:

Recently I read that sixteen American Senators who have questioned President Johnson's policies in South Viet Nam have stated that they are opposed to any unilateral withdrawal of American troops from that country in the absence of a mutually acceptable settlement. Since I feel that it must be made clear to Hanoi that the United States has no intention of leaving those South Vietnamese who have supported our efforts there to be slaughtered by the Communists, I approve of this statement. At the same time, however, I think it may be necessary to somehow convince the leaders in Hanoi that such a settlement would to dome degree be acceptable to them.

It has been my fear for some time that President Johnson is not serious about negotiation and that what he means by an "honorable settlement" is the complete surrender of the Communists to the independent South Vietnamese government that is to go into operation this fall. I have no doubt that such a government would best serve the people in South Viet Nam. However, I feel that we in the United States have neither the right nor the power to expect the settlement of the war to be in exact accord with our wishes. That we have not the right is a matter of opinion. That we have not the power can be shown by analogy with the Korean war.

At the time when this conflict was settled there was evidence that the United Nations' forces could and would recapture all of North Korea in spite of the Chinese intervention. This fact provided the bargaining power which gained South Korea an independent democratic government. It seems clear that we can gain no such bargaining power in Viet Nam without invading North Viet Nam and perhaps involving ourselves in another confrontation with Chinese troops. I think everyone is agreed that such a confrontation would be undesirable. It is thus apparent that we must make some compromise with the Communists in order to end the war.

I would like to think that the United States has made every effort to negotiate a settlement in Viet Nam, and that Hanoi was totally responsible for the failure of the talks which had been planned early this year. Unfortunately the information about these negotiations is so obscure that I can find no conclusive evidence that this is the case. Since I can not convince myself that my government is willing to make concessions to gain peace in Viet Nam, it is small wonder that Hanoi is not convinced.

It is thus my opinion that increased efforts toward easing tensions and not increased military action would be most effective in ending the war, and I wish to express support for the suggestion of Senator Joseph S. Clark that President Johnson order an indefinite American cease-fire in Viet Nam to begin after the one day truce this month.

Very truly yours,

J. B. (female)

[Editor's note: Senator Joseph S. Clark (1924–1984) was a Democrat from Pennsylvannia.]

48. "stop this murder"

York, Maine
May 21, 1967

Sen. Smith,

I would like you to know why the mailing date and the petition date are
not the same. [Recently], my brother . . . was killed in the vicinity of Da Nang,
South Vietnam. He was a Marine. . . .

I am asking you to read this petition and help to stop this murder—
please stand up for peace. It's to late for [my brother], but there are many,
many men yet to save.

I hold no bitterness against the N. Vietnamese, we are invaders in their
land, the American people are to blame for giving their verbal and silent approval for this war.

Sincerely,

H. P. (female)

[handwritten: Brother died, advocating for peace in Vietnam]

49. "stop this sacrificing"

Anson, Maine
May 29, 1967

My dear Margaret Chase Smith,

As our Senator, I hope you will use your influence to stop our sacrificing
of young Americans in Viet Nam.

I am not a mother and I have no relatives in the service, but for a long
time I have been bitter about sending our boys into such a foreign place to be
wounded or to die for a cause that means so little actually to our way of life.
I know Communism is a great threat; also that small countries will be over-
run, but are we going to "protect" every small nation against this threat, using
our soldiers when all other big nations are saying "We can't send men nor
money"? Are we the protectors of the whole world? I think we could better
use our money—& soldiers if we have to—toward making our own nation
once again a right-living Christian nation as it was intended to be by those
intelligent and Christian patriots of the early years.

I dare to write this letter after reading the enclosed article by Paul
Harvery; not only are the words I heartily approve of his, but the people in
high places he speaks of reflect my feelings exactly. And I realize that even a
simple and unknowing (?) woman like me is not the only one who would like
to save lives instead of "saving face".

Please consider all the words in the article, explore the wisdom, and use
your influence to bring American boys back to American homes, and Amer-

[handwritten in left margin: Communism]

ican dollars back to help clean up our own closets & cast out the mote in our own eye!

On a personal note:

Spring is slowly coming to Maine, and tho' we growl about the cold and the rainy days we look out & see the young leaves opening and big fat birds on the lilac trees. And we <u>know</u> Spring is here!

Sincerely,

O. T. (female)

Doesn't believe we should be fighting a war that doesn't benefit our best interests

[Editor's note: In his article "Not Every Viet War Opponent Is A Nut," Paul Harvey presents strong reasons for the United States to retreat from Vietnam.]

50. "I think it is terrible!"

Grand Lake Stream, Maine
June 27, 1967

Dear Senator Smith:

I would like to take this opportunity to inform you of my views concerning the current crisis in VietNam. I think it is terrible! American boys fighting over there for a cause that is a perversion of every American ideal in the history of this country. It is a mockery of ourselves and our fathers!

However, I do recognize some of the difficulties. As such, I cannot call for an immediate pullout. However, I would strongly advocate an immediate halt to the bombings of the North, and restriction of military activity to defensive positions in areas already held by this country.

The United States is wasting itself and its sons in a war for a country of little significance and less value. Let the people of VietNam run their own lives and let us run ours!

Sincerely yours,

P. F. (male)

51. "discontinue bombing"

Weld, Maine
June 30, 1967

My dear Senator Smith:

I am a resident of Maine. I am also a veteran of World War One (the war to end wars).

I take the liberty of writing this letter to you, to join, what I imagine is a large group of citizens who believe they have the solution of most of the worlds problems.

The following suggestion is in connection with the perennial dilemma in Vietnam which is responsible, as we all know, for the continued and increasing loss of prestige of our Government at home and abroad.

No matter what event in the world occurs, it sooner or later associates itself, detrimentally to us, with our present policy in Vietnam especially our bombing of the North which is, aside from any moral considerations and the fact that we are fighting ethically an undeclared war, costly in the loss of the lives of the cream of American manhood, not to mention the loss of our planes, 589 at last report, with its consequent cost of millions upon millions of dollasr in equipment.

All of this in spite of the studied and professional opinion of our military people that our efforts have not been and will not be effective in furthering the possibility of peace.

Mr. Salisbury of the New York Times after his recent visit to Hanoi, along with others, are of the firm belief that our bombing only brings about a determination and solidarity on the part of the North Vietnamese to resist our futile efforts in forcing them to the peace table.

At just about the time that there appeared some possibility of a détente between Russia and the United States, our policy in Vietnam raises its ugly head and precludes a better relationship between the two great powers, which is imperative if world peace is ever to be accomplished. Even the situation in the near East brings us in disrepute in the world, because of our Vietnam policy.

Briefly, my humble proposal is to immediately discontinue bombing of North Vietnam because of its futility, unfavorable home and world reaction and asininity.

As our military know, or should know, where the enemy from North Vietnam gains access to the South, plug the points of entry regardless of a possible increase in our forces and equipment.

It would appear obvious that should the bombing be discontinued, the immediate reaction at home and abroad would be a lack of an irritant of our policy. The demonstrations could then, should they continue, be directed against Ho Chi Min and Hanoi, for peace. In other words, we would eliminate the ammunition now being used against the United States by many of its citizens and that of the other countries throughout the world.

It would seem that this proposed course is worthy of thoughtful and serious consideration.

Yours for Peace,
Sincerely,
H. Z. (male)
Copy to Senator Edmund S. Muskie

52. "the dumest person"

Gardiner, Maine
June 17, 1967

Dear Madam,

The only way the people has to express their feelings is to write to there Senator and as you are one of the arm forces I would like to tell you how I feel. If you would send to Iseral and get the dumest person they got, he would be a lot better than the ones that is running our war, we are preaching peace and we have 73 000 killed or injured, our boys is searching the enemy and when they find them they are shot down like nine Pins, we will make a good target for the Communist when we loose our soldiers and material our leaders cant control the U.S.A. how can they in Vietnam
Sincerly,
J. C. (male)

III. WAR STRATEGY

Senator Smith continued to receive letters from ordinary Americans stating their opinions on how best to gain victory over communist aggression in Vietnam. Suggestions included more bombing, redoubling military effort, and bringing in Chinese troops from Taiwan. One correspondent demonstrated his disgust over the reports of defective rifles. All in all, Cold War ideology remained strong in a number of small-town households throughout Maine.

53. "continue to bomb"

Guilford, Maine
April 17, 1967

Dear Senator:

This is to inform you that it is my honest opinion that we should continue to bomb north Viet Nam. I have made it a point to ask a great many people in this area and especially some young men of the draft age and so far have not found one person who does not feel the same about it as I do.

I believe if we were to stop bombing them we would lose a great many more American lives.

I also believe MantinLuther King is interesting in helping Communism rather than the Negroes.

I am trying to get more people to write in and say what they think about this but find it is hard to get them to write although they agree that it would be a good idea.

Without doubt the ones against the bombing are being trained to write to their Congressmen especially out in some of the other states where the civil rights marches are.

I believe our President and Secretary of State and our Congress, also our Military men are strong enough to stand firm regardless of the demonstrations.

Best wishes,
R. L. (male)

Advocating the continuing of bombing to protect American lives,

54. "pursue the war"

April 19, 1967
Gardiner, Maine

Dear Senator Smith:

Christianity/ Religion

Recently a group of clergyman from Maine were in Washington supposedly on a fact-finding mission but what actually appears to have been a protest against our country's struggle against further Communistic take-overs and, specifically, our gallant and altruistic stand against Communistic aggression in South Vietnam.

One of those clergymen was an American Baptist and a member of our State Convention's Social Concern Committee. . . . I am afraid he may have given some misleading impressions about the American Baptists in Maine.

To clear the issue personally, I wish to state that I am whole-heartedly behind our government's policy to resist further Communistic take-overs and I do support our government's commitments in South Vietnam. I feel that we must pursue the war there with a will and a determination to inflict upon the Communists a sound military defeat. I am sure this is the only kind of language they are likely to understand.

I am concerned over so much talk of trying to find some halfway peace settlement. I am afraid we are giving the false impression that we are not committed to our way of life and have no will to finish what we have started in South Vietnam. Also, I am concerned about the various periods of cease-fires. They appear to be nothing but Communist tricks to gain opportunities to repair damages and build-up troops and supplies. . . .

I am concerned, as I know you are, about the image a few churchmen are creating of the whole church and the embarrassment it must cause you and the other legislators at times. I want you to know that, I, for one, stand solidly behind all, like yourself, who are dedicated to the American way of life and who are dedicated to the stopping of further Communistic take-overs and enslavement of peoples.

Please don't take time from your busy schedule to answer this letter unless there is some service I might be able to render.
Your very sincerely,
W.D. (male)

55. "We talk and talk."

Norway, Maine
April 28, 1967

Dear Senator Smith,

In the May issue of Reader's Digest you should read, "Let's Fight to Win in Vietnam." Also the commentary by Fulton Lewis 3d last week (Apr. 17–22) and this week (Apr. 24–28) should interest you. Particularly the last letter received by the family of a Vietnam casualty. Have we waited too long? Korygin has promised Hanoi he will see we don't win. We have a "Jeanne Dixon" in Maine. In her lectures she states she has twice seen our defeat. As for a treaty—February 2, 1919 Zinoviev stated "We are willing to sign unfavorable peace with Allies—we should put no trust whatever in the bit of paper we sign. We would use the breathing space so obtained to gather our strength" This has been proven.

This Congress is as weak as the Executives. No law to prevent the loss of our gold, no law to prevent the President sending troops to Rhodesia (how about their freedom) or other countries. This country is on the verge of anarchy and no law to stop riots started by the communists. Only talk of free speech and actions.

Lenin wrote: "the United States will be the hardest to take over, but it can be done by infiltration encouraging immorality, and stirring up the Negroes." They accomplish their objectives. We talk and talk.
Sincerely,
J. P. (female)

[Editor's note: Grigory Zinoviev (1883–1936) was a leading Bolshevik and Vladimir Ilyich Lenin (1870–1924) was the first premier of the Soviet Union.]

56. "playing to win?"

Gardiner, Maine
April 20, 1967

Dear Senator,

As I recall, as a girl you . . . used to play basket ball in that red wooden building (Armory) I think with the intention of winning correct?

In Vietnam are we playing to win? When areas with migs—anti aircraft
guns missiles etc are off limit as was the Yulu River in Korea, are we playing to
win, or do we give the enemy the signals while we have to play their game.

When MacNamara says "we will lose less lives this way. Even one life lost
is to many if only we are trying to prolong and keep the U.S. economy going. Do
we say, if in a year we lose 500 pilots rather than 1000 we are better off. Would
it not be better to take the risks stop shaking in our shoes—stop worrying about
our image. As Winston Churchill said? "Let us get on with the business at hand"

[We] have numerous boys we know well, all enlisted in the service, some
are there and some who will later. If they must die, let it be while playing the
game to win, not to draw a temporary truce line like in Korea.

As you know I was to young for War I to old for W2 yet I tried to do all I
could. Was in US.C.G.R.T. as training officer—did recruiting and gave hours of
time. I believe in our Country—our flag—and don't understand—Pinks—egg
heads—crackpots etc.

[We] just had to sound off. Any thing I have had to do I tried my best to
win, (not always) but gave it all I had. Our country should do no less.
Sincerely,
one who you and Clyde attended our wedding. . . .
G. D. (male)

[Editor's note: While in high school, Senator Smith played and won many high
school basketball games. In her senior year, she was the captain of the team that
won the state championship.]

57. "should try to win"

Wells, Maine
June 2, 1967

Dear Senator:

First of all I want to express my thanks to you for your fine record in the
Senate and your faithfulness to Maine.

We are getting more and more concerned over the war in Viet Naam
which it seems we have no intent to win.

This question baffles us—Why is Chiang Kaishek and his well trained army being tied up in Formosa by American restriction? It seems if he was allowed to go into China Mainland it would tie down some of the Red Chinese to fight at home. At least, what help they are sending the Viet Cong would be somewhat halted. It seems as though we should try to <u>win</u> this war.

The enclosed came to my attention recently.

I know your time is limited and you may not be able to answer this letter.

Anyway we of Maine love you and pray that wisdom will be given you in every decision.

Sincerely,

L. G. (female)

58. *"stop the Communists"*

Rumford, Maine
May 4, 1967

Dear Senator Smith:

Just recently I attended a funeral of one who was killed in Viet Nam; and I am greatly concerned that this war drags on and on. I sincerely feel that we are in the right in trying to stop the communists there as I do feel that if we do not stop them there eventually they will be over here. Therefore I feel that we should use every means at our command to bring this war to a successful and speedy conclusion. I trust that you will continue to use your influence toward this end.

I also feel that to sell or make trades with the Communists countries is only helping them to kill our boys. As I remember it one of them said only a few years ago that when they were ready we would sell them the rope to hang us with and I fear that is exactly what is going on with the treaty agreements that some of our leaders are trying to put through.

I know you are a very busy lady and therefore have not written before but after thinking this through I wanted to let you know that I am with you on the effort to stop the Communists from any further territorial gains around the world.

Very sincerely your fellow American

N. F. (male)

59. *"weapons that really work"*

Skowhegan, Maine
May 23, 1967

Dear Senator Smith:

I was shocked, saddened and disgusted at the news of those unfortunate soldiers who died trying to defend themselves with worthless jammed rifles.

God, it's bad enough to have to go to war with its horrors, mud, dirt, and danger. But to face death and be cut down by an enemy, and nothing but a bayonet and bare hands to defend yourself, must have been horrible.

Before our boys are sent into battle the weapons they are going to be forced to use should be tested under battle conditions such as mud, water, prolonged use etc. Better they should have older, reliable, perhaps not so fancy, weapons that really work.

I have a son serving in the war zone now and I am thankful he is on a guided missile destroyer rather than fighting in the jungle with a useless rifle to defend himself with.

If it were my son who was one of these boys, I would feel like getting someone by the throat who had a hand in causing him to be handicapped.

Did someone make a handsome profit deal at the expense of our soldiers blood?

Someone should have to answer for this, and it shouldn't take a year of hearings to get the facts.

Sincerely,   *Speaking in favour of better equipment for*
R. M. (male)   *US soldiers.*

P.S. Nothing can be done for the dead ones, but maybe something can be done to protect those still in danger from this condition.

IV. THE DRAFT

The contentious issue of selecting the necessary number of men for Vietnam duty had its roots in President Johnson's decision, in 1965, to use the draft rather than the reserves. The larger Selective Service System apparatus of civil service clerks and local draft boards had a number of loopholes that engendered class and race favoritism. Smith argued that it was a tragedy that "too many draft dodgers and too many high-salaried professional athletes" used the Reserve and the National Guard as a haven to avoid the draft. Although she questioned deferment preference for college students, she explained to her constituents that "deferment does not mean that they will not ultimately be caught by the draft." In the following section, letters suggest that many small-town working-class people were upset with the draft system that gave college students preferential treatment. The last letter in this chapter refers to the acts of antiwar protesters burning the flag and draft cards.

60. "universal military training"

Carmel, Maine
February 28, 1967

Dear Senator Smith,

I think it is time for the American people to give more than token support to our fighting men in Vietnam.

Our liberal minded politicians are horrified at the suggestion that we escalate the bombing of North Vietnam to more meaningful targets, so lets not kill anyone.

We could take three or four obsolete battleships out of mothballs, strip them of all materials useful to the enemy, load them with explosives at points that will sink them, man them with a skeleton crew of volunteers, run them aground in the main channel of Haiphong harbor, evacuate the crew and blow holes in them by electronics so that they sink, blocking the harbor. Once the channel to Haiphong is blocked, we could keep it blocked by strafing and bombing any attempts to raise or dredge around them. Lets not be too alarmed at world opinion of our trapping ships in and blocking others out who are supplying a country with which we are at war. Once the main harbors are useless for supplying North Vietnam, then the type of bombing we are doing <u>may</u> have some real effect.

While I am about it, I would like to state that I am opposed to lowering the voting age. We also should have universal military training without deferments except for mental or physical defects. Not only is the present system unfair to young people not going to college, but all of our youth would benefit by the experience and a small percentage of our young citizens could certainly benefit by being introduced to a little discipline. It would also be cheaper to train them in the military service than the Job Corps at $54,000. per graduate.

Sincerely,
R. S. (male)

61. "draft laws are unfair"

York Beach, Maine
May 4, 1967

Dear Mrs. Smith:

I saw in TV the other day the speech by General Westmoreland I can only say thank the Lord we have a man like him over there.

I have a nineteen year old son who was 19 last October he was drafted . . . and now he is on his way to Viet Nam.

I believe the draft laws are not fair at the present time. The boy who lived next to us is same age as my son he passed his physical also but is still at home. Could it be because his father is [a politician] and my husband is a [blue collar worker]? I do not know but I have my own ideas.

Also when my son was home on leave last month. He went to see his girl in N.H. and on his way home about 1 AM in the morning the policeman stopped him in York Village for a routine checkup, my son was doing no wrong. He said go home and get your orders (army) I'll give you 30 minutes. My son did this and still he did not believe it. He called some place on the phone than he said O.K. I thought maybe you were AWOL. This is a nice way to use a boy who is now in Viet Nam. When he comes back I recall personally show this officer his orders to prove he is home on leave and not AWOL. If he stopped him for something, disobeying the law but when you are doing nothing wrong and use you this way it just made me real angry. This was a policeman at York Village not here at the Beach. I could not ask for better policeman than we have here at the beach.

Thanks again for listening to me.

Sincerely yours,
R. L. (female)   *Unfair drafting and corrupt police*

62. "I do not consider the draft fair"

Temple, Maine
May 15, 1967

Dear Senator Smith.

There are a few questions I seek to have explained to me in regard to the Vietnam war. First why aren't there more allies helping out with the war? Second why is the draft taking all the youths of our Country? Why not send some older men to help the youth? I do not consider the draft fair to defer College boys. There are many boys fighting in Vietnam today who proudly would have gone to College had they been financially able. Seems to me its not going to boost the moral of the youth fighting in the jungles of Asia to feel they were considered the retards of the Country. The servicemen who carry the brunt of the battle deserve our support. I feel our leaders choose the wrong place to draw the line!! and we face the prospect of seeing our youth pour into a bottomless quagmire. With very little hope of success.

Yours truly,
F. B. (female)

College students exempt from service.

63. *"Cassius Clay can avoid the draft"*

Wiscasset, Maine
Nov. 3, 1967

Dear Senator Smith:

It is useless for one citizen to write to any member of Congress protesting the policy of the present administration, yet I write. Sorry this cannot be a pleasant communication, but I am filled with disrespect, distrust, and anger at all three branches of our federal government. I think John Kenneth Galbraith, former ambassador to India in the Kennedy administration was correct when he said "We are fighting in Vietnam to save the reputation of those men who made an investment in error."

1. When campaigning in 1964 President Johnson said, "We are not going to send American boys 9,000 or 10,000 miles away to do what Asian boys ought to be doing for themselves."

2. The members of Congress evaded their responsibility when in August 1964 they passed with only two votes opposed, the Southeast Asia Resolution as a result of the attack in the Gulf of Tonkin. Therefore without Congress declaring war according to the Constitution of the United States, the Vietnam war IS UNCONSTITUTIONAL. The Congress though evading the declaration of war, did not hesitate to pass the draft law, which for this war is wrong. (Robbing the cradle too!) To force our young men to fight Asia is morally wrong. My understanding and sympathy are completely with the "Conscientious Objectors". Where is liberty and freedom? We are experiencing the wickedness and tyranny of power by a few Americans who are in a position to wield it.

3. Our Supreme Court (also some of the lower courts) with their rulings relative to Communists in the U.S. (the Communist party protected), and also the police situation, are certainly not helping to reduce the menace of Communistic and criminal activity in our country.

A large and powerful nation such as ours, has no moral right to invade a tiny, uneducated, peasant type country to kill its people, destroy its property, nor to impose a form of government upon it, even tho that form of government may be desirable.

To date the Johnson administration is responsible for the killing of more than 13,000 Americans, the wounding of over 88,000 (almost a thousand missing), placing a tremendous debt upon the American people, and causing nationwide dissension, and disunity. Also the slaughter of many innocent Asian people.

I deplore the widespread horrible violence so prevalent in our country. I believe in responsible patriotism. My family relatives have always done their part in loyalty and duty to our nation—in both World War I and II—in France and In the Pacific (one killed). However I cannot and do not feel that this Vietnamese war is justified. I thank God every day that I have no sons to be forced into it. I consider that the war is morally wrong, that any and every young man who is a conscientious objector should have the right to refuse conscription, that his individual freedom to dissent should be respected, that he should be treated justly—not put in jail. Cassius Clay can avoid the draft—his money and his lawyers accomplish that. But the missionary's son or the poor young man goes to jail.

It would be interesting to know how many, or how few, sons of grand-sons of our Congressmen have been drafted as ordinary soldiers and sent to Vietnam.

If called up for induction what "rights" does a young man, who is a conscientious objector, have, if he is not a member of a pacifist religious organization?

I am very much interested in the matter, because I feel that the tyranny in a democracy can be just as evil as tyranny of a dictatorship.

Sincerely,

M. C. (female)

[Editor's note: Born Cassius Clay, Jr. (1942–), heavyweight boxing champion Muhammad Ali refused induction into the army on religious grounds (Nation of Islam). Clay's popularity in Maine (he had defeated Sonny Liston in a 1965 title match in Lewiston) plummeted and Governor John Reed stated that he "be held in utter contempt by every patriotic American."]

64. "burning his draft card"

Scarboro, Maine
April 24 1967

Dear Senator Smith,

Today I listened to Gen. Westmoreland say that people who are unpatriotic are truly hurting this Country of ours.

This afternoon the mailman brought my latest issue of U.S. News & World Report. In this I found on page 12 a picture of the United States flag being burned by some people looking like tramps you'd find along the railroad tracks.

At the top of the page is a picture of Gen. Hersey being burned in effigy.

My question is simply this: Are my relatives and friends being sent to Vietnam to make this country safe for the likes of these.

I feel anyone burning his draft card or the flag should lose citizenship. They do not intend to live a democratic way of life. Often the Japanese nationals were more loyal than these people are.
Sincerely Yours,
A. H. (male)

[Editor's note: General Lewis B. Hershey (1893–1977) was the director of the Selective Service System.]

• 3 •

Rising Opposition

I. FOREIGN POLICY AND OPPOSITION

𝒯he last half of 1967 witnessed an increase in opposition and antiwar demonstrations throughout the United States. All forms of media coverage of the war were more skeptical and critical. In graphic and disturbing detail, television brought the ugliness of the war into the living rooms of Main Street America. Unlike any other period in the Johnson years, antiwar views dominated the letters sent to Senator Smith during these months. Some wrote of the illegality of weapons and war, others demanded immediate retreat or presented passionate statements on a variety of issues. One female writer expressed her distress that Smith's assessment of antiwar demonstrations held in Washington unfairly focused too much attention on "less desirable elements" rather than the "brave young people" who believed the war was morally wrong. Another writer quoted from the Bible to highlight the failings of politicians.

65. *"considerable anguish"*

Medway, Maine
July 1, 1967

Dear Senator Smith:

Thank you for your letter of June 28. It was only considerable anguish that I signed the statement I sent to you and I certainly do not take it lightly. I have been trying to examine the Vietnamese situation for two or three years and I can not claim that my opinion is based on solid fact. However, I have been aware of one basic condition in my mind—persistent doubt, doubt which could not be allayed by any argument in favor of the United States' commitment. I do not think that I was inalterably prejudiced. Every single argument I have ever heard in favor of our military commitment has been less informed than almost any argument I have heard advanced against. This, in itself, is no proof; it is merely an indication.

Another "indication" is the way in which the opposition to our military commitment has invariably been cast in an oversimplified light by the administration. Henry Steele Commager hardly fits into the convenient category of "peacenik", or of dubious patriot.

Yet another indication is the fact that the administration has never, to my mind, even admitted the weak points of the legal argument for our intervention. Even if the administration is correct in seeing a positive commitment in the SEATO agreement, it should have the honesty to admit the presence of the counter argument—intervention in the internal affairs of a single country as delineated by the 1954 Geneva Agreement. In reading what I have on the subject, I never found the Secretary of State even admitting that such a position could honestly, if erroneously, be held. And this one sidedness casts another bit of mounting suspicion onto the administration's side.

Also there is the fact that the matter of a declaration of war has been notable for the silence which surrounds it. The Constitution is quite plain about the legality of a war in this respect. I have almost never seen this aspect mentioned by the administration spokesmen. Some might say it is a technicality. But this technicality seemed important to the authors of the Constitution.

Then, of course, there is the very difficult question of the matter of how many killed are civilians, how many non-civilians, and last, but not least, how many actually Communists. Figures are impossible to find here. But you know as well as I that in the absence of positive information, there is a great danger of undifferentiated violence which actually serves very little rational cause—on either side of course.

The use of anti-personnel bombs such as the so-called pineapple does not tally with traditional concepts of legal war. I'll omit napalm because it is such an emotional issue. But the pineapple is truly an anti-personnel weapon, a weapon which is more likely, within the conditions of war existing in Vietnam, to kill more civilians than terrorists or military. Even the use of a single illegal weapon, I believe, is enough to cast grave doubt on the cause.

Then too, there is the matter of the absence of trying every means possible to negotiate before hostilities. One of the pernicious things about "escalation" is that it permits one to ease into a war without facing the responsibility of making every effort to avoid the use of force beforehand. It is surely this that makes the declaration of war such an important legal consideration. A declaration of war is very serious. Before a democracy commits itself, it is likely to want to make every effort—as it right—to avoid war. But, where there is no need for a declaration—the task of trying every avenue first is sidestepped and the result is that the justice of the cause is so hopelessly confused that we have a situation such as the present one where the "spirit of confusion" afflicts our people. Most people just don't want to think about it.

Furthermore, if we are there to help the people of South Vietnam, I think that we should have made provision for immigration to this country for those who so desired. I am sorry that the administration has seen fit to allow virtually no Vietnamese into this country.

If a doubt persists, it may not be merely temperament. I know that in my personal life there have been periods of persistent doubt about a course I was following. Eventually the day came when I stopped pretending that it was just a "mood" and tried to find out what it meant. And invariably it was because there was something wrong in what I was doing, something I did not realize very well but which, once recognized and acted upon, made life much better, even if it meant a sacrifice.

Yours sincerely,

T. M. (male)

[Editor's note: Historian Henry Steele Commager (1902–1998) taught at Columbia University and spoke out against the war.]

66. *"immediate withdrawal"*

Emery Mills, Maine
July 19, 1967

Dear Senator Smith:

I would like to write to you about the foreign policy of this country, but I fear that I shall have difficulty making myself understood in a brief letter. Although I have not seen a copy of the Republican White Paper on Vietnam, I have read a bit about its contents. How can I get a copy of it? Could you send one to me?

As for my own views, I begin with a simple proposition: our policies are slowly in some places and rapidly in other places (especially Vietnam, but also in our own country) doing great harm. At least since 1917, and especially since 1945, we have sought through various means to prevent other peoples from having true revolutions. In the period since World War II this attempt has become increasingly futile, brutal, and disastrous. Our war in Greece turned out to be a mere foretaste of what was to come in Vietnam, and Greece itself seems headed for new disasters.

I have no desire to sit on other peoples' backs, and yet throughout the world I seem to be doing just that. As long as American troops are stationed abroad, it's going to look as if I am the one who's perched up there where I don't belong. As long as we continue to fight wars such as the present one against the Vietnamese, we are going to continue to destroy ourselves and many other people as well, and we are going to continue to risk a nuclear war.

If this country is to begin to get on a better path, the best beginning of it would be the immediate withdrawal of all of our military forces from Vietnam, Thailand, and elsewhere in Southeast Asia.

Sincerely yours,

W. S. (male)

67. *"Vietnam fiasco"*

Kennebunkport, Maine
August 8, 1967

Dear Senator Smith:

It seems to me about time that we profit from the experience of Great Britain, and withdraw from our self-appointed role as guardians of the world. Specifically, I believe we should withdraw from the Vietnam fiasco and strengthen our defenses at home so that no one will dare to step on our toes.

We should cease pouring billions down the drain in Vietnam and spend more for our own people. The meager increase of 2 ? % in Social Security is not enough. Neither should the younger generation be penalized by higher withholding taxes to pay for it. If we can raise billions for Vietnam, we can raise money for our older people in the same way. . . .

It is said in many places that the reason our troops were first sent to Vietnam was the pressure put upon Pres. Kennedy by Cardinal Spellman after the French withdrew, leaving the Catholics without government-support. After all, it was Buddhist country first, and the Catholics were intruders.

And we'd better cut down our National Debt and deficit.

Very sincerely yours,

G. H. (female)

[Editor's note: Francis Joseph Cardinal Spellman (1889–1967) was archbishop of the Roman Catholic diocese of New York.]

68. *"cut our losses"*

Mt. Vernon, Maine
August 19, 1967

Dear Senator Smith:

. . . I am glad to have your own statement of your position on the war. I note that you speak of attaining peace on honorable terms. This expression, "an honorable peace", has been ·widely used by many people and most fre-

[handwritten margin note: American interests seem to be always prioritized over humanitarian interests]

quently by Johnson. It sounds well but it is never defined, and as a rather vague generality it may mean something different with each user.

There seems to be a widespread feeling in this country, which you evidently share, that our government made a mistake in becoming involved as it has in Vietnam. In private life, when you have made a mistake, the manly, the honorable thing to do is to admit it, especially when your mistake is damaging to someone else; and the sensible course when it is damaging you is to cut the mistake short and not pursue it further. To so so may be embarrassing but that is the price you pay for the mistake.

I see no reason why this concept of honorable action is not as applicable in public as in private life. The most charitable view I can take is that our government has made a ghastly mistake. Wrong will not become right by pushing it further. Let us, then, pull out of Vietnam at once, admit our mistake, cut our losses. This would be retreat, if you like, but would be neither the appeasement nor the surrender you object to (if you will look closely at the meaning of those words). It is too late to save face, which is evidently what Johnson means by an "honorable" settlement. We have already lost face with most of the world. How many young men are you prepared to see die in support of this attempt at face-saving on the part of our government?

Very truly yours,

F. S. (male)

69. *"slow extermination"*

Southwest Harbor, Maine

August 30, 1967

Dear Senator Smith,

This is a letter of dissent from our Vietnam policy. While all Americans should be proud of the courage and enduraace of our young men fighting there, evidence is increasing that their sacrifice is benefiting only a small clique of South Vietnamese military leaders and war profiteers. We credit our leadership with sincere desire to help Vietnam, but any benefit to the common people seems to be negligible, and there is grave doubt if they want us there at all.

As a method of fighting Communism our policy seems stupid—its chief effect within this country is to prevent our making progress toward remedying the conditions which are already creating deep dissension here, and may be the cause of understandable left wing violence.

The policy we are pursuing appears to be to seek peace only after winning a victory by slow extermination—including the extermination of some thousands of young Americans. It seems that the position recently taken by Senator Morton might be considered for the Republican Party. I understand this to mean making peace a major issue instead of one which is subsidiary.

While I do not anticipate that your judgment will agree with mine, I do expect that you recognize that dissent may represent an equal loyalty to our country.

Very truly yours,

W. F. (male)

[Editor's note: Republican Senator Thruston Ballard Morton (1907–1982) served in the Senate from 1957 to 1968. Like other political leaders, Morton was reacting to the large antiwar demonstrations of 1967 and his response conveys the growing influence of antiwar protest in various political circles.]

70. *"be magnanimous and withdraw"*

September 3, 1967
Castine, Maine

Dear Senator,

A statement in the Bangor Daily News August 29th, gives your stand on the coming Panama treaty as negative and I am <u>most</u> <u>delighted</u> that you feel that way, I'm sure with more good reasons than I know of. . . .

I was briefly in Canada lately. I was impressed by the despair of Britains I met at the give-away of their empire. I was also given plenty of adverse opinion from all I met on our Viet Nam and other foreign policies.
. . .

If you have any literature on your stand on Viet Nam I'd like to have it. I write in encouragement to those Senators who are brave enough to oppose it. A gold Star mother a member of DAR I yet cannot condone what we are doing there and I agree with the French diplomat who suggests we be magnanimous and withdraw. That of course would save some splendid boys, too many of whom have already been sacrificed. I have been hoping you as a woman and at times bravely outspoken would join the little band of Senators I feel are devout patriots.

Very sincerely yours,

E. C. (female)

P.S. This letter seems to contain contradictions—for firmness in Panama—withdrawal in Vietnam. I do not look at the Viet Nam adventure as the interests of the U.S. and so without dignity—just stubbornness and in the view of friends here—a way to make some Americans wealthy

71. *"growing distrust"*

Falmouth, Maine
September 5, 1967

Dear Senator Smith:

Although I have for a long time been a very loyal citizen of this country and in general a supporter of the policies of our several administrations, I have in recent months come to feel a growing distrust for our current foreign policy.

I feel that our involvement in Vietnam, our intervention in the Dominican Republic, our handling of the Cuban situation, our refusal to recognize the Chinese mainland government: all of these, are unrealistic and out of date. It seems to me that we are failing to recognize great national forces, stirrings of the people that lead to the development of nations, the very thing which we say as a country we want to encourage.

I believe that we should recognize Red China and try to open bridges to her. . . . I believe that we should disengage ourselves from Vietnam and let the people there decide their own future. I believe we should seek to build bridges to the so-called communistic nations of Eastern Europe because the time seems to be ripe for easing of relations with these countries.

May I suggest if you have not already read them that you read . . . Jan Myrdahl's "Visit to a Chinese Village," and Senator Fulbright's fine commentary "The Arrogance of Power."

I know and appreciate your wisdom, your devotion to this country, and you open-mindedness, and I hope that you will think seriously of this matter as you address yourself to your very high duties in the months ahead.
Most sincerely yours,
T. J. (male)

72. *"military-industrial complex"*

Bar Harbor, Maine
October 10, 1967

Dear Senator Smith,

I wish to register with you my protest against the present policies in this country which you, in some measure, support.

Although much is said of the threat of Communism here and abroad, many of our actions promote rather than discourage it. Communism appeals to the dispossessed and, unfortunately, it has appeared to better their conditions in Russia and Asia as well as in Viet Nam. It is to be feared that it will soon get a firm hold on our Negro citizens here at home as they come to realize how badly we have dealt with them for so long. Force has been our only counter-measure and so far it is notably ineffective. In Russia Communism is beginning to wither away as Marx predicted capitalism would do in the west. Have we no faith that our system is better and will ultimately with men's minds, or do we think that our terrible weapons can bring light and hope?

The problem of poverty, racism, and civil rights at home and those of the war in Vietnam are indeed difficult and complex, but are we attacking them with as much lavish expenditure of human brain power, devotion, and genius (not to mention the vast amounts of money) as are being employed on the problems of space exploration and sophisticated weaponry? It is a sad thought that the military-industrial complex, as President Eisenhower warned us, enters into this picture.

I beg you to seek new ways of restoring peace and justice at home and in East Asia. Our coins still say "In God we trust"; however this is interpreted, it cannot be distorted to imply faith in instruments of death and violence rather than in ideals.

Yours truly,   *Argued Communism created better Conditions*
J. T. (female)

[Editor's note: This woman's reference to "poverty, racism, and civil rights" and the fear that communism would become more attractive to African-Americans correlates with Martin Luther King's statements of 1967 that linked the civil rights and antiwar movements. Seeing explicit connections between racism, economic exploitation, and the war, King wanted to fight all three at one time, a bold position that caused division even among his supporters. For example, in April 1967 the NAACP had voted against merging the Peace Movement with the Civil Rights Movement.]

73. "civil disobedience"

Falmouth, Maine
November 5, 1967

Madam:

On October 28 I read the front page article in the Portland Press Herald about your speech to the Grange in which you talked about the recent anti-war demonstrations in Washington. As I didn't hear your speech I would like to ask if this paper reported the tone of your remarks fairly?

After reading the article, I felt that you believe that, with the exceptions of a few sincere pacifists, the young people in this demonstration were a very unworthy lot. Is this true?

I was deeply upset by this. On that same day I read a letter from a college student who demonstrated written to his parents about his reasons for going and his experience. I have known this young man well all his life. He graduated with high honors from a fine Maine academy. He has worked hard to earn money for college where he is making a good record. He is not a pacifist but he sincerely believes the war in Vietnam is morally wrong.

If you could read his letter, I am sure that however much you might disagree with his reasoning or actions, you would not doubt his sincerity. I think you would also admire his courage. He was not beaten or tear gased but he saw many who were. He said many of the U.S. marshals were vicious but he had praise for the MPs who only tried to do their job well.

Two things bother me especially. First, that sincere and brave young people should go unnoticed while the less desirable elements (and I'm sure there were these) get all the publicity. Second, that instead of arresting many of those who engaged in civil disobedience, unnecessary brutality was used to try to break their spirit and make them go home.

My heart goes out to these young men, not old enough to vote, yet forced by our country to face a moral dilemma which is too much for many of us who are middle-aged. No wonder Senator Hatfield has called their situation a torment! Under these circumstances I think we should be more than tolerant when some of them don't act just as we might think best.
Sincerely yours,
M. M. (female)

74. "playing God"

Houlton, Maine
November 6, 1967

Dear Senator Smith,

When I read the enclosed letter in the Portland Sunday Telegram yesterday, I could not resist cutting it out to mail to you because it so completely expresses my own feelings on our involvement in Viet Nam.

I have never written to you before, nor to any government representatives and I hope you will accept this as an expression of my very deepest feelings and concern.

I have always had great pride in my country, but in this instance I am ashamed. No one would be more willing than I to fight for my home, my family and all I hold dear. My husband fought in World War Two and I am proud of that but I am not willing for the Viet Nam conflict to go on any longer. I am not willing for my now 9 year old son to fight in such a war where

I feel the United States has meddled and is playing God. I think that any other country's internal affairs are none of our business and I would and do resent interference in our (my country's) business by outsiders.

We have strayed far from the basis and ideals upon which our country was built and I hope that you, as my agent, will do all you can to right this terrible wrong.   *Favoring Isolationist foreign policy*

Sincerely yours,

M. N. (female)

P. S. Does one voice <u>really</u> make any difference?

[Editor's note: Obviously, the letters to the editor in the Portland *Telegram* reached beyond the city of Portland (Maine's largest city) and it population of 65,116. Small-town Americans, even if they had limited opportunities to express their views on a larger scale, were aware of the antiwar views expressed in larger centers.]

75. *"The Prophet Isaiah"*

Bath, Maine

December 6, 1967

Dear Senator Smith,

Almost a year has passed since I and other concerned citizens of Maine met with you in your office to express our concern and opposition to the Administration's dominant role in foreign policy as it pertains to the Vietnam action. I recall your clearly expressed feeling at that time that the President, having all the facts of the situation, was apparently doing all that could be done to bring an end to hostilities.

Since then a number of your Senate colleagues have entered the debate concerning our action in Vietnam, and it has been encouraging to note that the Senate has not completely abdicated its role relating to foreign policy and left the President to simply dictate what our relationship to this and other nations of the world should be.

Since my visit with you, countless innocent citizens of Vietnam and of the United States (drafted soldiers) have lost their lives because of the United States policy of military intervention in that country. To continue to give the administration a free hand in shaping our policy there, would seem to me to leave the lives of countless more Vietnamese and Americans in the hands of a politician who is surely never unaware that the justification of his past and present policy in Vietnam is a necessary prelude to re-election.

I suspect that Senators, like so many who carry heavy responsibility, do not find much time to search Scriptures. The Prophet Isaiah may well be out of date, but he might well be speaking a universally valid word when he says:

> Woe to those who go down to Egypt for help
> > And rely on horses,
> who trust in chariots because they are many,
> > and in horsemen because they are strong,
> but do not look to the Holy One of Israel
> > or consult the Lord! Isaiah 31:1

[handwritten margin note: Invoke the Bible as reason not to intervene in Viet nam]

With sincere wishes for peace in your heart at Christmas,
L. B. (male)

76. "Ugly Americans"

Cushings Island, Maine
August 26, 1967

Dear Mrs. Smith,

I can't seem to write out Maggie, and just Margaret doesn't seem enough.

I'm just dropping you a line of support. I hope I have found a complete change of view amongst <u>all</u> my friends with the exception of one or two men. Everyone who was not previously opposed to the continuation of the war in Vietnam is completely opposed now. I tried to convince myself, for a long time, that our overall intentions were altruistic.

Now—I see our governmental policies being made by the influence of military men—I see our inhumanity to our fellow man in an endless killing—We are "Ugly Americans" and we cannot lose any more "face" than we already have—by a planned—announced—gradual withdrawal of our forces following this coming dishonest election in South Vietnam. I feel we are wrong to try to impose our system on an unready—unwilling people—I hope you can do something—the unrest at home is a reflection of our distrust.

We're so proud of you

[handwritten margin note: unjust to impose our policy on the Vietnamese]

Sincerely,
W. T. (female)

II. POLICY OF BOMBING

One of the more important issues in letters discussed was the bombing campaigns. Bombers operating on a wide scale included the Boeing B-52 Stratofortress for high-altitude carpet bombing and a variety of dive bombers and fighter-bombers that allowed more accurate hits. In 1967, the rate of B-52 sorties flown was approximately 600 per month. There was mounting pressure to stop the bombing campaigns as a result of the greater awareness of the high human and financial costs or that it was a dangerous strategy that might enlarge the conflict. Consistent with her Cold Warrior image, Senator Smith favored unremitting bombing if that is what it took to force the North Vietnamese leadership to end the war.

77. *"recent raids"*

Wiscasset, Maine
August 14, 1967

Dear Senator Smith:

May I request your attention for a moment to one more protest about the war in Vietnam. (The number of such protests, as I am sure you know, is constantly increasing; as is obviously the number of people who may not protest formally but who are concerned about and opposed to this war.)

My particular concern at the moment is our increasing bombing of North Vietnam, especially recent raids near the Chinese border. This seems a dangerous and stupid policy, as is our whole policy of continued bombing. Surely we have courage enough to work for negotiations and peace rather than destruction. We certainly cannot lose more "face" than we already have lost in the eyes of the rest of the world. We might possibly gain some.

One more question, please: How or why has Congress allowed the President to wage war without its declaration by Congress, which is usually so much more careful and protective of its prerogatives, and rightly so?

Thank you for your attention and consideration.

Sincerely yours,   — Disapproves of Bombing
L. T. (female)   — Congress still has not declared War

78. *"cease bombing"*

Kittery Point, Maine
September 19, 1967

Dear Mrs. Smith:

I just want to put myself on record as feeling very strongly that we should pursue a moderate course in Viet Nam. By that I mean we should cease bombing the North, we should let the Viet Cong hold those jungle areas they now hold in the South because it is almost impossible to root them out and it is far too costly in men and materials. We should deescalate. No

one has ever won a war. It is difficult for us to withdraw because we are proud and because our economy would suffer. It is time we considered the future of the human race rather than the narrow minded expenditures of the moment. ✳
Sincerely yours,
E. R. (female)

79. *"stop bombing"*

Camden, Maine
Sept. 29, 1967

Dear Senator Smith,

My husband and I would like you to know that after much thoughtful reading and discussion and with full knowledge that this is a most difficult situation, we feel that the United States must make the offer to stop the bombing of North Vietnam unconditionally. The fighting in the Far East must be halted. We urge that the United Nations be given the authority and ability to stop fighting in any part of the world. If this means giving up some of our sovereignty we should be prepared to do it. We feel that the United States is on a collision course.

We also feel strongly that the problems of the cities must be solved with the greatest part of the help coming from the Federal Government.

We would urge cuts in the Space program. Who cares whether we're the first on the moon. The money is better spent on domestic problems such as education, urban blight, foreign aid too.
Sincerely,
R. B. (female)

80. *"homes burned to the ground"*

Ellsworth, Maine
November 24, 1967

Dear Senator Smith,

It does not follow that because a person is opposed to the Vietnam war that there is no concern for the welfare of the young fighting men, rather a question of whether they should be there at all. The costs of this war in hard cash is something we shall all feel for many years, postponed retirements, inflation, and a harder tax burden.

It disturbs me deeply when I see the films from Vietnam of the bombings, the homeless and maimed children, homes burned to the ground. Twenty eight years ago Hitler made the word German an obscenity, his bombing of open cities even to-day leaves a stench that will take many more

years to dissipate. Does Mr. Johnson wish to bring this nation to the same disrepute? If, as it seems, we have really reached an impasse and we are bent on total destruction of life and property, why not be humane and drop a hydrogen bomb on both North and South Vietnam and then pretend it never happened—I, as a christian wouldn't even kick a rabid dog slowly to death.
Yours truly,
A. T. (female)

81. "What now?"

Kennebunkport, Maine
October 19, 1967

Dear Senator Smith,

My sentiments regarding the Vietnam conflict have become gelled in my own mind to the point where I feel I must express them to those people representing me in government. I'm sure you've heard most of the opinions available uncountable times, but, who knows, perhaps one of us rather insignificant single individuals may have some new contribution. Thus, I offer mine.

I cannot pass judgment as to whether or not we should be involved there; I personally feel it can be justified. The problem is obviously, "What now?" Another obvious point is that the mounting pressure from many sources to cease bombing cannot be ignored. Yet, if this is to be done, it must be productive of something towards "peace." I feel that at some appropriate time in the near future, it would be well to announce that we are ceasing bombing and possibly all military action other than protection of present positions. Then, if "peace talks" have not begun within two weeks (or some other reasonable amount of time), we will use all our military power, short of nuclear weapons, to bring the conflict to a victorious end as quickly as possible.

It is almost axiomatic that conferences would not be started by the end of this unilateral truce. But it seems quite likely that it would not take many days of subsequent military action to get some willingness to start talking. It seems also that this would satisfy most of our critics other than those who feel we shouldn't be involved at all.

I suppose I'm as weary of this "war" as anyone, but I can see no satisfactory end to it until we deliver a reasonable and unyielding ultimatum—just as a parent must do with a child—act with very firm fairness. . . .

With the hope that genuine human understanding is the guide to your activities rather than political affiliations, I remain,
Yours truly,
E. F. (male)

III. POLITICIANS AND GENERALS

With the rise of frustration over the handling of the war, more Americans were singling out personalities for criticism, including the president. Referring to the loss of confidence in the president, Senator Smith herself publicly spoke of the "Johnson credibility gap" caused by his "failure to take the American people into his confidence." A greater number of people became more skeptical of the statements of political and military leaders even to the point that some ordinary Americans questioned the morality of specific individuals. It does appear that Smith's public criticism of the Johnson administration provided a catalyst for correspondents to speak out, so much so that some of the following letters provide additional evidence of a public fracturing of opinion among the leaders themselves.

82. "sinister overtones"

South Bristol, Maine
July 25, 1967

Dear Mrs. Smith.—

My neighbor . . . handed on to me the copy of the Congressional Record you were so good as to send him. I have read therein your remarks of last February 23rd, on pages S2498-2500.

I want to endorse virtually everything you said, and congratulate you on saying it.

I do not know that we can equate logic with wisdom, but I find that your speech leaves me with a grave question in mind.

How long can we continue to support a Commander in Chief who has made errors so great as those you describe?

This question is urgent at the moment. So far as one can tell from the news sources, Mr. Johnson, Mr. McNamara, and General Westmoreland have recently decided to send another hundred thousand men to Viet Nam. I have seen no indication that members of Congress participated in making this decision; indeed, it would appear to be a decision made by the President alone.

I am sorry to say that there is something sinister to allowing a single individual to make decisions on that order of magnitude. Especially in view of the fact that Mr. Johnson's authority to fight in Viet Nam rests on a legal basis which is both slight and shaky.

And if he has been wrong so many times before, are we not justified in wondering whether he is not wrong again?

I repeat what I have said to you before: The Congress must assert itself and seek to guide the President.

It is my personal judgment that further commitment in Viet Nam will be likely to leave the United States vulnerable elsewhere in the world. I doubt whether the recent conflict in the Near East would have been initiated had we not been tied down in Viet Nam. It is incongruous to reflect that the safety of this country depended upon the excellence of the Israeli army, but it seems obvious that it did. It is not our own doing that we have been so lucky.

As to the appointment to general rank of officers who are not competent, I have been with you in the past and I hope you will never fail to speak up.

With regard to the treatment of General Page (and the rotten motivation for it) I am also in emphatic agreement with you. Indeed, I think your remarks erred on the side of moderation. This narrative also has sinister overtones. If there have been bomb shortages and other shortages, certainly members of the Senate are entitled to the truth about the matter. If they don't get it, and get it at once, I am worried.

With best wishes,

Sincerely yours,

J. S. (male)

[Editor's note: In her February 23 statements, Senator Smith reaffirmed her support for Johnson and her opposition of an immediate pull-out of American troops in Vietnam. But she also listed a number of "tragedies" of the Johnson-McNamara policies that included: lack of military resources, allowing the National Guard and the Reserve to be havens for draft dodgers, and "punishing those officers, who dare, in the confines of the non-attribution halls of advanced military colleges, to speak of bomb shortages." While vice commander of the Air University and commandant of the Air War College at Maxwell Air Force Base, General Jerry D. Page allegedly criticized Defense Secretary Robert McNamara and war policy that resulted in bomb shortages in Vietnam.]

83. "Johnson-McNamara policies"

Christmas Cove, Maine
July 24, 1967

Dear Senator Smith:

I congratulate you for the remarks you made in the Senate on February 23, 1967 on the subject of the "credibility gap". You kindly forwarded the

Congressional Record of that date to me. I wish all of your constituents would read your remarks. I'll guarantee to you that my friends are going to hear about them.

In regard to the "treatment" which General Page received, it is my belief that President Johnson gave the same admonishment indirectly to all Americans including members of Congress when General Westmoreland reviewed before Congress our then-current position in Vietnam.

I formerly thought that we should fight to defeat the Vietcong. I now believe that we should pull out completely. I had thought that the great majority of Vietnamese wanted us there, but the more I read and hear the more I believe we are not except by our own puppets. We apparently don't dare walk the streets alone even in the territories we have "conquered". How can we ever win such a war?

Only one person among my acquaintances in Maine with whom I have discussed the subject thinks we have any business in Vietnam, and of my friends across the country I know of only two who believe so. I think the polls are not accurate in this regard, or perhaps more and more people are becoming afraid to disagree with the Johnson-McNamara policies.

Our country has enough problems at home to keep our minds and bodies occupied, and I think the Congress should eliminate the terrible despair which exists among our citizens over our Vietnam involvement. Add to this that there is not a country in the world with the exception of perhaps Australia and New Zealand which supports us.

It does not make too much sense to try to inflict our system of government upon a group of uneducated people when we are not doing such a good job at home. We had better get our own house in order and have others adopt our system because it is obviously the best. And, incidentally, I believe we are playing right into the hands of the Russians.

Respectfully yours

J. H. (male)

84. "McNamara"

South Windam, Maine
September 20, 1967

Senator Smith:

I probably write to my Congressmen on an average about once in ten years. I am doing so now because I am upset and angry. My pet peeve is Mr McNamara.

Is it true that our newest aircraft carrier was built as an oil burner at his insistence, and against the advice of our naval experts?

Is he a virtual dictator who has to answer to no one? If Mr. Johnson has the power of control, why doesn't he exercise it? Can Mr. McNanara be replaced, and if so, why hasn't this been done? After all, where did he qualify as a military expert, with the Ford Co.?

Why is the Vietnam war deagging along. Most people cannot understand why a country like ours which defeated Germany in WW 1 and both Germany and Japan in WW 2 is unable to defeat a small country the size of North Vietnam. And I think I am one of the very large group who believe we should not have become actively involved in the first place. . . .

Yours very truly,

L. G. (male)

85. *"mutiny"*

Belfast, Maine
August 12, 1967

Dear Mrs. Smith,

I have never met you, but remember you presenting a medal [in 1946]. . . . You also made a short speech in front of the Damariscotta Baptist Church.

I felt impressed that you were a sensible Maine person at that time.

I have gone to both so-called World Wars; impelled by patriotism. But this war in Viet Nam makes me feel I would even mutiny against going there.

You and I were pleased to read in our History Books how our woodsmen and other patriots could defeat the well trained British Soldiers.

Well it seems the Viet Cong are getting the best of our training Fighting Men and all our Modern Equipment.

The average Vietnam does not want to fight. They hardly cooperate.

I consider this present time appropriate to get out of this War gracefully unless the Viet Nam people are willing to do much more.

It seems there is no honor among the Leaders and they feel Uncle Sam is Uncle Sap.

If you read above, I would thank you to please sign enclosed card.

Yours truly,

P. A. (male)

86. *"bring them home"*

Freeport, Maine
August 24, 1967

Dear Senator Smith,

Isn't it becoming more and more clear that the American people want out of the war in Vietnam? And who is to get them out but their political leaders, especially their Senators, and especially you, who manifested such courage, intelligence and leadership in your memorable declaration of conscience against Senator McCarthy? Hasn't the time come for you to take another great stand?

The mounting anguish over the war comes in part, no doubt, from those who are beginning to realize that this gigantic fireworks display is not for free. The President has had to ask Congress for a 10 percent surcharge on income taxes. But Senator Aiken has said that this tax boost won't pay half the additional costs of the war.

Needless to say, I oppose any tax increase. The best way to support our boys is to bring them home alive, now! Instead of sending more and more of them deeper and deeper on this death march through Asia. How long must we continue to feed our national pride with the bodies of our young?

Indeed, a tax reduction would be possible if we brought the troops home and returned them to civilian life, at the same time wiping out the balance of payment deficits that our military adventures abroad are incurring. But any surpluses that result from a return to sanity in our foreign policies should be spent to reduce ignorance, poverty, political inequality and environmental pollution at home. Our cities could absorb any surpluses in the federal budget very easily and a lot more besides, if a sort of guerilla warfare is not to become endemic inside America.

D. G. (male)   *Using taxes as reason to oppose Vietnam War*

[Editor's note: An opponent of the war, Republican Senator George D. Aiken (1892–1984) of Vermont stated in 1966 that the best solution for the United States was to declare victory and get out of Vietnam, a statement that Smith viewed as frivolous and out of the question. Aiken and Smith were good friends and he was her first choice when she began asking other senators to sign her Declaration of Conscience of 1950. In 1964, he gave the nominating speech for her run for the Republican nomination for the presidency. On the four-year anniversary of her declaration to run for president, Aiken wrote a short note to Smith stating, "I still think this is a day to remember—and I do very well. We would be a lot better off if we had you down at 1600."]

87. "our dreadful blot"

Castine, Maine
September 11, 1967

Dear Senator—

Many thanks for the Congressional Record and two statements of yours on the Viet Nam war which I have read with interest. I was also delighted that you suggested a "Dove" as a Republican presidential candidate. I have been hoping the fortunate election of Mr. Eisenhower in a war situation would suggest the pattern for 1968.

My asking for your position on the war was partly motivated by articles sometime ago in the Philadelphia Inquirer which described you as one of the Senators Mr. Johnson could always count on and manipulate perhaps. I couldn't reconcile this with loyal opposition. However I think you covered your relations with the President in what you say yourself. I believe this gentleman is becoming a very hated man if I judge by a sampling around here. I'm afraid history will judge him one of our most unfortunate—for us—leaders.

If you have not read Ambassador Reichauer's article in Look, Sept. 19th, I wish you could find the time, particularly the last part. To me it offers a chance to do what we should have done in Viet Nam long ago—let them alone and withdraw all but economic aid to rescue what materially we have destroyed both North and South. The lost and ruined lives on both sides are our dreadful blot and disgrace. I hope we may have the grace to admit our mistakes and do what we can to atone.

Very sincerely yours,

E. C. (female)

88. *"a sense of guilt"*

Unity, Maine
September 7, 1967

Dear Senator Smith,

I just want to renew my plea that you use all possible means to needle the administration concerning its having by-passed the United Nations in going into Vietnam and the necessity of bringing the matter even <u>now</u> to the United Nations. I hope that you will say more about this in extension of your paragraph on the matter in your "declaration of conscience" of last April.

I admire your honesty and forthrightness in speaking of Mr. McNamara.

No demands upon the people at home are too great if they will save lives of our young men. I am oppressed by a sense of guilt and of the injustice of sitting comfortably at home while younger men die for us. Ending the war must be the uppermost task for everyone every day.

Sincerely yours,

D. M. (male)

89. "We need new thinking"

Kennebunkport, Maine
September 9, 1967

Dear Mrs. Smith:

The enclosed comment from last Sunday's New York Times moves me to write you. You do not speak for many of us in Maine when you endorse more or continued bombing of North Vietnam. In discussions around here I find very few opinions you could call so hawklike; most are deeply troubled by the conduct and developments of the Vietnam conflict.

General Gavin has been my spokesman ever since his televised testimony before the Senate Foreign Relations Committee. His proposals for action suggested a very different course from the one which has led us to today's dilemma, and whether viewed idealistically or pragmatically, his ideas still seem the wiser course.

Our motives are called peaceful by Rusk and Johnson in every public statement. But how can the champions of freedom, Seato or the Geneva Conference pursue peace by means of monolithic, unilateral violence? We are the only major nation to stage so large a war since 1945, yet we only escalate instead of reconsidering our untenable and unsuccessful course of action. We need new thinking, not more bombing!

Presently we are proving that deplorable man, H. Rap Brown, correct that violence is "as American as cherry pie." Is there no other answer for American world leadership than committing war in the name of peace? Apparently not by generals, many senators or our present official policy.

You are quoted in today's Portland Press Herald as looking for a "peace seeker" for the GOP nominee, but you endorsed unrestricted bombing in the Armed Services Subcommittee report. I know you conscientiously consider your mail and the views of your constituents. Please represent us by reflecting more of General Gavin's thinking and less of Secretary Rusk's in your endorsements and votes.

Yours sincerely,
P. T. (female)

[Editor's note: General James M. Gavin (1907–1990) sponsored the enclave theory of American forces in Vietnam withdrawing to fortified locales rather than continuing a strategy that he viewed as flawed. H. Rap Brown (1943–) was a black activist who also declared, "If America don't come around, we're gonna' burn it down."]

90. "lost face"

Cape Elizabeth, Maine
September 13, 1967

Dear Senator Smith,

Recently the papers carried articles on a hearing your Armed Services Committee had with the Pentagon. In none of the articles did I read of any question your Committee asked the officers or the Secretary why after more than two years of fighting an inferior foe we have not won the conflict.

As you and the Committee a are aware we supply our troops with unlimited equipment, i.e. food, clothing, ammunition and medical assistance. In addition they have the distinct advantage of air support, artillery, tanks, troop carriers etc. The Vietcong and the North Vietmanese troops in South Vietnam do not have their own air support, tanks, artillery troop carriers or navy. Yet our troops are still fighting the Vietcong in the suburbs of Saigon, Hue, and other locations in the south. It would appear to me that if with all the superiority that our troops hold they should have ended the war long ago. I can not believe that man for man our troops are inferior to the Vietmanese. Therefor it would appear that the fault would be with those who are responsible for the war plans. The Pentagon can not say that they have been limited in how they can fight the war in the south. Therefor I would suggest that your Committee suggest that a change of top officers in Saigon, and Washington would be in order.

Those who are in favor of this way say that we can not withdraw as we would loose face. May I point out that we have lost face as our troops have been unable to win over an inferior foe. I hope that we withdraw our troops taking with us all South Vietmanese who would wish to come.

Very truly yours,
A.C. (male)

Asking with American Superiority how haven't they already killed the Viet Cong

91. "plain tommyrot"

Round Pond, Maine
September 19, 1967

Dear Senator Smith:—

According to last night's TV you have presented to various Senators and to the President what is called "the Wisconsin plan" to deal with the Viet Nam War. As I understand it you are not sponsoring this plan. However you are certain to receive many critical letters. For that reason I am writing this letter in support of the plan. To me it seems to be a practicable way of getting out of a very bad mess. If space permitted I could write pages in condemnation of our policies in international affairs pursued in recent years. The world is certainly not ready for collective security against war. For us to take up the job alone because the others can not be depended on is sheer folly in my opinion. We are not the policeman for the world. Neither is it our duty to see that the people of all nations of the world are well fed and well take care of. For us to assume such responsibilities is megalomania pure and simple. Let's come out of the clouds and reduce our committments to a more realistic plateau.

Laying aside the problem of our mistaken attitude in international affairs, we must face up to the one facet, the war in Viet Nam. It seems to me that we got into it because of a series of misconceptions

ONE. That the existing government in South Viet Nam was the choice of the people of that country and that it was a stable healthy government of free people.

TWO. That the Viet Cong represented only a small part of the population of South Viet Nam, but were pawns controlled by outsiders called, "aggressors", actuelly the Communist government of North Viet Nam.

THREE. That Ho Chi Min and others of the North were themselves pawns controlled by Communist China.

FOUR. That bombing from the air would shortly bring these aggressors to terms and then they would give up their Communist plots and leave thepeople of South Viet Nam to continue to develop their country in peace and freedom. Actually air bombardment is only a specialized form of artillery action subject to the limitations which artillery has always been subject to.

FIVE. That our armyorganized, trained and equipped for conventional warfare and perhaps the best in the world could easily put a stop to guerrilla warfare.

SIX. That having taught the Communists a lesson we could withdraw from the region and pursue our own peaceful ways.

SEVEN. That, if we fail "to do our duty" in South Viet Nam, country after country would fall to communism and we would finally have to fight the Communist world alone possibly ourselves falling prey to some menace. I think this is just plain tommyrot. Communism is a very inefficient system. Every over-populated poverty-stricken country taken over by Communism is another mill stone around their necks. Instead of wasteing the lives of our young men in a futile war against the imaginary enemy, Let us get out as soon as we honorably can. I think the Wisconsin plan would offer us a good way to accomplish it. Let us turn our attention to real problems—the population explosion especially in the slums pollution of the air and streams—better education for those not now getting it—waste of our national resources—crime—inflation, etc., etc., etc. These are the problems which should occupy

the best brains of the country instead of tilting at ideologies which we do not approve of, or trying to make the world over in own image.
Cordially yours,
F. D. (male)

92. "immoral acts of the present leaders"

South Windham, Maine
October 29, 1967

Dear Margaret Chase Smith,

I have just read, with disgust, your comments to the Grange concerning the anti-Vietnam march in Washington.

The <u>real</u> sheep are those who blindly follow the immoral acts of the present leaders in our government and this will have to include you when you make blanket statements such as the one refered to.

I have participated in similar marches and have noticed that if <u>one</u> flag of the National Liberation Front is displayed, dozens of photographers threaten to trample to death in an effort to get a picture of a small, non-representative minority to make headlines in a newspaper such as the biased Gannett papers in Maine. Newspapers of this caliber have kept the backward populace of Maine in ignorance for years.

Your attitude in this matter does not bespeak that of a woman of compassion. The <u>real</u> supporters of the boys in Vietnam are those of us who protest seeing our young people go forth to fight an imaginary enemy, kill countless innocent civilians, support an evil and corrupt South Vietnamese government that does not have the support of the people in pursuing this war. We will continue to pressure to extricate ourselves from this deplorable mess so that these young men will be able to return to their homes to continue education, raise families and pursue their life work.

My sixteen year old daughter participated in this march. We are proud that she is not one of the "sheep". We are proud that she went with a group of students and teachers from the Meeting School in New Hampshire to register their opposition to the crime committed by our government against the youth of America and theinnocent abroad.

Please do not bother to send one of your formal reply letters to me. (You accidently sent me a reply which implied that I advocated the government policy recently.) Instead please get in touch with George Bliss at the Friends-Committee on National Legislation, 245 Second Street N.E., Washington, D.C. I believe that this Committee can help you. You do need help as do many of our leaders in government. Has it ever occurred to you just what you

will say to the mothers and wives of young men killed when this war is finally declared to be immoral by <u>all</u> right thinking people?
Sincerely,
D. A. (female)

93. "*old LBJ*"

Rockland, Maine
November 6, 1967

Senator Margaret Smith—

Now that Vietnam <u>has</u> organized its' own government, is it going to be shown what it can do? Can they settle their own differences, I do not ask <u>why</u> we are there, it's a fact that we are, but why are <u>our</u> forces bearing the brunt of this war, which has been escalated all out of proportions by the U.S.—and apparently the U.S. will stop at <u>nothing</u>. Why <u>now</u> are previously restricted areas open to bombing? It has been a cat-catch-mouse <u>game</u>, at the expense of <u>thousands</u> of our boys and men—Why didn't LBJ order an "all out" to win in the <u>first place</u>, seeing as how he got us <u>all</u> involved. It seemed to please him to send our men to a foreign land—and <u>Asia</u> at that—to be slaughtered for a senseless cause. These are our <u>sons</u>, not cattle. Sometimes it makes you wonder just <u>what</u> old <u>LBJ really is</u>!

I sympathize with the demonstrator's cause. A great many thousands of us do. They are not being unpatriotic; they don't have the answers, they don't understand all this, (and neither do I, although I've seen two world wars that I <u>could</u> understand) and it is their right to make their voice heard. Leading magazines, newspapers, etc., all carry the reports—men of <u>high</u> repute, call it JBJ's "colossal blunder"—who wants to fight for that? Who in Vietnam gives a damn how many of our lads die for them? Will my son have to? If he does; I, too, will take my life. I believe in the American way of life. I don't understand the Asian way—neither does my son. There is such a thing as loyalty, but just how far does this go.

Loyalty is not <u>mechanical</u> obedience. It has to be given from a person's heart and soul for a principle he <u>believes</u> in. It becomes a serious problem when there is a conflict of loyalties. True loyalty never requires the destraction of another person's loyalty. What is going to become of these scared and frustrated teenagers I don't know. They are being driven to it. The Supreme Court proclaimed that "no official is empowered to prescribe what <u>we</u> should <u>believe</u>, or to punish us if we do not accept the dominant beliefs." Loyalty is not conformity. And today the United States of America <u>is</u> striving hard for human dignity, trying to exercise some control over their <u>own</u> destiny, which is essential to human dignity, under the worst chaos of mixed feeling & frustra-

tion that I have ever seen in all the years of my life and I wonder where it will all end—here—and abroad!! For a man to be enslaved in chains violates his dignity, and it seems to me, that <u>that</u> is a cause of demonstrations. If has never happened here since the Civil War. We were to build a greater <u>America</u>—<u>for our boys and girls to grow up in</u>—thats what I told mine! Now, I don't know what to tell them—"the Great Society our popularly-elected leaders, make a mess—<u>you</u> go and die for it."
E. R. (female)   ✳ lots of good quotes ✳

IV. AMERICAN COMMITMENT

Despite rising opposition to the war, Senator Smith held firm against any American withdrawal from South Vietnam if such action could not be done on "honorable terms." Her position was typical of Cold War thinking: the United States had to make a stand in South Vietnam otherwise the communists would be stronger and the Americans weaker in other places such as Thailand. She found it frustrating that the Johnson administration adopted a "half-hearted holding action" that not only caused more deaths and injuries but prolonged the war. In her eyes, the bombing pauses symbolized appeasement and weakness and allowed the communists to gain strength as they poured more war supplies into South Vietnam. Smith wanted to see an all-out effort that would defeat the communists and end the war, a view that some correspondents supported.

94. "support our commitment"

South Windham, Maine
December 29, 1967

Dear Senator Smith,

These are difficult times in which we live. It requires a great deal of patience to live in a world in which numerous people, for reasons which seem valid to them, are bent on fomenting violence to accomplish their ends.

This past summer my wife and I left Windham to visit . . . Czchoslovakia. While in Communist Czechoslovakia we also met friends of my wife from East Germany. Everywhere we traveled in Czechoslovakia we met with sympathy and understanding for the American position on Vietnam. I am sure you are aware that Castro, Mao Tse-Tung and Kim Il-Sung have condemned the moderate attitudes of East European Communists towards the

West as "Revisionism." But in Eastern Europe there is a tremendous admiration for America. We encountered this every day. The people there see the Americans as prasticing restraint and avoiding a world war.

Please support our commitment in Vietnam. As long as you do Castro will not try anything in our hemisphere. He'll be afraid of us and know we mean business. Also as long as aggression is thwarted, Vietnam, the prestige of revolutionary, militant Communism remains low. As Israel remains safe, Nasser and the other Middle Eastern dictators will be afraid to snuff out that beacon light of democracy.

Please pay no heed to the highly articulate and vocal minority which advocates a sellout in Vietnam. This is the time for long-standing patience and fortitude. If we continue to hold in Vietnam, I see the rest of the Communist world turning revisionist eventually and world peace secured, and the pipe dream of successful violent Communist world revolution held by Castro, Lin Piao, etc. passing from the thoughts of men. *Contradictory* *to many*

My Sincere Best Wishes for a Happy New Year,

G. G. (male)   *Pro-War for purposes of scaring ideas of Communist take over of other Contries*

[Editor's note: Fidel Castro (1926–) became premier of Cuba in 1959. Mao Tse-Tung (1893–1976) ruled Communist China. Kim Il-Sung (1912–1994) held power in North Korea. In China, Lin Piao (1907–1971) was the second-ranking member of the Communist Party in the late 1960s.]

95. "stand against Communism"

York Village, Maine
September 8, 1968

Dear Senator Smith;

We are most concerned about the conduct of the war we are losing in the Far East. If we send men to battle, to fight and die or to live for ever maimed we should at least give them the support they need.

More attention and publicity seems to be given to the rabble rousers and paid protesters than to the tax payer who is losing money and patience. We have talked enough in Paris. It time to act. We have not made a mistake by taking a stand against Communism. The mistake the Administration is making is by not letting our military win.

Very sincerely,

H. F. (male) and M. F. (female)   *Voice of Support*

V. WAR OPPOSITION IN 1968

Almost a year earlier, General Earle G. Wheeler, Chairman of the Joint Chiefs of Staff, told the president that "the adverse military tide has been reversed, and General Westmoreland now has the initiative. The enemy can no longer hope to win the war in South Vietnam." Media reports of the Tet Offensive made this and other optimistic predictions appear ridiculous. The dates of the final two letters are after the Tet Offensive, an event that unfolded with devastating results, psychologically for the United States and militarily for the Viet Cong and North Vietnamese Army. The communists, however, would bounce back. The letters dated before January 30 did not need the Tet Offensive for their characterization of the war and American involvement as insane, naïve, and immoral. The angst that many Americans were experiencing in larger urban centers existed in the small communities and towns of Maine. It was a stressful period for Senator Smith, but she did not alter her hard-line position.

96. *"How insane must we act!"*

Palermo, Maine
January 17, 1968

Dear Senator Smith
    Near the time of President Johnson's Johns Hopkins speech on Vietnam, I wrote to the President, yourself, and Senator Muskie expressing my view that our nation was capable of solving the Vietnam "problem" without continuing warfare. All three replies were essentially in the same vein: you and Senator Muskie backed the President and he was following a difficult and prudent path. All of which I deeply respected.
    Since then I have sought knowledge of Vietnam, its history and lately the current history of U.S. involvement in Vietnam. All my reading may be summed up effectively in one book "The United States in Vietnam" by George Kahin and John Lewis.
    If you still back our President's policy towards Vietnam I pray you to seek your own council in this matter, that our Nation may soon recognize the horror of its committment to a cause which is in direct apposition to our basic political tenets. People now have the right to seek freedom thru Communism just as we once sought it through a Whig medium. Factual history advises me that our presence in Vietnam is not in our National interest—certainly not in the Vietnamese interest.

We still follow the course of lack of understand regarding China. How insane must we act!

Hopefully,

H. F. (male)

[Editor's note: Explaining America's mission in Southeast Asia, Johnson gave his "Peace Without Conquest" speech on April 7, 1965. George McT. Kahin and John W. Lewis were specialists in Southeast Asian history who presented a "dove" perspective in *The United States in Vietnam*.]

97. *"so naive"*

Cape Elizabeth, Maine
January 24, 1968

Dear Senator Smith,

This letter is the first I have written to any of my political representatives. The subject is one that not only my husband and I, but many of our friends, feel very strongly about. I have chosen to write you, because I consider you a person of great integrity; and, one who is interested in serving the people whom you represent.

Since we first heard Hanoi representatives had said they would be willing to discuss peace, if the bombing stopped, we have waited for our government to take the nest step towards talks. Yet, days and weeks have gone by, and our leaders have done what seems to us to be very little in implementing this meeting, save reporting "We will stop the bombing when Hanoi agrees to no troop build-up during the halt, etc., etc., etc."

It is a very frightening thing to even think—but we all are wondering more and more if our leaders really do want peace in Viet Nam now. As the weeks go by, this question grows, bringing other thoughts and questions to mind. Are our government officials brushing this over with the hope still clinging of a military victory? Are they convincing themselves peace talks aren't possible, in order to MAKE this a military victory? It also becomes understandable why those in other countries have so much hate for us. If we can turn our backs on peace, and toy so with the possibility of a third world war. And what of our best, maimed and dying every day in the jungles? Is time so cheap?

It seems so naive to demand a promise from the enemy that there would be no troop build-up (if peace talks were to begin, amid a truce). We have halted the fighting before, for what seemed trivial reasons, and build-ups and violations occurred then, even after promises from the enemy. No doubt they would occur again, with or without a promise from Hanoi, or anyone else.

Why, then, waste time and take the chance that Hanoi will change its mind, while quibbling over these things?

I am asking you to use your influence to help convince the President, and the Secretary of State, and all those in decision-making positions, that we depend on them to do EVERYTHING—not just as Secretary of State, Dean Rusk says, "Our share",—but EVERYTHING POSSIBLE to get the United States and Hanoi to the conference table.

It would not be surprising if, when the United States finally does decide to talk peace, Hanoi will turn a dumb ear, and I pray this doesn't happen. If it should, there will be many here and abroad who will say the fault lies much with the U.S., for stalling and playing games of politics. And, would they be right?

Sincerely,

J. O. (female)

98. "immoral, futile"

St. George, Maine
January 13, 1968

Dear Mrs. Smith,

We do not favor the President's suggested "travel tax" on pleasure trips outside the Western Hemisphere. Inevitably, such measures are circumvented by those travelers who spend the most dollars abroad, and the tax falls most heavily upon thos of us who must save for years for that once-in-a-lifetime trip abroad. Is it fair that we pay for the jet set's "business trips?"

The President does not deceive us with his concern for the dollar outflow. If he were as anxious as he appears, he would make a genuine effort to negotiate a peace settlement in Vietnam and bring our troops—and the dollars in which they are paid—home where they belong. So far LBJ has only proposed what he knows the opposite side cannot accept.

We are also opposed to the Vietnam war on the grounds that it is immoral, futile, and not in the long range interest of the United States.

We urge you to cast your votes for measures which will bring a speedy end to this dreadful war.

Sincerely yours,

R. S. (male) and A. S. (female)

[Editor's note: The "travel tax" was a small item compared to the serious debates on the rising costs of the war and President Johnson's fight for a major tax bill that he believed was essential to prevent damaging inflation and dangerous deficits.]

99. "the blood guilt"

North Haven, Maine
January 25, 1968

Dear Senator Smith:

I hope you will excuse my duplication of the enclosed credo which I have finally prepared hoping, as a concerned citizen, to absolve myself in some degree of the blood guilt which is on the hands of all of us. If the product is not very professional, this is one of the few (very few) disadvantages of living on an island ten miles from "civilization".

I have worked long and hard on this between [other projects], and hope you will be able to give serious consideration to at least the first two pages. Very truly yours,

E. B. (male)

(attached)

Protest and Vietnam

Reports from Vietnam make it clear that many of our troops are baffled and hurt by the protests here at home, which seem a deliberate attempt to repudiate and discredit them and disrupt the undertaking on which they are staking their lives. They cannot understand why this is even permitted, as it appears to them sheer perversity, aberration, or irresponsibility without any sense or meaning. In short, they do not know the reasons for this protest. But the fact is that the protesters feel they have good reason for their stand. Why is it that these reasons are not made clear to our soldiers? Does the Pentagon fear they would quit the army if they knew the whole truth? That our men are so unaware bespeaks a suspiciously parochial attitude on the part of our information services overseas. Is this still-young nation already suffering hardening of the arteries which does not permit circulation of thoughts and ideas?

An essential of Democracy, for which they are fighting, is an informed people at least aware of the alternatives in important questions. What more partial than a judge and jury which may hear only one side of a case, what more inept than an electorate which knows only one version in a controversy, and what more ominous than a military, like the youth of Nazi Germany, which is fed a single slanted doctrine?

Why don't the protesters state their reasons, you ask? They do state them, and these reasons are common knowledge to large numbers of people, those who search for the truth outside the mass media and Government handouts, who read more than the commonest periodicals and local paper. Why don't they try harder? They do try harder. They write, they talk, they sing, they shout, they march, they demonstrate, they even incinerate themselves; they risk abuse and vilification, injury and imprisonment. Who listens?

Callous hecklers urge them to go ahead and burn themselves alive, but would not, even so, listen to their reasonings. They are disadvantaged, like one trying to hold aloft a lighted candle in a raging storm. Theirs are often fragile arguments, the appeals to reason, justice, and pity, and are no match for the whips and clubs of patriotic fervor used by militarists of all history to brutalize the people and keep them thirsty for blood. When forceful at all, their arguments exceed the bounds of credibility and good taste, when restrained they seem pointless and insipid. Either way they lose. The Big Lie, as Hitler demonstrated, is unassailable, invulnerable.

The call to arms is always more thrilling, more stirring and romantic, than the invitation to reason together or the plea for sanity and moderation. The voice of the lynch mob is always more strident, compelling and infectious that that of the pacifist. The psalmist said, "Blessed are the peace-makers" knowing well that theirs is the difficult, unspectacular, thankless role.

[margin note: Christian appeal]

The writer is in no way qualified to speak for the protesters nor attempt to catalogue their arguments, but will venture nevertheless to submit to the following examples illustrating six broad categories of thought, together with two pages of quotations selected from hundreds of statements by public figures in substantiation of their views and vindication of their stand, from St. Peter up through John F. Kennedy, U Thant, Senator Fulbright and Robert McNamara.

Categories of Protest

1. They believe the War is illegal and immoral and that this war is particularly unjust, being basically a civil war in spite of the Administration's frantic effort to focus attention on North Vietnam's intervention, which they themselves provoked. They believe that the war flouts the Constitution of the U.S. in never having been declared, and that the affairs in Tonkin Gulf were mis-represented, and the Senate involvement dis-ingenuously planned for a predictable result now regretted by many.

2. They believe that the strategy of this war is militarily unsound, morally bankrupt, and politically disastrous; that our aims are already lost and that we shall be shamed forever by our rape of this small nation and by our pitiless employment of ghastly devices. They believe only a twisted mind could fail to lump the horrors of Napalm, the horrors of Hiroshima,, and the horrors of Auschwitz in any moral argument. They believe it is a mockery for Gen. Westmoreland to insist that for a halt in our bombing (which itself flies in the face of all sense and morals) the enemy should promise to abandon all movement and supply while we continue to build up unhampered our own vast warehouse guaranteeing 20, 000 tons of materiel daily to our own forces, ten times their requirement.

3. They believe in the Credibility Gap, the juggling of facts and figures to give any desired impression; the bad faith and lack of candor which has characterized this Administration in its forecasts, its promises, and its reporting; particularly they condemn the duplicity of the Administration for its pretense to seek negotiations while taking every calculated step to avoid them, and its dissembling in the matter of escalation.

4. They believe that instead of preserving Vietnam we are destroying it, and instead of even advancing our own best interests we are wrecking our economy, disrupting our own desperately needed social programs, inviting dissension and chaos here at home and presenting ourselves debased and discredited at the court of world opinion, with the probable result of retarding world understanding and the final risk of pulling the whole world down around us.

5. They believe the Saigon regime is not genuinely Democratic nor truly representative of the people but basically a dictatorship like that of Hitler whom Ky admittedly admires; a regime fastened on the people by the military and bolstered by U.S. arms, treasure and propaganda tosuit our own purposes. They believe that Viet consensus is not behind our presence and conduct of the war, that few except those now in power are strong advocates of our methods or even our help, and that Viet unity, purpose and morale have been shattered.

6. They believe that Man's conscience owes allegiance to an Authority higher than the laws of any State, including our own, and that their protest is in the finest American tradition. They believe that our peace-time Conscription is an abomination, that it is inequitable and discriminates against the poor and disadvantaged. They believe that punishment of protest by Draft Board action equates service in this country's armed forces with penal servitude, and is a denial of civil right.

. . . "I must obey God, not man" . . . Saint Peter.

---

100. "this nation's transgressions"

Old Town, Maine
February 23, 1968

Dear Senator Smith,

I wrote you once last summer about my concern about the war in Vietnam. At the time, you thanked me for my concern and pointed out that I did not have access to all the facts. I admit that I do not have all the facts, but during the last few months, I have come to the conclusion that no matter what the things are that I do not know, that this nation's transgressions have become too flagrant for me to feel that I can condone them at all. The U.S.

has become the most imperialist, aggressive nation in the world, and I wish I thought that my vote, recently acquired, would do any good.
Sincerely,
V. H. (female)

101. "how is it possible"

Burnham, Maine
February 17, 1968

Dear Madam:—

The law that was just passed by the President, saying there will be no more deferments on collage graduates, is a grave injustice to our nation, if not a critical one in this day and age. It should have never been alowed. But it does tell one thing our present administration is thinking in terms of a longer war possible world war three. Which we both know would destroy our nation and the world.

I would like to ask you one question.

How is it possible for the Viet Cong, North Vietnam's troops to come right into to Sigon where we are suppose to have some three hundred thousand troops there & South Vietnam has some 600, 000 troops in and around there. It looks to me as tho there has been many more of our boys killed then has been let out.
Sincerely,
J. (male)

Part II

THE NIXON YEARS, 1969–1971

TIME LINE

November 5, 1968	Richard Nixon defeats Vice President Hubert Humphrey in a close election
April 3, 1969	Americans killed in Vietnam (33,641) exceeds the number killed during the Korean War
June 8, 1969	President Nixon announces the first troop withdrawals; 25,000 by the end of August
September 16, 1969	The U.S. government announces the withdrawal of 40,500 troops
October 15, 1969	Moratorium antiwar demonstrations take place throughout the United States
November 3, 1969	President Nixon's "silent majority" television and radio address
November 13, 1969	Major antiwar demonstrations begin in Washington, D.C.
November 19, 1969	Congress passes the military draft lottery bill
April 30, 1970	Nixon announces "incursion" of U.S. troops into Cambodia
May 4, 1970	National Guards kill four students at Kent State University, Ohio
May 9, 1970	Senator Smith at Colby College to face students
June 29, 1970	American troops exit from Cambodia
July 12, 1971	The number of U.S. troops in Vietnam is 236,000, a reduction of over 300,000 since Nixon's inauguration (on January 31, 1969 there were approximately 542,000 US troops in Vietnam).

$\mathcal{T}$here were more than 14,500 American troops killed in Southeast Asia in 1968. The year on the home front was a disturbing one of protest, urban riots, and the assassination of civil rights leader Martin Luther King, Jr. Richard Nixon returned to politics in this turbulent year that also witnessed Johnson's surprising withdrawal from the race for reelection, the assassination of Senator Robert Kennedy while campaigning for the Democratic presidential nomination, and the nomination of Vice President Hubert Humphrey at the Democrats' Chicago conference where unprecedented confrontations between the police and antiwar protesters occurred in front of television cameras.

Nixon's campaign promise to get American troops out of South Vietnam gave him just enough support to defeat the team of Humphrey and running mate Senator Edmund Muskie in the fall of 1968. The new administration's foreign policy in Southeast Asia was similar to that put forth by Johnson. Nixon sought an honorable peace that saw the withdrawal of both American troops and the communists from South Vietnam and the maintenance of a separate, independent non-communist nation for the South Vietnamese. The communist leadership in the north and the Viet Cong in the south did not waver from their insistence for a so-called "democratic" government in South Vietnam that, of course, would be communist. Soon after Nixon's inauguration, the North Vietnamese accelerated their military operations in South Vietnam. Nixon wanted to put more pressure on the communists, but an increase of American troops was out of the question. He outlined the plan of Vietnamization, the buildup of South Vietnam troops to replace the reduction of American troops in South Vietnam. In early 1969, there were approximately 540,000 troops in South Vietnam and the goal was to reduce this number in stages. To buy some time while the South Vietnamese army gained strength, Nixon initiated an escalation of bombing, including more targets in North Vietnam but also sites in Laos and Cambodia. The bombing of the latter by B-52s took place without the knowledge of Congress and the American people.

The pace of any significant change from the Nixon administration, however, was slow in coming. On October 15, 1969, millions of Americans participated in the Moratorium, a large nationwide antiwar protest. In November, organizers of the Moratorium also threw their support behind other antiwar events, including an antiwar rally at Washington Monument that attracted approximately 750,000 people. The "silent majority" mentioned in some of the letters sent to Senator Smith after 1969 refers to Nixon's speech given in November 3, 1969. Reaching out to "the great silent majority of my fellow Americans," Nixon asked for patience as the government dealt with the

Vietnam issue. Polling of those who watched the speech indicated a favorable response and, thus, Nixon appeared to shore up support from his Republican base and conservative Democrats who tended to embrace one or another form of Cold War ideology.

Smith maintained her hard stance against communism, a position that had been politically effective for her from the beginning of her years in the Senate. Her response to antiwar letters was that the president was on the right track in reducing American troop involvement. A good number of the letters sent to her before April 1970 covered issues separate from antiwar arguments. Nixon's speech of April 30 changed this. On that evening in a live radio and television broadcast, Nixon informed the American people of an incursion in progress by American and South Vietnamese troops into Cambodia. The stated objective was to destroy enemy sanctuaries without occupying Cambodia.

A significant number of Americans did not accept Nixon's arguments and there was a spontaneous reaction across the nation, especially at colleges. Antiwar hostility erupted with deadly consequences. In response to acts of property damage and the burning of the Reserve Officers' Training Corps building, the National Guard took up position at Kent State University in Ohio. On May 4, tragedy struck when the Guard fired sixty-one rounds in a crowd of students and bystanders, killing four. Violent images added much to the despair of this period. Smith received numerous letters from distraught Maine people in the following weeks and the dominant antiwar message and Smith's response, demonstrates that the month of May represented a watershed for her political life. The tapering off of letters concerning the Vietnam War in the months after May 1970 correlates with changes unfolding in both the antiwar movement and Smith's own political life.

• 4 •

Nothing New under the Sun

I. WAR POLICY SUPPORT

Senator Smith consistently upheld a position that aggressive communism was at fault and that the justification for American involvement in Southeast Asia was "to stop the communists from conquering the world." As for her relationship with the new president, Smith and Nixon had a history of distrust for each other. In particular, her experience with Joseph McCarthy in the early 1950s caused her to view Nixon as a McCarthyite. On the issue of the Vietnam War, however, Smith publicly supported Nixon, believing he was on target to find an honorable way of ending the war without retreating to the communists. The letters in this section indicate not only support for Nixon and hawkish strategies, but also a conservative backlash to the actions of various antiwar protesters.

1. "unleash the full offensive power"

North Whitefield, Maine
December 8, 1969

My Dear Madam Smith:

The farcical propaganda oriented "Paris Peace Talks" as executed so skillfully by the North Vietnamese and Viet Cong conclusively have proven that Admiral U.S. Grant Sharp, USN (Ret) was and is correct on how the United States should conduct the Vietnamese War to <u>Win</u>! The attached article from the May 1969, Readers Digest is worth reading again by the Senators in Washington.

Certainly any pullout of U.S. Troops will result in a more horrible blood bath initiated on the South Vietnamese by the depraved communistic led

121

North Vietnamese and Viet Cong than was ever perpetrated at Hue. Do we want this heaped upon our heads also?

Won't you please heed the military counsel and do all in your power to unleash the full offensive power of the great nation to bring these cruel North Vietnamese butchers to their knees and thus insure the freedom of self determination of all peace loving people.

I also implore you to counteract the communistic plan to weaken our Armed Forces from within by the initiation of courts martial against patriotic men who were doing the job we instructed them to do. I am certain that the exploitation of the horrors of war involved in fighting a non identifiable enemy composed of men, women and children is a master plan to discredit our great nation. Knowledgeable Americans know that non identifiable Viet Cong men, women and children have murdered hundreds of American Servicemen. I wonder how our misled Americans would have carried out the assignment that was undertaken by Lt. William L. Calley, Jr. (particularly in a known Viet Cong stronghold held in their vice grip for many years). Lt. Calley implemented well defined tactics which when carried out are one of the few means available to defeat an enemy who has no mercy for any living creature.

I note with great displeasure that the News and TV Media are exploiting the biased spectacular side of this affair also thus further weakening our military and political position. God bless Vice-President Agnew for setting the record straight. It is of interest to note that the facts presented by the Vice-President were known to be factual by members of the News Media. . . .

In conclusion, I strongly request that your thinking and decision in the Senate not be influenced by the boisterous and deceptive opinions voiced by the militant and misled minority. I assure you that these opinions are not held by the majority of the American people and in particular those patriotic Americans who reside in our State of Maine.

Bless you Madam.

Respectfully,

R. J. (male)

[handwritten: We should be in Nam to win; should not be pulling out]

[Editor's note: Ulysses S. Grant Sharp (1906–2001) was the commander-in-chief, United States Pacific Fleet, 1964–1968. His conservative revisionist article in the *Reader's Digest* is entitled "We Could Have Won in Vietnam Long Ago." William Calley, Jr., was the American soldier charged and convicted for the murder of more than 300 Vietnamese civilians, mostly women and children, near My Lai. The My Lai massacre that took place in the middle of March 1968, but was only exposed the following year, was the most notorious American atrocity of the war. An army investigation resulted in fourteen individuals charged, but no convictions with the exception of Calley who received a sentence of life imprisonment. He was free on parole in 1974. Faithfully serving the role of administration lightning rod and provocateur, Vice President Spiro Agnew (1918–1996) and his combative statements on student demonstrators, intellectuals, and the media polarized the nation. He blamed the liberal media for undermining the American military campaign in Southeast Asia.]

2. *"This is war"*

Tenants Harbor, Maine
May 1, 1970

My dear Senator Smith:

I am as opposed to the Vietnam War as anyone but I fully support the President in his policy of terminating the with honor to all parties.

I hope you will support him in his present efforts and oppose the proposed efforts of a number of senators to restrict his course of action.

This is war and no commander can properly conduct or direct it with his hands tied.

I firmly believe that hasty withdrawals without proper guarantees by the other side will result in the lose of many American lives and divide this country at is has never been divided before.

Sincerely,
W. W. (male)

Opposed to Nam War but don't think they should withdraw hastily

3. *"liberals have been brain-washed"*

Sorrento, Maine
May 27, 1970

Dear Senator Smith,

We are so astonished at your short-sightedness. Pres. Nixon has acted in the best possibly way to hurry the war on to a close. American liberals have been brain-washed by communist propaganda, until they are acting to help the enemies of this country! We expected more of you. We wanted politicians with courage, who face up to reality. If we don't have them, we shall slide slowly down into another great war—for communism understands nothing but strength.

With sorrow and alarm from two old-timers who have given many ancestors in the cause of freedom, and who have themselves been to Russia and know what the challenge is today.

Mr. and Mrs. L. H.

4. "disgusted with my generation"

Gorham, Maine
May 8, 1970

Dear Senator Smith:

I have never written to a Senator before, but with all the talk about "write your Senator" I thought this was as good a time as any.

I am deeply disgusted with my generation (the group in college. I am 22). These young adults, if you can call them that, seem to think they know everything, etc. etc.

Look what happened at Kent State. I believe the National Guard were in the right, and think it will be a disastor to this country and its government if these men are prosecuted for doing their job. No wonder the young men do not want to go into the Service. If they refuse to go, they are put in jail. If they go and protect themselves and our country they are put in jail. A pretty reward I'd say.

This is no time to stop the younger generation; things have just gone too far. Congress and government in general should have taken direction action seven or eight years ago.

All anyone in politics can think of is not to say or do anything that will hurt their votes in the next election. Government just does care what this does to this country and its people.

I could go on and on for pages on this matter it makes me so mad. I have just one thing to say in closing. I am a direct descendent of John Adams, and I am very happy that he isn't here to see what government as well as people have done to this country. It just makes me sick.

Sincerely,

G. C. (female)

5. "over-aged spoiled brats"

West Buxton, Maine
May 28, 1970

Dear Senator Smith:

This will be a long letter, but please bear with me. I have not written to register an opinion since 1964, but in the last few weeks so much has happened to make me feel indignant and outraged, I feel that I will burst if I don't write.

. . . What might be pertinent is that my fellow [co-workers] are in agreement with my opinions. We range in age from twenty-one to fifty. While two of us are from Maine and two are from the South, the rest are from the Pacific Northwest. As far as I know I am the only registered Republican in the group.

First of all, I am horrified by the stand taken by some U.S. Senators with regard to the action in Cambodia. How can our military commanders in S.E. Asia act quickly, if approval must be received from Congress before they can take action against the Viet Cong or the North Vietnamese? I am sure the enemy will know of our future troop movements before our troop commanders, if that is going to be the case in the future. These senators seem to be more anxious to embarrass the President than to see the war in S.E. Asia brought to a favorable conclusion for us. If we are going to withdraw, helter-skelter, from S.E. Asia, we will find ourselves withdrawing from bases much closer to home in the near future. Eventually, like it or not, we will have a "Fortress America" policy, but without the fortress, for if this very same group of senators have their way, we will have no means to protect our missile bases which may be our only defense; as a deterrent or by their use. These very same senators who proclaim loudly that we should get out of S.E. Asia, seem to be anxious for us to get more deeply involved in the Middle East. The most charitable thought I have regarding these senators is that they must implicitly trust the Chinese and Russians not to attack us. But some times I wonder what the "J" in J. William Fulbright stands for. Could it be Judeas?

. . . A final thought about S.E. Asia; if we can maintain pressure on the Chinese to keep them out of that area, won't they be more liable to attempt to expand in the direction of Russia?

. . . As far as the student "unrest" in the States goes, I can feel very little sympathy for the youngsters, though in the final analysis, the fault lies with the parents for not bringing up their children properly. I am not so old but what I can remember my own childhood. I remember that the only thing that kept me out of mischief was the certain knowledge that I would be punished if I misbehaved. In the last thirty years with both parents working, they, the parents, are too tired to bother with their children. When the children want something, no matter how outrageous, it is easier to give in to the children than to say no. If the children are disobedient, it is easier to ignore it than to discipline them. Eventually, these children grow up and get out in the world. They find the society they live in doesn't permit them to have their way always. So, they rail against the "establishment". I feel that our student rioters are nothing more than over-aged spoiled brats. And yet, on the radio, I have heard these students described in glowing, idealistic terms! Are they really mature enough to be allowed to vote?

Also on the radio I heard that Senator Muskie, and others attended the funeral of a student at Jackson, Mississippi. Our opinion here, formed from the news coverage, is that Senator Muskie and his friends used that funeral for publicity purposes. Our junior senator may be making progress in solidi-fying the "dove" vote behind him, but he will need more than that in order to become president. . . .

Thank you for reading this. I shall try not to bother you again for a long time.
Respectfully yours,
W. E. (male)

[Editor's note: In a similar event to the Kent State University tragedy, police killed two students at Jackson State College, Mississippi, on May 14 during a demonstration at the predominantly African-American institution.]

6. "student radicals"

Mount Vernon, Maine
May 15, 1970

Dear Senator Smith,

My reasons for writing you are twofold:

1. I am <u>against</u> the "amendment to end the war," as advocated by Mc-Govern, Church, et al.

2. I am asking you, as a member of the joint committee, to restore the appropriations in Title II to at least the FY 1969 level to HR 16916 for col-lege library assistance and library training. These funds are very important to the faculty and students at the small, young Augusta campus of the Univer-sity of Maine. . . .

I am an independent voter. I have always voted for you. I will continue to do so unless it appears you are getting soft on the subject of student radi-cals and their equally addled elders who persist in thinking with their emo-tions instead of their brains, and who practice political expediency at the ex-pense of our country's long-range future the way our super-ambitious Senator Muskie has been doing these past few years!
Good luck to you,
Sincerely,
K. W. (female)
P.S. I have never written you before. Call me one of the "Silent Majority."

II. WAR POLICY OPPOSITION

The political maneuvering and election in 1968 and the transition of the Nixon administration in 1969 appeared to offer distractions for many ordinary Americans. Senator Smith received only a modest number of antiwar letters in this period. After April 1970, there was an avalanche of letters sent to Smith displaying a high degree of emotion concerning specific Nixon decisions that appeared to expand rather than limit American military involvement in Southeast Asia. Like the agonizing letters sent in the Johnson years, the following antiwar letters give evidence of frustration, helplessness, and sadness. Rhetoric such as "crises," "horror," and "tragic deaths" spoke volumes.

7. "I am appalled."

Hallowell, Maine
April 28, 1970

Dear Senator Smith:

Since the President's speech on last Monday night, I have tried to think hard and clearly about our situation in South East Asia. In spite of the many words from many people I have never been able to justify our military presence there. Now, after five years of constant combat with the death of so many young men, plus the many increasingly evident dislocations to our society, the President asks us to reconcile ourselves to still another year of war. It is true that during that year he is promising (perhaps) to reduce the number of men exposed to the war, but at the end of that time there will still be a quarter of a million of our men there with no indications of an end in sight. And he says this as though we should be grateful to him for an accomplishment. I am appalled.

Seldom have I been willing to base my support or opposition to my legislative representation on a single issue, but at present this one seems to me to be of such over-riding importance that I will actively support anyone who will take a positive position favoring immediate withdrawal, and I will oppose anyone who favors a continuation or acceleration of this present policy.

If the leaders of the American people cannot find a better solution than that offered us by our President, we are indeed a sorry lot.

Yours very truly, *Favours immediate withdrawal*
M. O. (male)

8. "the two crises facing America"

Damariscotta, Maine
May 9, 1970

Dear Senator Smith:

I suppose that over the years you've come to believe that a form letter like the enclosed is "better" than no acknowledgement at all . . . but it seems to me that the difference is minimal.

Be all that as it may, please realize that the two crises facing America— the war and the Administration's handling of it, and the frustration and bitterness of Our college youth (not the lunatic fringe of the Left or the Right) but the earnest, dedicated and confused majority, the majority, the vast majority,) and not Nixon's silent majority either—these crises are going to cease to be crises and become national disasters, unless a great deal more than the present administration seems willing to do, is done.

Please do everything you can to get us out of Viet Nan and to stop the polarization of our people. Agnew is an unmitigated national disaster all by himself, and I'd like to have more confidence thatn I have that our president doesn't agree with him.

Most sincerely yours,

J. B. (male)

* This waspish comment to the contrary not withstanding, you were great on Carswell— and great on McCarthy, like Agnew a vicious national danger, 15 plus years ago.

[Editor's note: Senator Smith, again, demonstrated her independence by voting against Nixon's choice for Supreme Court judge, G. Harrold Carswell (1919–1992) of Florida. She was supportive of Nixon's Vietnam War policies, but she was not afraid to oppose him when he selected a Supreme Court judge who had a record of mediocrity and racism.]

9. *"the horror there"*

Old Town, Maine
May 21, 1970

Dear Senator Smith:

I write to you out of concern for our country and its people. Because I feel it is important for you as lawmakers to know the feelings of the mainstream of Americans, I give you this background information.

Having been brought up in a small Maine city, subsequently attended college in upstate New York, accompanied my husband to [outside America] . . . we have been back in Maine some fourteen years now, and are trying to contribute in whatever ways we feel we can to the betterment of America. Normally, I am sure I would be considered a part of the "silent majority", for I find it difficult to express myself and fearful that my feelings may be misinterpreted, particularly where the issues are not clear cut.

However, there comes a time when we all must stand up and be counted—not only on issues concerning us, but in making decisions as to through what groups we will work toward what we consider worthwhile goals for our society.

My first moment of truth came when registered as an Independent (though from a family of staunch Republican background), I decided that I wanted some voice in the primaries as to who would run to represent Maine in Congress. We were in Morocco at the time; and a dedicated worker on our local Republican committee was interested enough to help us with arrangements for absentee balloting. Since then my husband and I have become increasingly active in working for good government and also in encouraging young voters to join in. They so desperately need inspiration and guidance.

That is one reason why I was so disappointed not to have you with us at our recent state convention. I do realize the limits on time your work imposes. Convention trappings as such may seem unimportant, but we Republicans in Maine desperately need all the help we can get to show our young people that our elected officials do care and are working hard for what we consider the right course for America. You can greatly help us because you are much more conversant with many areas than the average layman can be.

Last night I was with a group of University of Maine students, including one who has recently returned from a tour of front-line duty in Vietnam. These were not radicals, but dedicated, peace-loving young people who are seriously seeking direction for ways in which they can best work for the good of our country. I was saddened at their sense of disillusionment because they feel so many of us adults turn them off without listening.

I feel that we must listen—though not necessarily agree—and then to the best of our ability guide them along the paths we feel best for our country. For if we, who feel we arrive at decisions after searching and thoughtful deliberation, will not listen to them and guide them, who can?

This brings me to my main concern in writing. I try to search out answers for the terrible conflict in Southeast Asia. Realizing that none of us laymen can know all the considerations involved in our leader' decisions, I try to give President Nixon's stand the benefit of the doubt. But all within me cries out that there must be an end <u>soon</u> to the horror there. It might well be that that part of the world just might have to go it alone and work out their own problems for a while. <u>Our presence there over too many years has not seemed to contribute to any happy solutions; and I for one very seriously decry any more American blood being expended there.</u>

I believe it is time for us as a nation to reassert our determination in positive ways to work for the good of the world.

This letter, Senator Smith, comes from the heart, and my hope is that you will regard it as such from a very concerned citizen who loves her country and its people.

My thought is that all of us must do what we can, where we are, to better the United States of America. My prayers are with you as you work for the good of our country.
Yours truly,
A. L. (female)

[Editor's note: Colleges, students, and faculty across the nation went on strike in early May as a response to the invasion of Cambodia and the killing of four students at Kent State University. The University of Maine was no exception and the arts and sciences college faculty passed a motion by a two-to-one majority to support student protesters. There were rallies on campus, cancelled classes, and teach-ins. Some faculty and students who opposed campus recruiting efforts by corporations profiting by the war took their protest to President Edwin Young's office.]

10. *"pretty bad shape"*

Cape Elizabeth, Maine
May 12, 1970

Dear Mrs. Smith
I am writing to you because I believe, that at the moment you are the only Senator Maine has who is working for the good of Maine as well as the Nation, not running around trying to get yourself elected the next President of the United States.
I go to Cape Elizabeth High School where I am in the ninth grade. This letter is in reference to the murder of the four Kent State students by the Ohio National Guard. When it comes to the point that students can not hold a peaceful demonstration to show the President that he is not acting to the wishes of the people without the National Guard turning their demonstration into a riot, and then murdering four students because "there was a sniper.." this country is in pretty bad shape.
Earlier this year the Army charged a man with the murder of over one-hundred South Vietnamese civilians. These "South Vietnamese civilians" were probably for all intents and purposes Viet Cong, people who were feeding and sheltering the enemy and very probably fighting the allies. Yet this man will be brought to trial and will probably receive a prison term. In other words, In fighting a war and killing what was probably the enemy a man can be sent to prison. If this can be done to a man who is risking his life twenty-four hours a day, I certainly think it can be done to the National Guard for killing four American students who were trying to show the President that he

was not acting in what they felt the best interests of Americans. Thank you
for your time.
Yours truly,
C. W. (male)

11. *"stop the war"*

Fort Fairfield, Maine
May 19, 1970

Dear Senator Smith:

I am a resident of the State of Maine and a citizen of the United States.
I am unmarried and work as a secretary earning less than $5,000 per year. . . .

I am writing to state that with the high cost of living such as food, clothing, fuel, utilities and taxes, life is becoming more and more difficult and com-
plicated for us to endure.

I feel that we should stop the war in Viet Nam and Cambodia at once
and bring our troups home in order to solve our major problems in the United
States. Certainly, I don't want my sixteen-year old nephew spilling his blood
for a senseless cause in Southeast Asia in a few years time.

Never have our issues been so grave. With the money that is being spent
on a meaningless war effort, let us care for the needs of the American people.
Let us care for the needs of pollution, racial equality, our sick, our poor, our
elderly and our young people.

I thank you for this opportunity to express my opinion.
Yours very truly,
M. A. (female)   Domestic issues > importance than Viet Nam
                   Conflict

12. *"the power the Pentagon wields"*

Yarmouth, Maine
May 29, 1970

Dear Senator Smith;

I am a new member of your constituency. My husband and I came to
Maine at the beginning of this year, mostly for environmental reasons. Maine
is by no means removed from our intense national problems, but its pines and
birches and seacoast and virginal space give us a little breathing room for one
to think and act with a minimum of depression and indigestion.

So young people, and parents-to-be, we want very much to be active
in solving national problems, and at the moment, the most critical of these problems is the attainment of peace. I believe campus unrest, urban explosion,

minority injustice, pollution, and economic "downs and downs" all hinge in one way or another to U.S. involvement in Southeast Asia and the power the Pentagon wields in forming foreign policy.

With regard to the possibility of a U.S. in peacetime, I would ask you to support the following four bills, the first two concerned with the immediate problem of peace in Southeast Asia, and the last two with a permanent peace in the future.

1. The Church-Cooper bill insuring the secession of U.S. involvement in Cambodia by the end of this June.

2. The Hatfield-McGovern resolution to end the war by the end of 1970.

3. Senator Brooke's resolution (Sen. Res.211) for an immediate mutual suspension of MIRV testing pending the outcome of the SALT talks.

So I understand the MIRV tests, once they have been fully tested, there is no chance to reverse the race towards annihilating mankind. Surely our present capacity to destroy Russia's fifty largest cities fifteen times over does not need to be improved upon! President Nixon's science advisor, Dr. Lee DuBridge, has affirmed the safeness of Senator Brooke's resolution.

Joining Brooke in this resolution would be a very positive contribution on your part toward world peace. Please consider how precarious the chance of permanent world peace is, while MIRV testing goes on.

4. Finally, Representative Halpern's bill for a Department of Peace with a Secretary, Under Secretary, and four Assistant Secretaries. In view of the overwhelming strength of the Department of Defense (once upon a time more honestly titled the Department of War) and the Pentagon in the formation of national and foreign policy, it would seem logical that such views leaning towards military solutions of problems should be balanced by people who actively seek peace and believe in peaceful methods of settling disputes between people and between nations.

I hope you will at least consider these four bills and perhaps advise me as to your stand on them. If you have already signed any of them, thank you very much for your part in making the future a credible possibility for the younger generation.

Sincerely,

A Mother-to-be for Peace

M. N

[Editor's note: Presented by Senators Frank Church (Democrat) and John Sherman Cooper (Republican) in May 1970, the Cooper-Church Amendment sought to limit presidential powers during war. The McGovern-Hatfield "Amendment to End the War" stipulated the withdrawal of U.S. Troops from

Vietnam and the suspension of all U.S. military operations in Southeast Asia before January 1972. All Republicans, Senator Cooper (1901–1991) represented Kentucky, Senator Edward William Brooke III (1919–) represented Massachusetts, and Representative Seymour Halpern (1913–1997) represented New York. Dr. Lee DuBridge (1901–1994) advised the president in 1969 and 1970. The MIRVs (Multiple Independently Targeted Re-entry Vehicles) were missiles equipped with multiple warheads. SALT refers to the Strategic Arms Limitations Talks between the United States and the Soviet Union; the first SALT agreement came out of a summit meeting in June 1972. It is unclear whether the above author was a member of the group called "Another Mother for Peace." Founded in 1967, AMP encouraged members to write and notify politicians of their opposition to war.]

III. INQUIRIES

While some letters sent to Senator Smith consisted of straightforward questions on practical concerns and other issues, a number of writers used an inquiry to make a particular point about American involvement in the war. Letters here were for, against, or neutral concerning American involvement in Southeast Asia. In one case a nurturing mother worried over American boys not having access to an adequate supply of fruit. Among the most powerful of letters were those from frightened parents as seen in the first two letters of this section. A mother from Joy, Maine, wrote of living "one month in hell" when she desperately sought information concerning her injured son in South Vietnam.

13. "enough?"

Rockland, Maine
June 20, 1969

Dear Mrs. Smith:

My son . . . is in the Naval Reserve and in the Seebees. He has served eight months in Vietnam and is due to go again in July.

With all this talk from President Nixon of troop withdrawal from Vietnam why is it that my son and apparently many others have to go again to that God forsaken country when they have already served there once.

I know how you feel about this deplorable situation and I hate to trouble you as a busy as you must be; but don't you think if any young man is sent there once, against his will of course, that it is enough?

I hope you are feeling much better and may God give you the strength to do what you think is right.

Very truly yours,

D. R. (male)   *Individuals should not have to serve two terms.*

14. "How much is one family supposed to take."

Joy, Maine

Sept 21, 1969

Dear Mrs. Smith,

I have a question. How much is one family supposed to take. First our son 19 years old is drafted. This we excepted as duty. After 16 weeks training we are informed he is to go to Viet Nam. A war in which even our government does not call a war. Next we receive a letter from our son saying he has hurt the muscles in his right hand and got hit in the head with motar fragments. This after one month in Viet Nam. We wait for one week for word from the government to notify us of his health and welfare. Nothing comes so we ask help from the Red Cross. After four days of not hearing from them I call again and they say they can find nothing. So I went to one of our State Representatives. After two days we find out that the government is to busy to report to the parents about their children. They are not to busy to draft them though. After two and one half weeks we gave up. We received another letter from our son one week before giving his hospital address in Japan so we tried calling him only for him to tell us he is going back to Viet Nam in two more weeks. We have lived about one month in hell worrying when just a little word from our wonderful government we could have been spared this. We try to bring our children up with honor and love for their country. How can anyone keep honor when you take a 19 year old boy away from home and after he gets wounded, send him back to get killed unless he agrees to sign a paper for one more year of service then he can have a job on the back of the lines. If this is the American way then I must have been brought up under false pretenses and have lied to my children. Now I would like to know how much money it takes to get out of Viet Nam. When a government is to busy to report an injury to one's parents. I think it is time for us all to pray for help or drop a big bomb and end it all. It is beyond help. I believe there is a lot of people in this country who feel as I do just are not so scared as I am so don't write to you. Why can't my son and a few others of the wounded be sent home instead of replacing the ones who are able to be sent home in good health because it is good politics.

Just a scared Parent

R. J. (female)

15. "Don't you think you could contribute to that change?"

Kennebunk, Maine
May 7, 1970

Dear Senitor:

I am writing you, because I am so very disturbed at the one sided coverage on T.V.—Radio & News papers, regarding the Colledge upheavals & riots.

The students & outsiders who invoke the trouble are getting away with murder. And that's no idle statement. They were directly responsible for the 4 deaths at Kent Ohio. Not the Nat. Guards. But who is getting all the blame? Pres. Nixon & the V.P. Not one voice is raised, to put the blame where it belongs.

Why are not his party teammates in the Senate & House, coming out as strongly against those who are really to blame, as those who are mis-directing the blame on him? Yourself included?

I believe with your record & influence you could bring to bear, that you could be a powerful help to the side which does not approve of condone the awful mess.

We all know that the news media is all <u>one</u>-sided and only for what is sensational, & makes news.

Wouldn't it be wonderful, if <u>some</u> one, some how, changed the <u>sensational</u> to Patriotism, & loyalty once more?

Don't you think you could contribute to that change?

I am a woman your own age, who am very active in civic betterment. Not welfare or charity. But in doing things for other's benefits, I find most folks I talk with, are very co-operative when it comes to Country. I believe we can out number the radicals, if we all pull to-gether. I hope you can be a leader for the good of the Dear old U.S.A.

Sincerely,   *News is on the Viet Nam*

V. L. (female)

16. "We expect you to reply"

North Edgecomb, Maine
May 7, 1970

Dear Senator Smith,

We are returning your letter as entirely unsatisfactory. We refuse to believe that our concern could be handled in such an off hand manner.

As our representative in Washington, We expect you to reply and give us your views or at least the courtesy to inform us why you disagree.

May we remind you that in a democracy an informed citizenship is the government and you are its representative.

We should know your way of thinking about matters that concerns our country, and you should avail yourself of the opinion of your constituents.

There is no doubt a "silent majority" is an ideal citizenry for a dictatorship of the right or the left. I hope you are not in favor that this government should stumble into this category by default of its citizens.

Your first responsibility as a senator is to the people.

Please do not add to our distrust of the president by further disillusioning us about the congress of the United States.

Sincerely,

E. S. (male) & L. S. (female)

[Editor's note: Smith's written response (below) was unusually brief. One possible explanation is that she was experiencing considerable pain; she had her right hip replaced soon after.]

Mr. and Mrs. E. S_____
North Edgecomb, Maine

Dear Mr. and Mrs. S_____:

I received your telegram of April thirtieth with regard to sending arms to Cambodia.

Sincerely yours,

Margaret Chase Smith

United States Senator

Expected to hear her thoughts

17. *"wondering if you might enlighten me"*

Milo, Maine
May 14, 1970

Dear Senator Smith:

I am wondering if you might enlighten me about a matter that has been brought to my attention by several of the servicemen who are serving in Viet Nam from our area? We write to two young men regularly and of course ask what we can send in packages etc. The biggest request and it comes frequently is canned fruit. I was very surprised. These boys claim that they receive no fruit what so ever with meals.

I found this hard to believe so I inquired around. Boys who served there as far back as '64–65 through ones who have just returned all said the same. Little or no fruit. One young man (he is now 28) said his mother had sent him a can of fruit cock-tale and a 12 year old VietNamese boy ran off with it.

He said he had his rifle to his shoulder and ready to pull the trigger before his buddies stopped him.

My husband who is some what older than these men served his time from 1955–1959. He said at that time all rations issued had canned fruit in them. He too was very surprised that our men are not getting canned fruit.

Is it possible that fruit just isn't available? Or does the man in the field or in areas near the DMZ just have to take a back seat to those in Saigon and the more built up areas.

I don't mind sending packages of fruit to these boys—but what about the poor fellow who has no one to send him some. I think that the moral of these boys might be helped some if something was done about this situation.

Could you informed if there is reason for this situation and if anything is or can be done about it.

Thank you,

Sincerely,

K. C. (female)

18. *"We are a nation of equals or are we?*

Hallowell, Maine
May 21, 1970

Dear Senator Smith,

Events of the recent weeks have finally egged me on to write this letter and the final push was given by my son . . . a student at the University of Maine.

[He] came home after the academic disaster that has graced many of the edifices of higher learning. Throughout this week, [my wife] and I offered no advice and left the decision up to our son on the strike issue and am proud to say that he voted against same. The following weekend, [he] came home and said the major support for the strike was the lower classmen and the upper classman particularly the seniors were against the strike and exhibited their mature judgement in negating the idea. My son supports the President as I do and realizes that the best defense is an offense. People have forgotten the 20th Maine at Gettysburg attacked an Alabama Regiment and won when they were so decimated that they should have been taken prisoners. Today I wonder if we are not losing our intestinal fortitude. We have a great country but I wonder if greed and avarice have not taken over plus neglect on the part of parents. In our case we came out with a real American, although I must admit, I could have given my son more time.

I would like to say also that I believe the draft should be changed to include the college crowd when they get out of high school. I can not see why the availability of tuition and a college ticket exempts many prima donnas that we saw perform over the last weeks. Failure to go to college should not be punished because of funds or lack of desire. We are a nation of equals or are we? Does the dollar bill take precedence over equality?

I must admit that I have nothing but shame for my Bowdoin College background and feel that Bowdoin as well as many other Universities should examine their faculty members and hire some loyal Americans. I seriously wonder and am concerned as a citizen, especially The State University that operates by my taxes, that I should be supporting some communistic leaning in our instructor staffs. It is time that we stopped "Pussy footing" around and called a "spade a spade". I wonder whether Kruschev is not laughing in his beer after he said they would tear America up from the inside at The UN in New York. Americans have short memories. Please pardon me for so long a letter, but I have a son that has a few years ahead and I would like to think there would still be a United States in his lifetime. Russia's gain in the missle arsenal as well as other military endeavors coupled with the obvious or unwitting communistic supporters in the United States is a matter of great concern.

Thank you for your indulgence and patience and despite the uncertain times, I don't feel that I have to apologize for being a straight laced American with a little pride in our country. I can still claim no shame for shedding a few tears when I see the National flag. I wonder how many Americans can do this today? Again we have a large house and an open door if you should come up to Maine. Congratulations on your speech in Colby and I proud to be your constituent. If the other half of the Senatorial team from Maine would should signs of being a Senator and not a Presidential candidate, Maine's efficiency would increase fifty percent.

Respectfully yours,

J. B. (male)

[Editor's note: At the all-male Bowdoin College (Brunswick, Maine) of approximately 950 students, most of the faculty opposed granting students any credits for the Army R.O.T.C. In early May 1970, Bowdoin President Roger Howell and the faculty sided with Bowdoin students protesting against the war. The Brunswick Town Council condemned the resulting student "strike." Estimates claim that on campus there were a small and equal number of active members in both the Students for a Democratic Society and Young Americans for Freedom (a national conservative youth organization). The Colby College incident mentioned receives much attention in chapter 6, I.]

19. "Whose war is this"

Gardiner, Maine
May 25, 1970

Dear Senator Smith,

I am a registered nurse who used her holiday on Monday to visit with you and my other representatives in Washington. I was extremely disappointed that neither you nor your legislative assistant were available for me to talk with. Maine is far enough away so that I am sure you are not often visited by your constituents. However, I feel that when someone, such as myself, comes that far with the express purpose of talking to my representatives, there should be someone available who is in a position to at least speak for you.

I was there with a group from the Harvard Medical community in order to urge you to support the Hatfield-McGovern Bill. I realize that in the past you have not tended towards voting for such a measure, but at this critical time I feel that immediate and total withdrawal of our troops from Indochina is mandatory.

Whose war is this, ours or the South Vietnamese? How long can one afford to polarize and split the country to the point of violence as a result of frustration and anger? Our prestige in the world cannot help but decline as others view the split inside the country, the decreased value of the dollar, and the health, education and welfare systems that are starving for funds and reorganization.

It is time to review the priorities of our nation. We can no longer afford to fight in a purposeless war, such as the one we are in in S.E. Asia, at the expense of our vital domestic needs.

It is also time for Congress to reassert its control over the president. Mr. Nixon's decision to enter Cambodia was inexcusable in many ways, but particularly in the way he ignored the opinions of anyone in Congress.

I strongly urge you to vote for the three bills before you; the Cooper-Church, the repeal of the Tonkin Gulf Resolution, and the Hatfield-McGovern Bill. Help us to make a firm step towards peace.

Sincerely,
H. G. (female)   *Importace Domestic > Vietnam*

[Editor's note: The following letter is one of Smith's longer responses to a constituent. Written at the end of a difficult month of nationwide protest and turmoil it is particularly revealing and informative of Smith's understanding of the Vietnam War issue and her defensive attitude toward those who questioned her integrity.]

May 29, 1970

Dear Miss G:

I regret that you were offended. There were several other members of my staff available to talk with you in the absence of myself and my legislative assistant. It is unfortunate that you did not ask to speak with any of the other capable members of my staff.

I have seen hundreds of students expressing the same views that you do in your letter and raising the same points that you have in your letter—many of whom have been from Maine.

I shall vote for repeal of the Gulf of Tonkin resolution—but I shall vote against the Church-Cooper Amendment and against the McGovern-Hatfield Amendment.

I have faith in President Nixon and I believe his record is far superior than that of President Kennedy or President Johnson. President Kennedy sent our first troops into Vietnam for combat duty. President Nixon reversed that policy in his first year as President by bringing back 115,000 of our boys—and will bring back another 150,000 within a year. He ordered the Cambodian incursion not only for the protection of our troops but as well to aid in the planned withdrawal of our forces from Southeast Asia.

President Johnson increased the number of our troops in Vietnam to over 500,000. President Nixon reversed that policy by bringing back 115,000 in the past year and ordering another 150,000 to be brought back within a year. I think his record is clearly superior to that of President on extricating us from Southeast Asia.

I refuse to say that he is lying when he says all of our troops will be withdrawn from Cambodia before July 1, 1970 and I am not going to discredit him before he has the time and opportunity to keep his commitment.

If my support of him results in causing retaliation from you, then that is a penalty I accept without any hesitancy whatsoever.

I extend the respect and courtesy to you believing that you are expressing your sincere views—regardless of whether you reciprocate or not.

I regret that you found that your holiday was spoiled by my not being present in Washington on that holiday.

Inasmuch as no votes were scheduled in the Senate on that holiday, I had gone to the Columbia-Presbyterian Hospital in New York City that day that your were here as that was the first opportunity I had had for some time to seem my orthopedic surgeon for a checkup on the arthroplasty surgery he had performed on my left hip. I have been having severe pain for several weeks.

I am sure that you would not deprive me of doing this. Should you have the slightest distrust of me, I welcome you to write Doctor Frank Stinchfield at the hospital to investigate if I am telling you the truth.

Sincerely yours,
Margaret Chase Smith
United States Senator

20. *"Could your office kindly locate and send me . . . ?"*

Alfred, Maine
September 17, 1970

Dear Senator Smith:

Could your office kindly locate and send me an up-to-date list of our Service Hospitals in South Vietnam with correct APO numbers? Not names of C.O.s or Chief Nurses as they change as year's duty is done.

. . . we have been sending packages of paperback books to those hospitals we know of . . . .

You will be interested to know that the wonderful people of this town of Alfred, Maine have contributed over 3,000 paperbacks to date. We are all anxious to let our nurses as well as our men out there know that we in the most far away state are still think=ing of them.

The books have come with very little effort on my part. I was kindly permitted to place labeled cartons in our library, our one store, our one restaurant and one hairdresser's and the books poured in. My husband (also a WW2 vet.) has cheerfully packaged and paid for mailing in lots of 20 to 25 each. The chief nurses tell me they are truly appreciated and passed from hand to hand until fall apart and help pass the tedious hours our injured spend there.

Your assistance with the up-to-date list will be very much appreciated.
Sincerely,
E. S. (female)

III. RELIGION AND VALUES

As was the case in earlier years, Senator Smith heard from ordinary Americans and a few church ministers who used religious rhetoric to express a diversity of opinion. The varied positions meant that there could be no consensus on the issue of the war and several letters in this section suggest that Christians who held a biblical perspective at odds with the liberal theology of elite antiwar clergymen tended to show greater support for a more forceful foreign policy when dealing with communism. The first letter, however, is a long, powerfully disturbing account of rape and murder that occurred in South Vietnam and how such evil activities, in the eyes of the author, had ties to atheistic and satanic beliefs within communism. Another letter is of a mother lamenting that her son has lost his Christian faith. In the Vietnam War, issues of morality had many contexts and some of the following letters are examples of more direct piety.

21. "satanic beliefs"

Calais, Maine
March 18, 1970

Dear Senator,

This will be a long letter because increasingly of late some very disturbing bits of information have been coming to light, facts that should concern every loyal United States citizen because they have to do with the honor and integrity of our Nation.

On page 70 of the February issue of Christian Herald magazine, at the top of the page, an item appears about the book "Casualties of War", written by Daniel Lang, printed by McGraw Hill of New York. I have not yet read the book but this item says, "On November 16, 1966, a reconnaissance patrol began a mission in the central highland of Vietnam. The sergeant in charge told his men they were going to get themselves a girl, and for five days 'avail themselves of her body, finally disposing of it, to keep her from ever accusing them of abduction and rape.' The patrol found a pretty Vietnamese teen-ager in a near-by village and began to carry out the plan. One member of the patrol was Sven Eriksson, a Lutheran boy from Minnesota who refused to take part despite jeers at his lack of virility and threats to make him a KIA (killed in action). After the girl, Mao, had been repeatedly raped <u>at knife point</u>, <u>stabbed and her head blown off</u>, Sven thought the army would do something about the crime. His lieutenant and captain advised him to keep quiet. When Sven persisted, trials were finally held and his four companions were given <u>light sentences</u>. As soon as the last two GIs get out of jail, Sven knows they may kill him for revenge. He wishes he could forget what happened to Mao, but he cannot. '<u>It had been preceded by any number of similar occurrences.</u> <u>'In one form or another, he said, they took place almost daily.</u>'" (Underlining is mine.)

In war, of course, we expect fighting and killing of some soldiers but the armed forces of supposedly civilized nations are not expected to indulge in needless killing. Much publicity has lately been given to a massacre of some civilians in South Vietnam a few years ago, and the part that Sergeant Callay may have had in it. Here in "Casualties of War," it would seem that some U.S. officers deliberately <u>plot</u> to abduct attractive teen-aged girls, abuse them sexually, and after a few days kill them—premeditated kidnapping, premeditated sexual abuse, premeditated murder, deliberate crimes by members of our armed forces, with the apparent unconcern of their superior officers. This is a shocking revelation of the low moral standards apparently held by numerous officers in charge of our armed forces in South Vietnam; a permissiveness which allows kidnapping, sexual abuse of those our armed services are supposed to be helping, and premeditated murder with little or not attempt on the part of superior officers to stop it. In other words, the officers become accessories of the murderers. I do not believe this has won the respect and confidence of the South Vietnamese people for our nation. It will not win the respect of the morally decent citizens of the United States, or their confidence in the officers in charge of our armed forces. No wonder that some of our young men return from the war zone disillusioned with the actual value of this no-win war as it is being conducted by our government leaders.

Incidentally, while Mr. Lyndon Johnson was president I remember one news item which reported that he was advocating government controlled houses for prostitutes to be opened within easy reach of camps, on the excuse that venereal diseases could be avoided or greatly reduced. In other words, Mr. Johnson was putting his personal sanction on easy immorality rather than on moral integrity for the armed forces of our country. I have never heard or read that Mr. Johnson's suggestion was carried out, but of course it may have been one of the hushed-up bits of business that has been kept from public knowledge.

Our Presidents and all members of our Congresses must know that alcoholic beverages damage both the body and mind of those who drink; and that immoral practices do not develop proper thought or high ideals such as create wise legislators—Presidents, Senators, and other government leaders, or a truly great national army, navy, and air force—and yet many use such drinks, and some, no doubt, injure themselves with immoralities. Apparently no lesson was learned on the need for constant preparedness from the tragic unpreparedness of the armed forces on the morning of Dec. 7th following the party on the night of Dec. 6th at Pearl Harbor where lots of free liquor had reportedly been available, thanks to the genial but potentially hostile hosts, the Japanese.

The greatest enemy to our country today is said to be communism not only in communist countries but also within our own United States, and yet for years, especially during and since the presidency of Mr. Franklin D. Roosevelt, our Presidents, many members of Congress and the Federal Supreme Court have been very soft toward communism both inside and outside of our nation's boundaries. Infiltration by communists, with their atheistic and satanic beliefs, their lawlessness and violence has been permitted, resulting in the perversion of many of our inexperienced and immature youth.

Hobnobbing socially or trying to do business with those who boast that they are going to "bury" or overthrow our nation—and whose actions prove that they mean it—is no solution to our national problem. The years that have increasingly demonstrated the inability of the United Nations to cope with the Communist refusal to co-exist in peace with non-communists nations, should have taught out nation's leaders the futility of depending any longer on the United Nations. Russia produces both defensive and offensive weapons without publicity and without world protest, but Russia accuses the United States of handicapping the arms talks when our nation considers defensive measures. Russia does not honor such pacts as she makes when she prefers to disregard them. Her work is of no value whatever; she constantly is aiding and abetting the communist activists in ways that will cause trouble all over the world; she wants to cause discord and dissension in the United States and weaken the cause of national freedom wherever it exists. Many of our Congressmen and other leaders seem to be cooperating with Russia's designs.

No wonder so many of our youth feel insecure; no wonder that they consider something to be radically wrong in our country; no wonder there is great unrest, lowered personal ideals and standards, even reaching into the armed services. Apparently our youth has found no signs of high morality, or deep patriotism; little indication of genuine "Trust in God" emanating from many of their superior officers or their governmental leaders. The murderers among our armed services in Vietnam are the product, are they not, of the actions and influences of the educational, social, and political activities of the past twenty years? Communism has had its subtle effect upon that. Is our nation about to sell itself out to atheistic, satanic, massacre-approving communism? One of your deeply concerned constituents,
J. H. (female)   *Attack at the moral of the Army*

22. *"Holy Bible"*

Calais, Maine
April 15, 1970

Dear Senator,
Thank you very much for sending me the letter from W.J. Chilcoat in reply to my letter quoting from the Christian Herald items concerning the content of the book, "Casualties of War" by Daniel Lang. I appreciate your aid in bringing me this information.

All war results in many tragedies, and most especially so the prolonged no-win wars such as in Korea during the Truman administration and this South Vietnamese war begun in the Kennedy administration and escalated during the Johnson years in office.

The most authentic and best book ever written concerning the relation of men toward each other is the Holy Bible. I can not find an "no win" directives from God, I can find, instead, the "go out and don't be afraid because God will be with you to help" -directive . (Deut. 20:1) Also Jesus sent His disciples into many cities to tell the people that "the Kingdom of Heaven is at hand", but He warned them to leave any city where the people did not care to listen. The disciples were even to shake the very dust from their feet. (Matt. 10:2, 14). Doing business with Godless communist people and nations, helping them to greater prosperity and power has not brought about the desire for honorable cooperation. Both communism and Big Business seem determined to cause the overthrow of our "nation under God", and some congressmen and government leaders appear to be aiding and abetting them. Why is this permitted without active protest?

Yours truly,

J. H. (female)

[Editor's note: The same author wrote the previous letter.]

23. "a President who relys on God"

Eastport, Maine
May 19, 1970

Dear Senator Smith:

In as much as I feel you are the only real representation we in Maine, have in the Senate, I am writing you about my concerns. Let me also say the criticisms I have to make are in no way personal either, as I feel confident, though I may not have always agreed with your decisions, in my opinion you have always acted in the way you felt best for our country. We in Maine, irregardless of party affiliations love and respect you.

I am concerned with the present trend to curtail our President's powers and I feel at this time it would be detrimental to the well being of our country. Certainly the dissention in our higher eschalons of government, which is always given wide coverage by the news media, lends stimulus to the youth marches, strikes and even violence. While our boys are giving their lives, our politicians are for a great part aiding and abetting the enemy—so why should they give up when receiving such loyal support from representatives of our government? Much of this has political overtones, which is apparent by the loudest voices of dissent who were "rubber stamping" for the past two administrations but suddenly have all the answers for an end to the war. They are also great proponents of air pollution but constantly polluting the air with maligning statements and divisive ones. Where have all our statesmen gone?

Naturally we are not always right but this is our country and we should have her for what she is and stands for and defend her even unto death.

We are fortunate to have a President who relys on God for his decisions. Who is willing to sacrifice himself for the sake of his country, while one of his chief adversaries and critics neglects his duties in the senate to race around raising money for his own party and hoping to insure his own political future. It's time to follow our President and humble ourselves and pray. God says "When a people who are called by My Name will humble themselves and pray then they will hear from heaven". There is nothing more practical or effective than prayer in solving problems of any kind.

Thank you Sen. Smith for giving me a bit of your time and be assured you as well as our President and the whole Senate are being remembered each day at the Throne of Grace. If we seek His face in faith believing, He will do the exceeding abundantly on our behalf.

Respectfully,

V. B. (female)

24. "a fine Christian man"

Jacksonville, Maine
May 30, 1970

Dear Madam:

If I am one of the so called Silent Majority, who are supposed to agree with all our elected officials say in public I go on record now as no longer a member of that group. I think it is a shame & affront to the people of Maine and the Nation, to listen to, or allow even certain high elected officials of this State to snip away at our President. I can only conclude these voices have the next years election in mind.

I think also it gives aid and comfort to the enemy which only serves to prolong the war.

Our forefathers would have called this Treason.

I believe our President is a fine Christian man and a Patriot and I thank God he is at the helm.

Let us all remember, and some memories are very short in election years especially, that our Chief inheireted this mess and is doing everything humanly possible to end it with honor and dignity.

Let us then give all support to the man who has the most difficult and thankless of jobs rather than to discourage and discredit him.

Personal

Dear Mrs. Smith:

I sent this letter to the "Letters to the Editors" of the Bangor Daily News. These comments are not directed at you. I think you are a wonderful

person and dedicated to your job. I only wish some of our elected officials had your good qualities.
Yours respectfully,
M. B. (male)

25. *"we silently pray"*

Bucksport, Maine
May 10, 1970

Dear Mrs. Smith,

It cannot be legal or right for the faculty members of a state University to let the students not attend classes for the rest of the year while they will receive their present grade average in June.

It is not possible that these professors be allowed to convert classes into workshops to educate and mobilize opinion against the decision of our government and our president who are trying for a quicker peace.

Many of these students must have received State Grants and Federal Loans to help them. A statement must be signed by the student on at least some of these as to their allegiance to their country in order to receive these.

Violence is deplorable. Rock throwing can be lethal—Standing in such a crowd is encouraging such action, which demands the use of troops or police.

Too many people are closing their eyes and ears and saying these peaceful (?) student dissenters should have their chance == even as some dissenters openly shout of revolution.

We silently pray that the President's decision—which we consider right—will accomplish a quicker peace.

We silently pray for those who sit with long faces—for those who dare to desecrate the American flag.
Sincerely
R.W. (female)

Interesting thoughts almost speaks against Freedom of Speech.

26. *"lost his faith"*

Springvale, Maine
May 23, 1970

Dear Mrs. Smith:

I need help and don't know what to ask for in the Library and haven't too much time to read books. Thought of you and hope you can suggest something.

One of my sons goes into the service [next month] and he is very bitter about Vietnam and the administration. I wrote him I thought President Nixon did right in sending our men into Cambodia. In fact, I felt sorry for our military leaders that they could not do it before. It must have been hard on them to have the enemy hit and run to Cambodia and to have supplies hidden there.

Yesterday he sent an article on Vietnam prepared by the staff education committee of Join Community Union, 4553 N. Sheridan Rd., Chicago, Ill. 60640. It is all for Ho and his policies and his plans for South Vietnam.

All I know is what I have read in the papers and magazines. I know the French went there to profit. We have misused the negro and Indian here. But I felt we were there to help the South Vietnamese and to try to stop the Communists from taking over that part of Asia.

[My son] went to Sanford High School and I was shocked when he came home and told what his history teacher told them about the American Revolution. He said it was started by rabble rousers and men who wanted to get rich quick. We gave him our ideas of the men we admired, Washington, Jefferson, Hancock, etc.

However, he has [years of undergraduate and graduate university] behind him and as he is coming home for two weeks before going in the service, would like something to back up my beliefs.

Does the government have anything giving a brief resume of their stand similar to the six page propaganda on the peasant's view [he] sent me?

Our oldest son spent four years in the Air Force and . . . [w]e had high hopes for [the youngest boy]. When he went to [college] he was ambitious, a hard worker, and a Christian. He did not like the worship service on the campus and went to the Baptist Church [near the college]. (Was glad of that as [our older son] had gone there when he was at [college] and it was a good church). Now he seems to have lost his faith in the church as well as his country.

I suppose I should be happy he did not turn to drugs and to the militants.

I suppose the war upsets the plans of the young and we who are older don't understand.

The country has so many problems. I feel sorry for President Nixon and you who are in Congress and pray that you will be given the wisdom to make things right.

Sincerely yours,

J. M. (male)

27. *"pervert our youth"*

Brownville, Maine
May 16, 1970

Madam:

You probably have seen the excellent editorials in the Bangor Daily News, of which these two clippings are samples.

I feel that we are not very far from a revolution, which has been carefully instigated by Communists to pervert our youth. For the past twenty years, or more, it has not been popular to be patriotic. The ills of our country, instead of its many good points have been played up in the press and media, and text books have been "revised" with the same aim, until now we have a generation some of whom are eager to desecrate the flag and openly work for the defeat of their own country. Lenin said, you remember, that by working at the youth of America, in one generation it would fall like ripe fruit in the Communist lap. We did not believ him. We were so sure that when both sides were presented, freedom would prevail.

It may be too late, already, but it seems to me we have failed to do our utmost to show North Vietnam as the agressor, to hammer away as the Communist sympathizers have, to refute their harangues, to follow their inflammatory speakers with others who tell the truth, and, of course, to crack down <u>hard</u> on violence, burnings, occupation of buildings, and other acts of destruction and indignity.

And where is the United Nations? We never hear about it in the press any more. Granted that it has no teeth to act, it should be a rallying ground for opinion—or have we let all the opinions there, too, be slanted to Communism?

You, I realize, have to act through legislation, and probably can do little. We have the legislation, but it is not implemented. Criminals get all the breaks—suspended sentences, or none at all. But I know you are a conscientious and brave Senator, and I hope you will speak out, as you have before in lesser crises.

Your very truly,

L. F. (female)

28. *"men become alcohol drinkers"*

Fryeburg, Maine
November 5, 1969

Dear Senator Smith,

Thank you for contacting my request, that something be done to try to bottle water for the Vietnam soldiers, with the Department of Defense officials.

I had to smile at their answer that it is "not economically feasible" in the face of the many ways the money is spent.

Any returned soldiers and others over there that I hear from do not call the water program successful as this Department wrote it is. This is something some of us can continue to work on.

I was talking with a returned soldier yesterday and he said many of the men become alcohol drinkers when they return from using the beer in Vietnam.

Thank you again for your effort and you may be able to do more on this subject of bottling water to send.

Yours truly,

S. B. (female)

· 5 ·

Cambodia Fireflash

I. OPPOSED

$\mathcal{N}$ews reports of April 29 and President Nixon's televised announcement the following evening that American and South Vietnamese troops were launching attacks on North Vietnam army sites located in neutral Cambodia galvanized the antiwar movement. The contested terrain of what constituted the proper direction for American foreign policy was again on the radar screen for many Americans as they witnessed the escalation of military engagements in Cambodia. The widespread explosiveness of this episode is obvious from the following poignant and spirited letters sent to Senator Smith from people living in small towns. Two letters include messages addressed to Nixon.

29. "deeply shocked"

Burnham, Maine
April 29, 1970

Dear Mrs. Smith

I was deeply shocked to see that we have been comitted to Cambodia and I feel its a very bad mistake on the part of the president of the United States

Now we are well on the road to world war 3, because now Russia, & China are obligated to send ground forces in to this area. So begans the first faze of world war 3.

Hasent there been enough mistakes without this?

Maby I am wrong in how I think but I believe its the worst mistake we as a people have done, now our country will be divided more than ever cause this now will take in all of Asia a divided people & country will not stand up.

This dosent mean I am a dove like some call each other. But I still we are in the wrong.

I hope you will do something about what has happened. Or perhaps you cant, But I truly hope. . . .

Thanks for listing to me. But I do care what happens to this country very much & this was could be the ruening of our Economy & if this goes we as a nation are done like others before us. God Bless Our Country
J. H. (male)

30. "futile and pernicious"

> Jackman, Maine
> April 29, 1970

Madam:

We wholeheartedly urge you to do your utmost to restrain the Nixon Administration's effort to extend military aid to Cambodia.

We believe that this a futile and pernicious continuation of the tenacious theory that the U.S. can deal militarily with S.E. Asia, on the contrary, it can only further impair the possibility of any reasonable termination to the Viet Nam War.

The fallatious appeal to American commitment to freedom and democracy must not be allowed to continue. Rather, it must be made evident that further extension in S.E. Asia runs directly counter to the best interests of this nation: it is injurious on practical terms and further erodes the perpetual effort to actualize the ideals of freedom and democracy in their true form.
Sincerely yours,
N. F. (male) and R. F. (female)

31. "sinking deeper every day"

> Falmouth Foreside, Maine
> April 29, 1970

Dear Senator Smith:

This is the first time I have written a letter to a public official, but I feel that the time has come that I must protest. If I were not primarily occupied with earning a living, I would join the peace marches.

The news this noon was most disturbing. If the radio station is not misrepresenting the facts, it would appear that we are now heavily involved in

Cambodia. I, along with countless other Americans, have endured our involvement in Vietnam, but now the situation has the appearance of quicksand. We are sinking deeper every day, and I feel it is time to withdraw.

The nest item covered on this newscast was the announcement that the stock market has taken another plunge. The economy of our country is in jeopardy, and over and above the expenditure of lives in Southeast Asia, the monetary expenditure is more than we should be involved with. We have some pressing problems here at home, as I am sure you are aware of, that could use some of the defense money.

I have always voted a Republican ticket, but the recent actions of this administration have caused me to doubt the wisdom of my past votes.
Sincerely,
L. S. (female)　　Domestic policy more important than foreign war

32. deeply disturbed

Skowhegan, Maine
April 29, 1970

Dear Senator Smith:

I am deeply disturbed by the news today that the United States has entered upon the soil of Cambodia with members of our Armed Services. I see this as a direct contradiction to our efforts to extricate ourselves from Southeast Asia.

I firmly believe that we must acknowledge that there is no fight for freedom in Southeast Asia. Rather there is a battle between opposing forces having no desire for freedom: the Communist bloc on the one hand and the equally totallitarian, if rightest, governments of South Vietnam and Cambodia. In this battle we have no part, save to leave and allow them to settle the real arguments as to which system of non-freedom shall rule in that part of the world.

I hope that you will actively oppose this new step by us into Cambodia.
Sincerely yours,
R. S. (male)　　NO Freedom in Communism of American system

33. "deeply disappointed"

Boothbay Harbor, Maine
April 30, 1970

Dear Senator Smith,

I am opposed to the action that the President of the United States of America has taken in sending troops into Cambodia. I have been deeply disappointed in the apathy among members of the Congress of the United States to curb the overwhelming power of the Military and the Executive branches of our government. Either the system of checks and balances is an outdated and unworkable system in the Twentieth Century, or the members of both parties of both Houses of Congress are unwilling to do the job they are elected to do.

Either take the necessary legal action to curb the unrelenting power of the Presidency and the Pentagon or declare War and let this battle become an open and legal battle that can be fought to win. The battle is already being fought on the streets of America and there is no more time for delay and evasion. The next step will be too late, if that time hasn't already arrived.

I oppose the action of President Nixon, President Johnson and President Kennedy in taking us into Asia with our military forces. I equally oppose the do nothing attitude of their Congresses that have given them such a free hand to pour our resources and manpower into a far away cause while most Americans see such a dire need for all that ability here in our own Country.

Sincerely yours,

M. W. (female)

34. *"warlike stance"*

Falmouth Foreside, Maine
April 30, 1970

Dear Senator Smith:

Just to beg you to take a firm stand against the current Cambodian involvement. Your voice is a strong one . . . one that will be listened to where it counts . . . and I want you to know that we are depending on you to try to stop the madness. The country cannot withstand this further violence, particularly at a time when we had been led to believe that Mr. Nixon was "stopping" the war and withdrawing our men.

I cannot believe that we are right in this warlike stance, and in the knowledge that it makes no difference to the White House what I believe, I'm turning to your good offices.

Sincerely,

A. B. (female)

35. *"very much grieved"*

Temple, Maine
April 30, 1970

Dear Senator Smith.

I am very much grieved to hear the news that the U.S. has become involved in Cambodia. It is most disturbing to realize that we have a President who is so concerned with his own image that he seemed unconcerned with our countrys needs. It would also seem that our Congress is not made up of dedicated men. It seems as though that President Nixon or Congress are not conscientious enough not to deal in blood. As of today with all the authority given the President that its almost unnecessary to have a Congress. Mr. Nixon has turned about face in his champaign he agreed to end the war in Vietnam. Now he is escalating it. It would seem Congress surrended its power by permitting an ill-advised undeclared war.

Yours truly,

F. B. (female)

36. "Are we un-teachable!"

North Edgecomb, Maine
April 30, 1970

Dear Mrs. Smith:

Last evening we, the citizens, were informed that the president has sent ground troops and advisors into Cambodia—perhaps against the wishes of the nationals of this country.

I must now add my small, and probably unheeded, vote of protest to this further involvement.

Are we to be forever compounding former mistakes? Are we un-teachable!

Have we become so feeble that we can only react and are unable to choose a course, hopefully right, and stick to it till the race is run?

Can a just and honorable solution be found to what seems to be a dishonorable operation? I doubt it.

Mrs. Smith, I feel that the military (pentagon) are much too generous with the blood and lives of my young countrymen.

Yet he who speaks out, even in a rational way, against this worsening situation runs the risk of being branded unpatriotic or worse.

We were told that we were not involved in Laos but the facts proved to be what?

Do you wonder that our nation is in a state of unrest?

Is the credibility gap widening? Perhaps it's time for another "declaration of conscience" from a very much respected member of the senate.

Thank you for reading this.

No reply necessary.

Respectfully yours,

R. C. (male)

37. "outrageous"

Cape Elizabeth, Maine
May 1, 1970

Dear Mrs. Smith,

Enclosed is a copy of a letter we are sending President Nixon. We urge you to support those Senators who are searching for ways to curtail our participation in these outrageous adventures.

Sincerely,

Mr. and Mrs. C. S.

Dear Mr. President,

We strongly protest the commitment of American forces to actions in Cambodia. For a decade we have watched operations, which the military promises will shorten the war, lengthen into frustrating and murderous quagmires, and each Thursday we hear the grim casualty figures. There is no evidence that we have brought any measure of democracy to any countries of Indo-China, but we have brought an incredible measure of human misery to the people of those countries as well as to countless families in our country.

For a decade we have heard speeches like yours last night, full of promises to defeat the enemy; to save American lives, and to end the war honorably. We do not accept these promises—the war cannot be ended with a military solution, and our honor has been irredeemably tarnished, not only by isolated incidents such as My Lai, but also by our unconstitutional military presence in southeastern Asia.

However, most outrageous of all, is the promise to protect American lives. American lives will only be protected when our soldiers are removed from the areas of warfare; it is a measure of how confused our policies are when we send men to battle in order to protect them!

We are appalled by your rejection of the opinions of the elected representatives in the U.S. Congress, and we support their moves to curtail Vietnam funds.

Sincerely,

Mr. And Mrs. C. S.

[handwritten annotation: War cannot end w̄ military solution, We are not currently protecting American troops]

38. "I am appalled"

Hallowell, Maine
May 1, 1970

Dear Senator Smith,

I am appalled at the president's latest and most provocative move. I am appalled at his attitude about our country and the need to show U.S. power and importance. I am appalled about his assertions about humiliation and defeat.

To me every one of his statements is morally wrong in the world of today. His undercover and aggressive attacks, which he labels as defensive moves, are not only wrong and against all principles basic to freedom in today's world, but they are bound to make an already bad situation undeniably worse.

The situation today demands of nations that they learn to live <u>with</u> other nations, other peoples, other cultures. <u>The president is increasing the idea of our place in the world as one of imperialism and aggression. His incredible need to avoid defeat and humiliation, and to show our pride and arrogance, has only led to more and justified hostility.</u>

In addition, the constant demand on our young men to fight in a war that is incomprehensible and useless, is adding immeasurably to the conflicts at home, and reasonably so.

I should like to know exactly where you stand on this issue. I feel that this move must be reversed immediately, and that there is no way to handle the southeast Asian situation but immediate and complete withdrawal of our troops. <u>War, declared or undeclared—with no legitimate cause behind it—is not</u> my idea of the American dream. ✳✳✳

Sincerely,

R. O. (female)   *The War is about Pride and arognce*

Division in America

39. "impeachment if necessary"

Skowhegan, Maine
May 1, 1970

Dear Senator Smith:

The military adventure in Cambodia is totally indefensible. Not only does the President dishonor the country by a public invasion of a neutral country without even the token approval of the American-supported leaders of Cambodia; he also has shown a dictator's disregard of the wishes of the people of America and their elected representatives which reveals that he doesn't give a tinker's dam for the Constitutional limits of his authority. It would be a grave mistake to assume that success, however complete, could justify such murderous conduct.

I voted for the President because he promised an end to the war. This week, he has repeated in a few hours the course of perversion and duplicity which it took Johnson several years to perform. It would be an act of charity to suggest that he face the same fate. Two wrongs don't make a right — they make a criminal act.

It is not enough that he eventually be stopped; it is not enough that some future president promise a program of Cambodiazation and withdrawal; <u>he</u> <u>must</u> <u>be</u> <u>stopped</u> <u>instantly</u>. The people of the nation as well as of Maine look to you to bring your customary good sense and enormous prestige to support whatever measures are necessary to stop these criminal acts: repeal of the last military appropriation, or impeachment if necessary. This will be stopped; and I would much prefer to see you stop it than Abbie Hoffman.

Very truly yours,

J. H. (male)

[Editor's note: Embracing radical political action, Abbie Hoffman (1936–1989) was a countercultural figure.]

40. *"war without a cause"*

> Hallowell, Maine
> May 1, 1970

Dear Senator Smith:

The enclosed letter to the President states my reaction to last night's chauvinistic speech as well as I can explain it in a letter of reasonable length.

To me it seems obvious that in addition to the killing of our young men <u>this war without a cause is at the root of many of our very disturbing social problems at home.</u>

I most ardently hope that you will use every means at your disposal to bring this pointless horror to an end.

Where do you stand?

Sincerely,

M. O. (male)

Dear Mr. President:

You listed in your speech last night three possible choices. Obviously you do not consider complete and immediate withdrawal a choice. After listening to the rhetoric of our leaders for five years as to why this is not a realistic choice, I still think it is the only honorable and realistic course.

We made a tremendous and ghastly error when we permitted ourselves to become involved and it now seems that we must remain involved and vastly increase our involvement because our leaders, Mr. Johnson and yourself will not admit to the error. <u>Certainly it is difficult to confess to an error after it has caused the death of 40,000 of our young men but increasing the total of deaths will not improve the matter.</u>

You said that you were not asking for the support of your audience and you certainly will not have mine. You will get the most determined opposition that I can find the means to muster. You did ask us to support our men in South East Asia and I submit that the best and most effective support that we can give them is to bring them home.

I am not competent to judge the lawfulness of your decision, but I certainly question your moral right to lead this nation further into a pointless war against the wishes of a great mass of its citizens.

Last night's speech certainly changed the war from Mr. Johnson's War to Mr. Nixon's War, but it is pointless and futile regardless of who it belongs to.
Sincerely,
M. O.

[Editor's note: Nixon's three listed choices were: to do nothing, "provide massive military assistance to Cambodia," or "go to the heart of the trouble. And that means cleaning out major" enemy "sanctuaries which serve as based for attacks on both Cambodia and American and South Vietnamese forces in South Vietnam."]

Wbr Ccsusing Domestic problems

41. "hypocritical mouthing"

Albion, Maine
May 2, 1970

Dear Senator Smith:

Please do something to stop the foolish war policies of our President. Couldn't you somehow enable him to see that the mistakes of the past 40 years, and our mistakes of 10 years in VietNam, won't be corrected by the initiation of a wider war nor by the reinstatement of policies (like bombing in the North) which have proven failures?

Worst of all, the President and Secretary Laird, etc. appear eager to pull public opinion samples into the same status over Cambodia as a new Tonkin Resolution. This nation is tired of a fruitless undeclared war. President Nixon's hypocritical mouthing of peaceful words and pretense of leaving Asia alone are contradicted on every newscast and in every new announcement.

Now is the time for the senate to take every necessary step to stop our new illegal "undeclared" war on Asians in Asia.
Sincerely,
R. L (male)

[Editor's note: Melvin R. Laird (1922–) served as Nixon's first secretary of defense from 1969 to 1973.]

42. "very much opposed"

Cape Elizabeth, Maine
May 6, 1970

Dear Mrs. Smith,

I am very much opposed to Mr. Nixon's decision to fight in Cambodia. From our involvement in Vietnam I do not see how we can enter into more war in another country, and expect any different results such as Mr. Nixon says that we will be through in 4 to 6 weeks.

I am particularly concerned about these wars because of the draft and no draft deferrements. I am 18 years old, and can foresee many of my immediate friends being kept from college plans to fight in a foreign undeclared war. We are the most directly involved and yet have so little say in the affair.

I am very concerned in opposed to the war, and wanted to express my views.

Sincerely,

M. V. (female)

43. "absolute opposition"

Round Pond, Maine
May 9, 1970

Dear Senator Smith,

We deeply regret that no one was in your office today during this time of national crisis. We have come from Round Pond, Maine to discuss the current Indo Chinese situation with you.

We wish to make known to you our absolute opposition to the present Cambodian adventure. We call for immediate withdrawal of both American and South Viet Namese troops from Cambodia. We call for a continuation of an orderly withdrawal of all American troops for Viet Nam.

We also support the sentiments re youth as expressed in Secy. Hickel's letter to the present.

Basically, we have lost faith in the White House. After the President's two recent speechs and one news conference on Indo China we feel we can no longer believe White House statements. They change from day to day.

Specifically, we call for the reassertion of the traditional American value of a strong Congress in the spirit of the original Continental Congress. Please do your utmost to effect this purpose.

Again, we regret that your office was closed today.

Very truly yours,

J. E. (male) & J. B. (female)

[Editor's note: On that day, Smith missed the Washington visit of her Maine constituents because she was back in Maine meeting with students at Colby College. Walter J. Hickel (1918–), secretary of the interior (1969–1970), wrote a private letter to Nixon that was critical of the administration's hostile approach to young antiwar protesters. Leaked to the press, the letter caused quite a stir and led to Hickel's resignation later in the year.]

44. "cannot be the World's policeman"

Skowhegan, Maine
May 26, 1970

Dear Mrs. Smith:

In recent weeks public opinion has become increasingly antagonistic to Washington because of the Cambodian affair and the painfully slow pace of troop-withdrawals from south-east Asia. Because of this I wish to express my opinion.

Perhaps the greatest source of mistake in failure to change once-proper policies when the reason for these policies no longer exists. At the end of World War II there was a power vacuum in many parts of the world. Only North America among the advanced nations had not been decimated by the ravages of the war. American aid under these circumstances frequently succeeded in stabilizing the situation. Today, however, this situation no longer exists. There is certainly not a lack of power or political purpose in south-east Asia. It may be that we feel this policy and power is misdirected but never-the-less that it exists cannot be denied. Because of this fundamental change, it is no longer our responsibility how the people of this part of the world conduct their political affairs. It is therefore, my opinion that we should leave the people of south-east Asia the weapons to defend themselves but that we must not fight their battles.

As far as the long-term struggle with Communism is concerned, a strong and viable local situation is far more important than to rule south-east Asia. At the present time our wealth is being wasted and our youth alienated by our involvement on the Asian Continent. These things must be set right in order to maintain a strong and free America. The young men who dodge the draft are not unpatriotic or cowardly. They will gladly shed their blood to defend our Country if it is attacked. To hold the belief that Communist expansion in south-east Asia is a threat to the United States seems to me as far fetched as Hitler's claim that Poland was about to attack Germany at the beginning of World War II.

The concept expressed by Mr. Nixon in his television appearance to explain the Cambodian affair; that we are responsible for events in south-east

Asia must be abandoned. It no longer applies. We simply are not and cannot be the World's policeman.

I see references frequently in the news media to return to isolationism. This is a mistaken idea. What is needed is to go forward in all peaceful relations with countries but not military involvement.

I hope this Country is still the government "Of the People, by the People, and for the People." If the people's will can be heard, I feel that the War in south-east Asia will be stopped.

Sincerely,
W. J. (male)

[handwritten: Sees War as unjust as S. Victures Not really a legitimate threat to America]

II. SUPPORTIVE

While they were much fewer in number, there were strong letters that supported Nixon's position on Cambodia. Like Senator Smith, there were those who believed that Nixon deserved the support, if not the trust, of the American people, since he appeared to be doing what was necessary. Stating that Nixon had already drawn 115,000 American troops from South Vietnam, Smith continued to argue in early 1970 that Nixon was at least significantly reversing "the trend of the eight years of Kennedy and Johnson." Support for Nixon also had links to the popular perception of protesters and a couple of letters clearly state their disgust for the lack of personal hygiene of many young antiwar protesters.

45. "agreement with President Nixon"

Turner, Maine
May 4, 1970

Dear Senator Smith:

This is to verify my telephone call of May 1st, in respect to my agreement with President Nixon in his handling of the Cambodian problem and my inability to understand Senator Fulbright's stand against the same situation.

How one man elected to represent one state thinks he has the right to judge one man elected by the states is beyond me.

I don't believe President Nixon is infallible, but I do believe that no man should be condemned for making a decision. Right or wrong, at least he has faced the problem and attempted to solve it. We the people of the United

States have faced disillusionment too often in the past decade with our elected leaders in their inability to make a decision.

I would like to know if Senator Fulbright is one of those men who had rather live on his knees than die on his feet. If so may I remind him that once you start crawling you have to take more and more punishment because of lack of resistance.

Let me also ask Senator Fulbright if his neighbor's house was under attack, and if it fell his would be next. Would he still sit at home and let his neighbor be destroyed. I sincerely hope not.

Words are nice and properly used can <u>delay</u> action in regards to a problem. But that is all.

When the common person has been whipped enough he will stop listening and start acting. So please for me ask Senator Fulbright, why he will not face facts for what they are instead of trying to magnify a situation.

Now I know there is no way for me to know the complete situation in Cambodia, or any where in Indo China. Neither do I believe that Senator Fulbright does so why condem a movement that just might stop a third world war.

Thank you for your considerate indulgents.

Sincerely yours

G. P. (male)

[handwritten: Support of Cambodia because he views it as a threat to the United States]

---

46. *"support the President's effort"*

Gardiner, Maine
May 6, 1970

Dear Senator Smith:

I am one of the silent ones who has remained silent long enough. Please be advised that

(1) I fully support the President's effort to resolve the Vietnam conflict including the use of U.S. troops in Cambodia.

(2) I am sick and tired of watching television news reports and reading scores of magazine and newspaper articles in which many of your fellow Senators try to rationalize the irrational attacks on our society, and its judicial, legislative and educational processes, violence is <u>not</u> a justifiable means to an end in a country where there are other way if that end is desired by the majority.

Thank you

S. W. (male)

47. "I will stand behind Nixon"

Richmond, Maine
May 9, 1970

Dear Senator Smith,

As a student of the University of Maine, I was forced to decide whether to strike. I am very much against war and violence of any kind. President Nixon's decision to send troops into Cambodia stunned me. However, after careful research I have concluded that the President is doing what is necessary to save our troops and innocent citizens in South Vietnam from massacre.

I want peace and I want an end to this criminal war. President Nixon is working to achieve these goals. I will not strike. I will stand behind Nixon and work actively for peace.

What is your stand on this issue?

Yours truly,
C. C. (female)

48. "behind our president 100%"

Belfast, Maine
May 10, 1970

Dear Mrs. Smith,

I do not like what I read in the papers and see on T.V. But as a mother of 4 and two boys who have been in the service I want to tell you I'm behind <u>our</u> president 100% for what he is doing in <u>Asia</u>. I pray that when this Cambodia business is over his point will be proven right. Nobody likes death of kids but we don't want communism here either.

Now for the students this is awful. I think a lot of their beef is cause they think after college they will have to go to war. Are they any different than the poor boy who couldn't go to college to get out of going. I think they beef about everything just because they are stired up by a certain group of commies.

I feel sorry for the Kent kids and the parents of the killed ones. But what they are blaming on the National Guard is awful. The Kent kids are just as much to blame for those deaths as anybody.

Why dont these kids graduate from college and then when they get their education and live a little more knowledge then maybe their influence will help if they have the right brains.

Let's get rid of the kids who don't want to study and just want to keep things stired up.

Keep up the <u>ROTC</u> its good if you want it. The kids don't have to go to it so why knock it. They just don't like anything.

I didn't vote for Pres. Nixon but I wish I had. Keep him up with is good work I didn't realize what a great man he is.

Please excuse my writing as I'm writing on a book as I've a very bad broken leg and its awfully hard for me to write. I'm taking medicine and it makes me kind of shaky.

Thanks for listening to me,

A. H. (female)

A bath and hair cut might not hurt a lot of the kids I've seen.

49. "I wholeheartedly concur with President Nixon"

Falmouth, Maine
May 11, 1970

Dear Senators Smith and Muskie,

I write briefly to tell you I wholeheartedly concur with President Nixon & his Cambodian offensive. I <u>urge</u> you to <u>back</u> <u>him</u> <u>completely</u> & to vote No to any Senate plans to go in any other direction other than he has chosen, in reference to both Cambodia & the bombing above the DMZ in Vietnam. The move to wipe out supplies & supply routes is <u>long</u> overdue—supply lines have always been & always will be in war the main thing to control.

I also urge you, Senators Muskie, to stop being a politician looking to <u>your</u> future & be a <u>man </u>who supports our President & thus our Country & our state of Maine. Election year or not this is no time for "politics as usual."

You each are receiving the same letter—I pray you listen.

S. B. (female)

50. "Thank God for President Nixon"

Norway, Maine
May 11, 1970

Dear Senator Smith,

Thank God for President Nixon. He has the courage to look beyond the end of his nose, and beyond the coming election.

Doesn't any one in our House or Senate remember how unprepared we were at the time of Pearl Harbor?

Doesn't any one remember Neville Chamberlain?

Doesn't any one remember the "Oxford Oath"—the students who gave Hitler the go ahead with a war those students may never have had to fight if they had backed a Big Stick policy.

If we are to have peace we had better review our history. We had better get our students back into some history classes with teachers who can teach it the way it was.

Please add my one small voice to back Mr. Nixon on the Cambodian Move, arms to Israel, and any move he makes in his sincere fight for peace.
Sincerely,
K. G. (female)

*WWII happened because of appeasement—
We could have stoped it—*

51. "*he deserves backing*"

Wilton, Maine
May 23, 1970

Dear Senator Smith,

I was among the very few at our Democratic State Convention who disagreed with the direction of the party on the Vietnam-Cambodia situation.

I feel Nixon is my President whether I voted for him or not and as such he deserves backing and support especially in times of crisis.

I need information to help me hold my ground. I do not feel I am alone in my opinions.

Although I am State Committeewoman in the Democrat party I feel you are one of my Senators and the one I must turn to for the other side of the coin—so to speak.

Senator Muskie made statement his mail ran 2000 to 10? (latter figure was very small) one day asking that we "get out". I feel I know who the 1990 are and I also feel the "silent majority" is _not_ writing. I would like to know how your mail is running. Maybe the some 1990 are writing you and not the silent majority.

I hope you will not feel I am writing for any political purpose. I am writing just as [myself]—American and nothing more.

The only way I feel I can stick to my convictions is to become as thoroughly informed as possible. Right now my beliefs are based on personal feelings and I realize I have to reach to other levels.

If you have anything I could read I would be more than willing to delve a bit deeper.
Sincerely,
A. T. (female)
P.S. I also must add I think Agnew is great. He reminds me of one of my favorites—Harry Truman.

52. "the correct one"

Lisbon, Maine
May 27, 1970

Dear Senator Smith,

Since my previous letter to you it seems our "do nothing" President has finally made a decision—and the correct one too! I am refering to the raids on the sanctuaries of the enemy in Cambodia. I applaude your stand in this matter!

I watched the program with Senator McGovern & the four other Senators with great interest, regarding their amendment to end the war. It really gave one a great deal to think about, but still leaves me where I've always been, i.e. I believe we should either step up the war & win a military victory, or, as Senator McGovern advocates, end the war by withdrawal from it. I do not believe the North Vietnamese will commit mass murder of the South Vietnamese, nor do I feel we would "lose face" in the world if we withdrew but rather the opposite, we would gain the respect of the world for stopping the killing, the wounding, and destruction of property. And—according to the same report, America spends 23 billion dollars per year on the war in Vietnam and it was mentioned that this ✳ amount would clean America's water of pollution!! To me, this is much more important than aiding & abetting a Civil War in Asia!

Another area of Federal spending that angers me & my neighbors is the Space Program!! The fact that it cost us taxpayers 24 billion dollars to put a man on the Moon is unbearable! And—the fact that the program is to continue for years, using our tax dollars to "blow a hole in the sky", instead of cleaning our air, water and earth of pollutants is more than unbearable!! We are "Earthlings" and we have too many problems and ills here on earth crying out for a "cure" that should certainly have top priority over the stupid waste of money exploring Space!

Further, I am extremely concerned about the violence on our campuses and the striking of students. As I once wrote Senator Muskie, "if the students want to strike & not learn, then close the colleges and universities and deny the young an education"! They couldn't act any more stupidly than they do now!! I am sickened when I see how our young people dress and allow their hair & beards to grow. They look filthy dirty to me. Whatever happened to the sport-coat or blazer & grey flannel trousers for the boys & decent skirt and sweater and/or jacket for the girls? The young seem to have lost all their self respect and human dignity & now they want to vote at 18 when I'm not sure they should even be allowed at 21 to vote, at least not from their actions & ideas. . . .

Sincerely yours,
C. P. (male)

American money can be better spent elsewhere

III. DILEMMA

Not all letters that discussed the Cambodia issue were aggressively for or against Nixon's policies. A sense of anguish comes through in the words of some writers as they weighed the pros and cons of greater involvement of American troops beyond South Vietnam. Exhibiting restraint and humility, most authors presented a deliberate tone. The author of the first letter identifies himself as an opponent of the war who does not engage in the radical actions of burning draft cards and flags. Probably aware that Senator Smith had no patience with excessive civil disobedience, there were those who made the point that one could be both a dissenter and a loyal American.

53. "very reticent"

Yarmouth, Maine
April 24, 1970

Dear Senator Smith,

For a long time now I have been what could be considered a very reticent member of the "Silent Majority". However I feel, on the eve of a seemingly deepening committment in Indo China, specifically Cambodia, that I must speak out. Up to this point I have tacitly supported the Nixon administration in the belief that he, and his people, were sincerely dedicated to extricating our country from its military involvement in Southeast Asia. I am afraid that, at least in my view, that the evidence is steadily mounting to support a view opposite to this.

I am not a burner of flags or draft cards, but I am a loyal American and believe at this late hour I must state my feelings to individuals in places of responsibility.

Sincerely,

G. G. (male)

54. "hope I'm wrong"

Winterport, Maine
April 28, 1970

Dear Sen. Smith,

I hope you will not mind my writing to you on this subject. I feel it is importent enough but I don't know if it will do any good.

The subject is "Cambodia". I am so afraid the United States will become involved as we did in South Viet Nam. I have the feeling that the Congress

Everything America fought for in Viet Nam simultaneously was lost in America as a result

is either afraid to use its influence or for some reason is unable to do anything no matter how they feel. I sincerely hope I'm wrong. Would you please tell me if you can do something to prevent this from happening. I'm sure you must feel the same way about our involvement.

Thank you,

J. S. (female)

55. *"I really wonder"*

Northeast Harbor, Maine
April 28, 1970

Dear Senator Smith:

Please use all your influence to prevent any involvement in Cambodia—either arms or manpower. Such belligerent action (both in Cambodia & in Vietnam itself) is diametrically opposed to the will of the people. How can we continue to call ourselves a democracy when the last three administrations have involved us without our consent or approval? I am [older]—a conventional wife, mother, and school teacher. I hold no brief for the violence shown by some of our young people in protesting the Vietnam war; but if the president makes commitments for us in Cambodia, I can understand how extreme disgust and frustration will cause even most thoughtful and balanced of young people to "boil over". If I were 35 years younger and as idealistic as I was then, I really wonder what my reactions would be.

Sincerely,

E. F. (female)

56. *"discuss this matter"*

Winthrop, Maine
April 29, 1970

Dear Senator Smith:

Tonights Huntley-Brinkley television report to the country announced very dramatically President Nixons decision to inject our country into the delicate and serious Cambodian crisis. His actions, as well as the failure of Congress, the duly elected representatives of the American people, to declare a state of war, not only here, but in the conflict taking place in South Vietnam, compels me to write you, Seantor Muskie, as well as the president of our country, expressing my displeasure of the action taken by our Commander In Chief of our Armed Forces.

Without question there are many facets of this undeclared war that millions of Americans are very unfamiliar with. This could possibly create an attitude on the part of government officials that our voices should not be raised in protest to the deeds of our government under certain circumstances. I am one of these Americans not knowledgeable of the data and facts at your command. However, better for me, for our country, to raise my voice in indignation with reference to my dissatisfaction relative to the course the adminstration has pursued concerning the escalation of the South East Aasian problems, than to assume an air of militancy and with a few cohorts go out and attempt to burn down a college.

Our Congress, at least in my opinion, has failed the electorate in not assuming its full responsibility with reference to our present dilemma in Sputh East Asia. This failure on the part of our elected officials can be traced back to our engagement in Korea, which was our nations introduction to the type of warfare we are now engaged in. Democrats as well as Republicans can wear the cloak of shame for the negligence they have shown in not carrying out properly their vested responsibilities.

This letter is a difficult one for me to write for many reasons. One of the primary ones being my failure to understand why the Congress of our United States fails the citizenry so by not declaring a state of war. Without question, and again my personal opinion, if a declaration of war had been presented to the american people, and we had gone in and assumed the position of a world power and world leader, my confidence in the citizens that compromise our vast country would have been behind the Congress and the Administration, regardless of whether it was President Kennedy, Johnson, or our present president. Another disturbing factor to me with regards to international problems and undeclared war, affectionately today called conflicts, is the inability of the United Nations to not only prevent such happenings, but to bring them to a quick and conclusive termination. The american taxpayer realizing how much financial support this organization derives from his country wonders just what his tax money is accomplishing.

The elimination of hostilities between all nations should be the first item at all times on the agenda of this world wide represented orgainization. Nothing should preceed this need. It all can be done too without the eloquence of speechmanking that takes place in the halls of this august body.

There has been a tremendous amount of unrest on our college campuses over the last several yeras, which has been brought about in a large measure by the continuance of our position in South Vietnam, and I am afraid there will be a decided increase in this because of the entry of our forces, advisory and tactical, into the Cambodian situation. I strongly belive our country should prepare for strong rejection of the adminstrations policy regarding this matter, particularly from the militant and dissident student element who don't show the slightest hesitancy of burning down buildings on college campuses, court houses, and legislative halls of our government.

How long will the Rapp Browns, Abbie Hoffmans, and all those who flaunt law and order be allowed to descreate our american institutions? My disgust at these characters who riducle our judical system, who make a mockery of our courtrooms and judges, be allowed to roam the country venting their hate on those who love this country, who uphold its laws, and respect its traditions with infinite loyalty and devotion. When will permissiveness that allows lawyers like Kuntsler who represented the Chicago seven tried on conspiracy, be stoppped? These are but a few of the many, many things in our society that disturb all fine americans.

Another painful reason I find in writing this letter regarding our involvement thousands of miles from our own shores pertains to me directly. This week our son . . . a graduate of the University of Maine . . . unmarried, but anxious to settle down in this respect and raise a family. . . called us several evenings ago to inform us that it now appears he will drafted by May 12th unless a miracle occurs, which he doesn't expect because of past events that have taken place regarding this matter. He is no better than any other citizen, this we all readily admit, and during the years he was struggling to get his education, and at great sacrifice by all three of us, he did receive college deferment for which we were grateful for, as we were always hoping for the rainbow on the other side of the clouds. However, it can best be summed up by his words to me the other evening when he said, "its just two years of my life wasted". Here is a boy thats a credit to his family and country. A boy who says that those in college creating disturbances and denying those who want an education to receive it should be barred from this opportunity. His graduation last August brought us much pride and joy, not only in his accomplishments, but in our ability to give him the education we desired he have that will contribute to the betterment of our overall society. Our personal feelings concerning the escalation of the "conflict" are reflected in our sons attitude.

It would be deeply appreciated if you will discuss this matter with your colleague Senator Muskie.

Very truly yours,

E. S. (male)

[Editor's note: William M. Kuntsler (1919–1995) defended the "Chicago Seven," the activists charged for conspiracy to incite riots during the Democratic National Convention in 1968.]

· 6 ·

Winding Down Road

I. COLBY COLLEGE

$\mathscr{T}$he widespread protest in colleges that came as a result of the announcement of the Cambodian "incursion" intensified with the tragic killing of four students at Kent State University. It was a period of great agitation on college campuses. Hundreds of campus demonstrations and student strikes occurred throughout the nation in the early days of May. On the same weekend (May 9–10) that approximately 100,000 antiwar protesters gathered at Washington, Senator Smith responded to the request of student leaders from ten Maine colleges and the six campuses of the University of Maine to meet and debate the war at Colby College, Waterville, Maine. Colby was an elite private school that had been out of reach for a young Smith and most others with a modest class background. The overwhelming majority of Colby students were non-Maine residents including Steve Orlov, the student body president and resident of Massachusetts who played a major role in having Smith and Senator Muskie come to Colby.

Like other institutes of higher learning, there were divisions at Colby over American foreign policy in Southeast Asia. As early as November 1967, half of the faculty and administrative staff opposed the war. Greater signs of opposition unfolded in early May 1970 when faculty, with a vote of 71 to 21 (10 abstaining), and students, with a margin of 1040 to 117, approved a campus strike. There were marches, rallies, workshops, sit-ins, and other events. The Students for a Democratic Society presented the controversial *Salt of the Earth*, a 1954 boycotted film produced by blacklisted Hollywood radicals. President Robert Strider told an overflowing crowd that the Nixon administration "failed to take into account the deadening impact the war is having on young people and especially on college students." Into this politicized environment, Smith arrived on Saturday afternoon, May 9, to answer students' questions. Before a crowd of

173

approximately 2000, she stood on the steps of the Colby library and experienced 90 minutes of "taunts, invectives, and obscenities." Suffering intense pain in her right hip and receiving jeers from students who had no patience for her pro-administration position, Smith described the session as "perhaps the most unpleasant experience of my entire public service career."

Offering a valuable first-hand account, one of the letters in the following section states how a few at Colby inflamed the emotions of the students with subversive rhetoric. Many of the following letters reveal the divide that existed between the angry, obscenity-spewing, and radical component of the antiwar movement and the conservative sector of small-town Maine. Providing a point of reference, the final letter is a detailed and fascinating portrayal of protest at the University of Wisconsin that was sent initially to a relative living in the small community of Bath, Maine.

57. *"I applaud your stand"*

Fairfield, Maine
May 12, 1970

Dear Senator Smith:

Your firm support of President Nixon during your dialogue with Colby College students last weekend was most reassuring.

May I earnestly urge you to continue this support during the critical weeks ahead.

Many of us are becoming increasingly concerned for the future of our country and, frankly, alarmed at the apparent tendency of more and more members of Congress to legislate for a vocal and sometimes violent minority rather than for a law-abiding, tax-paying majority.

Let us not permit either the foreign or domestic policies of our nation to be formulated on the college campuses.

Again, I applaud your stand at Colby.

Yours sincerely,

K. M. (male)

58. *"commend you for your stand"*

Hallowell, Maine
May 12, 1970

Dear Senator Smith

I wish to commend you for your stand, as expressed earlier this week at Colby College, in backing up President Nixon in his decision no longer to grant the enemy the use of their sanctuaries in Cambodia.

After years of fighting in Vietnam, practically with one hand tied behind our back by reason of the enemy's advantageous use of these Cambodian sanctuaries, and many months at the conference table where the enemy has flatly and continuously refused to enter into any form of meaningful negotiation, a move to deny him the use of these sanctuaries would seem to be only a prudent step. I do appreciate your willingness to express yourself as you have done. . . .

Thank you for your consideration,
Yours very truly,
B. P. (male)

59. *"commend you on your stand"*

Skowhegan, Maine
May 13, 1970

My Dear Senator Smith:

At the risk of being banished from the ranks of the 'silent majority', I take my pen in hand to commend you on your stand concerning the issues of the day. The many <u>voices</u> in the wilderness must take action thru the democratic process if we are to retain our way of life. I'm not against change if its for the benefit of the many but—like most other middle aged Americans— I'm fed up to the point that I will fight the growing rule of insignificant minorities. All of our people should have their chance—(thing in modern lingo) . . . . I do not believe this gives anyone a right to ruin the Country.

Should there have been any doubt, you proved your right to be know as Woman of Courage by your recent response to the college group at Colby. It is my understanding that you didn't pull any punches—Many of them need to get involved in something good and face the fact that we do have an imperfect Eden but it's a lot better than the Hell that they seem to foster.

My [family] send their best wishes and we all will do all we can to keep you in the service of our Country for a long as it is your wish to do so.
Respectfully yours,
M. R. (male)

60. *"I am glad that you expressed yourself"*

Winthrop, Maine
May 12, 1970

Dear Senator Smith:

I am glad that you expressed yourself at Colby College as supporting this country's move into Cambodia. We have a son in Vietnam, and those huge caches of military supplies are no longer quite so accessible to the Viet Cong for use against him and his friends.

As for congressional action on Indo-China, it does not seem to me that we can "resolve" or legislate the conduct of our war, declared or undeclared, nor dictate to the commander in chief how he should best direct the war. We haven't his capabilities, his bases for judgment, nor his access to privileged information.

Furthermore, I deplore the political hay which our other Maine Senator is trying to make by appearing to support the unwise young. There are those who are former strong supporters of his (I am not) who feel he is letting us down badly.

As for giving the vote to 18-year olds, I do not believe we should. They have recently demonstrated their concerns, but not their good judgment. The very qualities that make the 18-year old a good soldier—recklessness, lack of concern for a far tomorrow and gradualism, extreme egotism—all mitigate against his being a voter charged with responsibility for you and me. (And we have four boys, [two teenagers and two young adults].) Returned Vietnam veterans are a different matter, no matter what their age. They have earned their votes.

You need not answer this letter, since there are many things you are probably doing in these harried days.
Sincerely,
R. B. (female)

61. *"forthright, courageous"*

Falmouth, Maine
May 10, 1970

Dear Senator Smith,

Mrs. [M. P] and I were at Colby Saturday, to talk informally with some of the students. We were guests of her son [P.] He and some of his friends wanted us to discuss with them the problems which are so exciting students today.

Unfortunately, we had to leave before you were through and were unable to see you. We might not have had sufficient time to give you our reactions to your presence and to the other events of the day. [M. P.] and I are in very close agreement on almost all political questions.

We were very proud of the forthright, courageous and dignified manner in which you conducted the question and answer appearance. Before you came and while you were explaining your position, we had hoped that your answers would help the students to think more calmly and to reach some rational conclusions. On the way home we began to realize that the meeting had been carefully staged to minimize your influence. After a night's reflection, I am more than ever convinced that you, [M. P.] and I were skillfully outmaneuvered.

[We] got to Colby about noon and picnicked with her son, another student and [J. C. of the Maine Times]. We were given to understand that there were to be some brief speeches after which the students would break into small groups at which [M. P.] and I would answer questions. Before the speaches started we did talk with eight or ten of the students. They were friends of [M. P.'s son] that particularly wanted our opinions.

The speaches were late in starting and then it gradually became apparent the speakers were determined to prevent the discussion period by stringing out their talks to cover all the time before your arrival. It was probably a compliment to us but one we did not appreciate.

[J. C.] was the first speaker. He told a long story about a councilman of Brunswick who was "frightened" to have Bowdoin students talk to Brunswick school children. He derided the police, the town government and the school board. He urged the students to increase their efforts to talk to school children, to talk to citizens and to continue their disruptive tactics.

[His] intent seemed to be to inflame the emotions to his listeners. He was followed by [G. M.] who was more incoherent, more inflamatory and more long winded. Then some hippy nonstudent babbled hippy phrases and was followed by a profane and foul-mouthed professor from UMP.

[P.] and I advised [M. P.] not to make a statement. The emotions of the crowd had been carefully built up. This was, I believe, a deliberate attempt to set the stage for your appearance so that you would meet a hostile, intolerant audience.

Those responsible for inviting you and, perhaps, the head of the student government who introduced you meant no discourtesy. They had earnestly wanted your considered opinion on the problems which are perplexing them. This was the feeling I got before the speaking started. During the speaking, the flag was lowered and groups began to gather by the flag pole and in front of the steps. I observed this but it was only after you began to answer questions that I began to see that there was a very definite plan to all the proceedings.

I believe that a subversive group stage managed the afternoon. It attempted to prevent all rational discussion, to keep emotions at a peak and to insulate the conservative and moderate students from rational thinking. I also believe the subversive leaders came from outside Colby and represented the SDS and Black Panthers. Some of them came from Bowdoin.

In the present emotional state, there is no hope that reason will prevail. I feel that the campus revolts are more serious than is generally believed because the emotion-based demands are non-negotiable. I feel that there is a very wide-spread conspiracy that should be investigated. [M. P.] does not agree with this last opinion.

I apologize for the length of this letter but wanted you to know my thoughts.

You were magnificent! I only hope that your efforts were not wasted.

Yours sincerely,

E. W. (male)

[Editor's note: UMP probably is University of Maine–Portland. One of the students from Bowdoin College was Brownie Carson, a former Marine infantry platoon commander who chastised Smith for her ignorance concerning American troops secretly sent on military operations in Laos.]

62. *"courage to speak"*

Wiscasset, Maine
May 10, 1970

Dear Mrs. Smith:

It was refreshing to read or your meeting with the students while in Maine. It seems you are the only elected official who has the courage to speak your true feelings. Most are only saying what these confused "children" wish to hear and totally disregard the complex answers to this terrible war.

Please use your prestige and experience to support President Nixon and try and get our country on the road to sanity again. Patriotism, safety in the streets of our cities, self reliance and common courtesy are just a few of the things sadly lacking in our lives lately. They continually harp on the frustration of youth but someone had better become aware of the frustration of we less vocal citizens

Thank you

J. L. (male)

63. *"Profiles in Courage"*

Kezar Falls, Maine
May 11, 1970

Madam:

I applaud and endorse the position you took with the students at Colby last week. Such a stand before such a group at such a time took the courage that belongs in a chapter of its own in the next <u>Profiles in Courage</u>.

I am writing to Senator Muskie as well, to ask him how peace-at-any-price can be more effective now than it was in the pre World War II situation; why protests are not directed against Hanoi, Peking and Moscow; how isolationism and survival can go together when a major power is determined to bury us; and if he would have taken the same position he has turned to under a Republican president if this had been a Humphrey administration directing the present course in Indochina.
Very truly yours,
N. R. (female)

[Editor's note: Published in 1955, Senator John F. Kennedy's *Profiles in Courage* focuses on the political courage of senators (from John Quincy Adams to Robert A. Taft) and other leaders in American history. The book won a Pulitzer Prize for biography in 1957.]

64. "my congratulations"

Winthrop, Maine
May 16, 1970
Dear Senator Smith:
Thank you so very much for your brief reply of May 6th relative to my letter of April 29th. As of this writing I have not heard from Senator Muskie pertaining to the subject matter in the copy of the letter forwarded to him. You are to be commended for the excellent manner in which you serve your constituents at home.

Let this letter also convey to you my congratulations on the fine way you handled yourself when appearing before the students etc at Colby College on Saturday, May 9th. The television medium brought to he viewer a small segement of your appearance as well as that of your colleague in the Senate. I was very pleased to hear you state in effect that you supported President Nixon with regards to the incursion into Cambodia. Lets hope that all his aspirations etc concerning this phase of his entire SouthEast Asia program is successful. God knows that he needs the support of every citizen at this crucial time. With conditions at home being as they are our president should have the prayers of every American who believes in our country and all it represents. . . .

As mentioned in my April 29th correspondence our only son, and the only [S.] left to carry on the name, was drafted into service [recently]. Its a sad day in the life of a twenty five year boy who eight months after graduation from college must give up his eleven thousand dollar a year position to "waste two years of this life." As a woman I am sure you understand fully his mothers feelings when they said goodbye to one another. There was very liittle I could do or say under the circumstances to alleviate the air of sadness that was prevailing.

May Gods blessings be with you as you discharge your duties in our nations capitol.

Yours sincerely yours,

E. S. (male)

65. *"agreed with you"*

Skowhegan, Maine
May 26, 1970

Dear Senator Smith,

First of all, may I express to you personally my deepest sympathy at the loss of your brother-in-law. It was a terrible shock & loss for your sister and for the town of Skowhegan.

I know that by now you must have received the letter that my father wrote to you. Please let me explain the background of that letter and this one. After reading the account of your appearance at Colby, I felt that some action on my part was called for. In that article you stated that most of the people that you hear from are opposing your stand on issues and/or the President's.

After also reading some of the answers that you gave to the questions at Colby, I felt that I should write. This is the first time that I have written to you regarding the issues & your stand on them.

I discussed the article with my father & mother. They both agreed with you & your position—as do I, most emphatically. I said then that I planned to write to you and express my support. My father said that he would, too & he wrote before I got the chance.

His letter was worded much better & more eloquently. However, I want mine to express to you simply and plainly that I fully support you. You have said things about the war, the funds for it, and the other problems that face us today. I am in complete agreement with your stand & actions & voting.

As I said when I first wrote to you six years ago, I am <u>very</u> proud to say I know you—very proud to live in your town & state & feel safer with you as a Senator. I know that you carefully study each problem & then vote in the way that you feel is best for the people. I am aware that other Senators do this too but I'm <u>sure</u> that you do.

I'm sure that I have rambled on enough now. But again let me say that I have complete confidence in your judgement and you have my <u>complete</u> sup-

port. As my father said, we support you in anything you do in the future. I hope I haven't rambled on too much. I know the letter was disorganized but I hope it somehow expresses the way I feel. Sorry it was so long in coming. Hope your hip is fine & hope you come home this summer.
Affectionately,
M. J. (female)

66. *"want to congratulate you"*

Skowhegan, Maine
June 3, 1970
Dear Senator Smith:
. . . After President Nixon announced his entrance in Cambodia, I mailed him a congratulatory telegram as a good move which was a necessary step and a hard step to make politically because if he wanted to please the voters he should not have taken this step. He however acted on the recommendations of the field commanders and not what was best for President Nixon.

Today, I am reading about your new speech on the Senate floor and want to congratulate you because of your well taken position. You have courage. You also had courage to come to Colby and speak and your speech was so refreshing to compare with other nauseatingly flattering speeches of the day.

Today, campuses have become the breeding places for leftists, anarchits and have become a diseased area full of cancerous cells which could ruin the entire body if not taken care of at this time.

I suggest, if we love the way Europe is going today and want to progress this way, that we do away with campuses. Today our campuses have violence and death and I feel that the students should live privately with people and adjust to people and understand people around them instead of becoming a boil and breeding place for professors to inject their poisonous thoughts.

. . . Today, it has been proven that campuses have outlived their usefullness. With modern transportation, etc, more students can afford to rent, live with relatives, etc. I would like you to think about this subject and discuss with other leaders this point I believe that this would protect our children from being consumed by the campuses and their problems. Universities should spend more money on better equipment, etc rather than on dorms. If it is not possible to close the campuses then the living expenses should be increased or taxation applied.
Sincerely.
K. K. (male)

67. "agreed to disagree"

Falmouth Foreside, Maine
June 4, 1970

The Honorable Margaret Chase Smith,

This must of necessity remain a short note, but I do feel a compulsion to write following your recent appearance at Colby College & your speech in the Senate on June 1.

Regarding the Colby affair, which I attended: I cannott imagine many other public figures displaying your willingness to field questions from a gathering peopled by those whose views you must have known would be hostile to yours. I do hope that you understand several points about that Saturday. First, many students, including myself, were & still are desperately upset by the events of the past few weeks. These events have been a truly heavy emotional drain—perhaps so heavy as to render our responses, at times, somewhat irrational. Still, by & large I felt the crowd was at least reservedly polite. Please realize that your style, indeed a courageous style, was not lost on many of us. If anything, we agreed to disagree & in light of many events around the country perhaps we ought to look at the Saturday at Colby as a healthy exchange of ideas.

I have nothing but praise for your speech of June 1. It has often disturbed me that people seem to ignore that the ultimate threat to our country comes from the political right. Certainly we all find the actions of the extreme left disgusting & even tiresome. But when will the hate campaign of demagoguery from the right (let's say it, Spiro Agnew, George Wallace, Lester Maddox, Ronald Reagan et al.) come to a welcome end? Even as a clean shaven student I am constantly finding myself in situations in which the venom of these men has been transmuted to otherwise rational adults. This not only sickens me, it causes me to wonder if those extreme leftists are not perhaps speaking my language. My hope is that your speech will reopen the paths of concilliatory moderation.

Mr. Nixon has not assuaged me. He uses the terms "Cambodia neutrality & territorial integrity" too loosely (forgetting the implications of our invasion into that country.

Peace,

D. L. (male)

[Editor's note: George Wallace (1919–1998) was a Democrat leader and segregationist. In 1963, as Governor of Alabama, he opposed the enrollment of two African-American students into the University of Alabama. Wallace ran for President as a Democrat in 1964 and as an American Independent Party candidate in 1968. In 1970, he was elected for the second time Governor of Alabama. A successful businessman, Lester Maddox (1915–2003) was another Democrat leader who supported segregation. In 1970, he was Governor of Georgia.]

68. "I felt you would appreciate the contents."

Bath, Maine
May 21, 1970

Dear Senator Smith:

I am [an employee] in the Bath School System.

Enclosed is a copy of a letter which my nephew, [N. W.], wrote to us from the University of Wisconsin. I felt that you would appreciate the contents.

Many of us in Maine greatly admire the tremendous work you have done not only for our state, but for the nation. You reflect an honesty which is gratifying to see in a public servant. I personally feel that you exemplify the qualities of statesmanship that we so desperately need. I don't always agree with you, but I never question your sincerity.

I do wish that could give as much support as your conscience would allow to Mr. Nixon. He has faced many problems with wisdom and courage, and I feel he will go down in history as an outstanding president.

It would be helpful if you could influence the news media to present fairly both sides of the picture?

God Bless you,

Sincerely,

G. W. (female)

May 9, 1970

There's a lot to write, and there are all kinds of ways of getting into this letter, and I've considered several but I guess it would be best to just describe a little bit of what has been going on here this week.

Last Thursday Nixon made the speech announcing the "invasion" of Cambodia, as they call it. Significantly there was no immediate outburst against the policy, except in a few scattered universities. It took the killings at Kent State on Monday to really get things going. The word arrived here about noontime, and at seven that evening there was a student rally to decide on a strike.

This school was pretty much closed down by a strike for two weeks before and one week after spring break. It was supposedly a labor strike by teaching assistants for better contract terms but most of the strikers saw it for what it was: simply a trial-run to see if the university could be shut down.

They nearly succeeded. Most kids didn't go to class, and they didn't walk the picket lines either. They just faded. About 15% of us kept going to class, through the picket lines. After spring break others began to go back to class too, and they gave up the strike.

At the Monday night meeting, they couldn't decide on a strike. The teaching assistants had shown that a good strike (like most anything) requires a lot of hard work and organization. On Monday night the Rads (radicals) didn't want to make that kind of effort; they just wanted to have a good riot. They went out and started breaking windows, and stoning police cars, and interfering with traffic. The police put down tear gas, and they broke up for the night. Sometime early in the morning, someone burned down a Kroger grocery store (supermarket really—a big building) a few blocks off the campus.

Tuesday morning it was clear that there was going to be a bad riot that day. There was a rally scheduled for 2:00 in the afternoon, and you could tell that they would riot afterwards. I had lunch in the student union, and the Rads were walking around like someone was standing flat-footed on the top of their shoulders, like they were holding up the worlds all by themselves. They wore long faces and were trying to make themselves angry, and they were very, very earnest. They were trying to feel sorry for the four kids who were killed at Kent, but they really couldn't, so they settled for feeling self-important.

I went to my German history seminar at 1:30, and at 2:30 the tear gas canisters started going off outside. Our classroom is on street level, and there is an open, outside corridor above it. Kids started pounding across that corridor a few minutes after the gas went down, and before long they were streaming along outside our classroom. One girl noticed us and yelled: "Look at those bastards in there holding [expletive deleted] class!" About then tear gas started, coming in through the ventilating system.

We moved upstairs three floors to the professor's office, and I had a good seat by the window. There were three police cars with taped windows parked on the street outside, and several policemen with gasmasks, helmets, and nightsticks formed a line in the middle of the street. As the gas dissipated, the students started to filter back in groups of two and three. They lined up along the buildings, and before long started to chant: "One, two, three, four; we don't want your [expletive deleted] war." They started throwing rocks at cops, and the latter just stood their ground, ducked the rocks if they could, and kept their hands in the bags where they carried their supply of tear gas grenades.

Another group of police hit the kids from a different direction, and broke them up with gas. While we had coffee after class, we watched the kids filtering through the open patio in the interior of the big Humanities building which takes up a whole block. They were crying, and chocking, and gagging into handkerchiefs. A lot were carrying rocks and wore red armbands. The armbands are more symbolic than necessary for identification. Their hair and clothes serve to identify them pretty well. I walked home with another fellow from the seminar, and the gas was pretty strong. They apparently used some kind of dust in tear gas these days because it persists for a long time. Otherwide we didn't have any troubles getting home.

I had dinner that night a few blocks from home in a quick-service restaurant about three blocks from the campus. As I was finishing, a small group of rioters ran by outside followed closely by police, and the area was gassed. A few of the kids came into the restaurant to recover. On the way home, I passed a column of six-bys that were bringing the first National Guard troops onto the campus. They quieted things down a good deal, although small bands roved around breaking windows and starting fires until early morning. A few Molotov cocktails were thrown at the homes of university officials and ROTC advisors.

By Wednesday I was convinced that the Rads had failed in their main objective of shutting down the school. They couldn't agree on how to do it, and they really only wanted to riot and "trash" anyhow. "Trashing" is breaking windows and burning down buildings in a purposeful, political way. [W. (female)] asked me in Indianapolis when they would start "trashing" people. It may not be long: I heard some far-out Rads at the union last week saying that it was about time for the assassination squads to get busy.

By Wednesday there were a lot of schools in the country closed down (Dartmouth was on the list), some of them for the rest of the year. Here the riots hadn't shut it down, and they kids got pretty angry but even where they're really angry, they can't think of anything more original to do than inchoat trashing. I was surprised that the administration here didn't cave in. I have thought that they were pretty spineless because they don't ever come out and say much. But they do keep the place open, and that wasn't easy last week.

One factor here is a kind of joint geographical-political split. The sciences and the agricultural branches are on the western half of the campus, and the humanities and social sciences are on the east. The latter are the ones who riot and strike while the others pretty much go about their business. So no matter what happens on this side, one half of the university in always open.

Wednesday morning I figured that something pretty bad would have to happen to close the place down. It hasn't yet but the Rads are threatening now that someone is going to get killed if they don't close the school. Wednesday afternoon there was a little riot with the Guard, just to try them out, and that night there was a skirmish around a group of dormitories in the middle of the campus. These "riots" are really pretty tame affairs: there's a lot of noise and milling around and enthusiasm but it comes down to a few people throwing rocks and a few shooting tear gas and the big majority just running around in circles or standing around in circles. So far the police have gotten the worst of it—about fifteen more or less serious injuries against none of significance to the students. One university employee may lose an eye after being hit by a rock on his way home after work.

Thursday it got hot, and it was fairly quiet during the day. There was a rally in the afternoon, and a mob tried to break off the campus for a little training on one of the commercial streets but they couldn't get through the cordons of police and the Guard. The local radio stations reported that they felt depressed after their failure, and that made the kids mad. They scheduled another rally for nine in the evening and on the campus that afternoon you could sense that they were really working themselves up for a major effort.

The rally didn't last long, and they broke through the cordons quite easily, moving in small groups by many routes, but all heading toward the state capital, about a mile from the main campus. Some of the groups went by this house. The Guard got there first and drove the kids off with gas. They were all over the place in little groups so the police gassed the whole stretch of State Street between the campus and the capitol. The kids started some fires, and the firemen had a little trouble getting them out because they had to gas masks. The kids were slashing hoses where they could.

For about four hours that night there was chaos. A couple helicopters with searchlights were flying around above all the time, trying to spot how the kids were moving. The papers reported the next day one of my favorite incidents: some of the rioting was going on along Langdon Street, where a lot of the fraternities are. When the gas went down, a lot of the kids would run into the fraternity houses to take cover. At one, a policeman came in through the back door, walked through the living room where he smiled, said "Hi", and dropped a tear gas canister on the floor. No one ran in there for a while. I spent that night typing out a seminar paper.

Friday was pretty quiet during the day. After Nixon's press conference there was a little sporadic rioting, especially near the famous Mifflin Street Coop, about three blocks from here. That's a little cooperative grocery store run by students where a lot of drugs actually change hands. Also a lot of the far-out Rads live close by. There was a bad riot there last year and a little one in April.

Friday about ⅓ of the faculty had a big meeting, and they voted to cease normal university activity for a week starting on Monday in order to study the issues more closely, or something like that. That's ridiculous. There can be precious little real discussion on this campus anymore. People will listen only to what they want to hear. Minds are made up, really closed down tight. So if the faculty has its way, there will be the same anti-Nixon, anti-war, anti-racism, anti-establishment, anti-pollution garbage all week long. One of the reasons the kids here are rioting is that they have heard too much of this before, and they want to do something else. The romantic thing to do nowadays is to take the streets and live in them.

I hope the folks in charge don't misread what's going on. They could bring all the troops home tomorrow, and the Revolution would still go on because the object is to destroy the military establishment. They could free all the Black Panthers tomorrow and let them run the streets, and the revolutions would continue because they want to destroy the courts and the "white-man's law". If all the pollution were brought under control, it wouldn't matter because the Rads want to destroy the capitalistic economic system. Nixon could resign tomorrow, and it would mean nothing because they want to bring down the government. Che Guevara himself could be President, and they would still try to tear it down. So don't confuse the demands of the Rads with their aims. And don't underestimate them. They have a tremendous following among the young, and their numbers are growing all the time.

Nevertheless, they aren't much of a threat to anyone but themselves. First of all, they are lazy. That was obvious here this week. They could have shut this school down before the Guard got here, but it would have meant a lot of hard work. They want it all now, right this minute. They have a lot that way as it is. They have a lot of money, so they can get food fast and a place to stay. They get sex easy too because it's getting tougher and tougher to get pregnant unless you really want to. They have instant happiness too—in the form of maijuana, and even some of the hard stuff. They have been told their whole life that they're the finest, brightest, lovliest, most wonderful people who ever trod the earth, and the silly asses have actually believed most of it. Most of it, because they know they're human, and for that reason they let their hair grow and wear strange clothes and things—they know that they are not as great as they've been told they are so they try to defile themselves and freak out their admirers (parents, teachers, ect). But every man jack of them still thinks he's pretty intelligent, good head and no hang-ups, that he's got the whole sordid world all figured out and knows all the answers and even more of the questions. So they don't listen to anymore, not even to each other.

That's why they'll never make it, despite all their brave words and posturings. They simply can't stand each other. Have you noticed that this movement has no leaders at all? They have their heroes: Che, Huey Newton, the Chicago 8, but they have no leaders. That would mean admitting that someone was better, smarter, tougher than they are, and one of our peerless revolutionaries are ever going to admit that. They want to have their revolution and make it themselves, all by themselves, alone. A good revolution demands organization and a transcendent morality, and the current Rads have neither.

They're confused. They're grasping for anything, and most of them are pretty scared and alone. They are only dangerous to themselves. Together they get pretty hysterical and try playing one-up in cynicism or they just blow their minds in a big or little group. This is the suburbia generation. They have seen their parents leading senseless lives and saying all the time how great it is, and the kids just can't put the two together and make any sense of it. Parents think their kids are turning against them but it's just the opposite: the kids are yelling and screaming for someone to help them and give them a few answers and nobody hears them.

Nixon did a good thing yesterday morning. The kids will never admit it openly but when they are alone the next time, they are going to think about it. He wanted to go and talk with them. That's all they're really asking. Maybe in the depths of his own uncertainty, Nixon got a brief, flickering insight into the hellish despair that a lot of the kids in this country are going through.

Right now the kids have one tenuous tie to reality left, and it's a pretty healthy one. They have fine music. Their parents can't hear them; the schools run them through a depersonalized sheep-run; sports, sex and drugs simply divert them for a while without giving any answers. But the music helps bring it together. That's the secret hope of the Woodstock nation, that the music still holds them to the world in a meaningful way. Listen to their music, especially Simon and Garfunkle, the Credance Clearwater, Bob Dylan, Johnny Cash and a few others. Those are the ones who say something in their music. The kids don't really groove with the Steppenwolf, Jimi Hendrix, Joe Cocker and the like, except when they're stoned. Simon and Garfunkle are the most important, and if you want to know what the kids are like, listen to the "Bridge over Troubled Water".

The kids talk a lot about love and joy, mainly because they've heard that a good revolution runs on love and joy. But they dogmatize both, they beat their thin chests and proclaim the wonders of revolutionary love and joy. Love means going down with anything that comes along, and joy is feeling good when you lay out a cop with a rock. When you have to be dogmatic about love and joy, then you don't know a whole helluva lot about either. What they are saying is that they have known neither, and they know it, and couldn't someone please make the music come true: can't someone please put down a bridge over troubled water instead of tear gas?

About five years ago this time of year, I wrote a letter about what was coming. It looked bad then, and it was worse than I expected. Now it looks better. You can see now where it's going. The Rads aren't going to tear it down. 'Course there's not a whole lot of good can be said for the system except that it's viable, and it's still got places in it where decent people can live.

And even enjoy the good things. Take care, and next time you see a real rad, listen to his music before you make up your mind about him.

[Editor's note: The statement "Nixon did a good thing yesterday morning" refers to his early morning, spontaneous visit to the Lincoln Memorial where he talked to protesters.] *Rant about hating hippies*

II. PROTEST

Antiwar protest was strong for several weeks, but college students went home and they, just like almost everyone else, faced the distractions of summer work and leisure. Protest activity simmered as a result of Nixon's promises of troop withdrawal and implementation of a draft lottery system that ended random call-ups. Antiwar organizations experienced additional setbacks due to internal divisions, vigilant law enforcement, government appeals for patriotism, damaging press reports, and a more visible backlash by the American public disturbed by the violence of antiwar radicals. Television shots of aggressive, foul-mouthed protesters who carried Vietcong flags presented powerful images to mainstream Americans. In May 20, 1970, approximately 100,000, mostly labor-union members, gathered in New York for a pro-government demonstration. Many other Americans simply found the whole war issue emotionally exhausting. While some Maine people continued to be supportive of college demonstrations, the letters that Senator Smith received from those expressing antiwar sentiments were fewer in number.

Visible Contrast

69. *"the kids are right"*

Livermore, Maine
June 1, 1970

Dear Mrs. Smith—

I recall you, alone, had the courage to stand up to McCarthy. Pray you can still rally your colleagues. Can't understand the apathy of the public—perhaps they're just not informed—or Congress who has abrogated it's responsibility. Perhaps, individually, people react when their prerogatives are threatened but, collectively, they don't seem to care!

I feel as if I had gone through the "Looking glass"—When I talk about the War, people say "You don't want them over here do you?" Which seems just about as realistic as the natives of Weld, Maine invading Viet villages.

The main issue, that the strongest prohibitions in our Constitution have been violated, is ignored.

I have even come to feel that the kids are right. Hamilton advised if there were continued collusion between Exec. & Legis. as to the direction of military power, the people should recall what powers "they have heretofore parted with out of their own hands". It seems this is what they are trying to do—Rashly and inexpertly, but at least they care—

I am frightened at the warmth and backing of big business was for the President—Hitler had the same—Disorders are fearful to property owners, who will go along with anything just to keep the lid on.

Are you aware there is a rumour that Rand Corp. "think-tank" has had a question asked it—carefully explicit—"in behalf of the president"—not by—The question, "What would be public reaction if '72 elections were postponed in view of national emergency?" Some one is interested—now—two years ahead of time to poll opinion, according to rumour, which has a dubious source—an underground newspaper, which one of my brothers students showed him in Connecticut several weeks ago—More disturbing to me than the rumour, is the present structure of our government that gives rise to such rumors.

Sincerely,

L. F. (female)

70. *"end the U.S. operation in Indo-China"*

Friendship, Maine
June 2, 1970

Dear Mrs. Smith:

Congratulations on your senate speech. I think you are just right to urge us all to speak up.

I would like to add my voice to the many which are, I hope, asking you to support the Cooper-Church amendment and other amendments designed to end the U.S. operation in Indo-China.

I feel less confused now about my attitude as the arguments against continuing seem to be snowballing at this point. I feel that the international political considerations are not more important than the domestic problems which the war has brought about. I am not able to judge the former very well, but I can tell you that I feel much more threatened by the possible consequences of our own tragic problems in this country. I still feel that many of our problems can be solved but I don't feel we can accomplish a thing of last good by fighting in Asia.

I personally will not be saddened by the event of a "defeat" or a lack of victory in Viet Nam under the circumstances. I would feel that reasoned withdrawal would be much more honorable than continuing—in fact, it might be the only action in which we can take lasting pride.

Weren't you alarmed to hear the President (in his TV address on Cambodia) imply that part of the justification for going to Cambodia is that this is a proud country that has never been defeated? Surely, this is the least acceptable reason for fighting any war, no red menace scares me as much as that kind of thinking from a national leader. I trust in his private conversations he shows more sophistication in his reasoning!

We are fortunate to be here in Maine, but there is no place to hide from the human problems of the world. I am convinced that the war cannot continue long because it is losing whatever toleration it has had in this country. Only the real "supporters" are willing to defend it. Congress should do what it can to bring it 40 as end as quickly as possible.

Respectfully,

C. F. (female)

[Editor's note: Senator's Smith June 1 speech in the Senate was her "Declaration of Conscience II" that warned: "Extremism bent upon polarization of our people is increasingly forcing upon the American people the narrow choice between anarchy and repression." She concluded that "It is time that with dignity, firmness and friendliness, they [the great center of our people] reason with, rather than capitulate to, the extremists on both sides—at all levels—and caution that their patience ends at the border of violence and anarchy that threatens our American democracy."]

71. *"our system of government stinks"*

Bridgton, Maine
June 2, 1970

Dear Senator Smith:

From today's papers I note that you have again "discovered the obvious". I suggest that you would do more good if you were to discover something a little less obvious, for instance, the conscience of the Senate, or the declining respect and confidence that Americans have in their Congress, particularly the Senate.

You might point out to your colleagues that their arrogance, in every Senator a General, for every problem an answer, for their failure of responsibility in distinguishing between the right to criticize and good judgment in when to exercise that right, for their callous disregard in weighing the consequences of their words to remove any risk of aiding the enemy, for their deliberate heating up of the fires of campus demonstrations for cheap political gain, and for their hypocrisy in fiscal responsibility, have all brought the Senate to a new low in esteem and contributed to the divisions you deplore.

The Cooper-Church Amendment debate is a good place to call your fellow Senators to the accounting they should make. Clean your own stables of the accumulated muck before you set out to warn the Country of the effects of your own slovenliness.

One of you calls the Premier (Vice) of an allied, sovereign nation "a tin horn Dictator"; another sneeringly refers to him as "an Asian Agnew"; still another says that he doesn't understand why we can't make the S. Vietnamese leave Cambodia when we do. This is the "retoric" the Liberals approve? This is the way to show the world that South Vietnam is not an "Imperialist Puppet"? No, this degrades the whole Senate and makes common cause with those who say our system of government stinks! Indeed, perhaps the Senate does stink!

Very truly yours,

C. M. (male)

72. *"opposed to violence"*

Lincolnville, Maine
June 2, 1970

Dear Senator Smith,

Thank you for your balanced & and sane remarks on the <u>Today</u> show yesterday. Today's Bangor paper "covers" you well & I assure you have secretaries to clip that part of thing or I would send you ours.

I guess I just want to say "Bless you—the voice of reason." My husband & I are opposed to violence as a change-agent but we sympathize with the students' disaffection. We feel the President is poorly advised, dangerously insulated from reality or sadly misusing his executive powers—Cambodia is a disaster and Vietnam just should not be taking so long to get clear of. What troubles us about a good country & good people infuriates our younger friends, apparently (we are 38.)

Please be aware of our opinion as you struggle with your responsibilities. We were grateful for your bravery 20 yrs ago (we were in school then) and grateful for the publicity given your reasonable presence yesterday.

I would be more helpful to you but, like my country neighbors, I am trying to plant a big vegetable garden this week.

Respectfully,

D. B. (female)

P.S. I forgot to say:

Anybody destructive frightens me—I have small children. But the choice between the repressive, fascistic (have you heard the analogies between the U.S.
in the 70's & Germany in the 30's that are going around? I heard them first
at a Unitarian Church conference.) syndrome on the right and the angry violence on the left drives me away from all media & right out in to the garden, qualifying me as a member of the Silent Majority, I guess. Some choices
are no choices. But we are what used to be called liberals so do not think of
ourselves as typical. It's a mess, isn't it.
D. B.

73. "not one cent for guns"

Falmouth, Maine
July 2, 1970

Dear Senator Smith—

I am sick to death of government by public relations—

I want to know and believe I have the right to know the facts about this
war—

If we captured weapons by going into Cambodia and gained time—we
also brought bombing and killing into a country that was not previously at
war—

What is different about our going into Cambodia to protect our national
interest than the Russians going into Checkosolvakia to protect their national
interest?

If we are fighting a legitimate war in South East Asia—why is nobody
else on our side?

If the North Vietnamese can win a war using only communist military
hardware and not Chinese or Russian troops why can't the South Vietnamese
win their position by the aid of U.S. hardware but not troops.

What is the cost in terms of Americans and Aisans dead and wounded?
How much money has been spent? How much good or bad will has been in-
cured for this country?

If we want to protect American lives—we can bring them home. I would
be willing to spend any amount of money to build hospitals—schools—
roads—in any country—but not one cent for guns in a foreign country.

Violence in this country feeds on these attemps to justify a position with
out giving the plain unvarnished facts.

Respectfully yours,
A. A. (female)

Pacifist Voice

74. "debating the merits"

Rockland, Maine
August 29, 1970

Dear Mrs. Smith:

I have watched tonite's CBS special broadcast with McGovern, Javitts, Stennis, and Tower debating the merits of the McGovern-Hatfield amendment and was more than ever convinced of the rightness of it. I would respectively ask you to vote yes on Tuesday when it comes up for vote. These people will never let us stop as long as we are willing to let our youth die for them. They are capable of defending themselves if we will let them. We will never negotiate when we can only decide the sizeof thetable in two years.

I recently read that there is a possibility of the scuttling of President Nixons programs for rejuvenation of the Merchant Marine to get revenge for his cuts in Educationand Health and Welfare. Could suchiresponsibility be possible? As the mother of a boy in the Merchant Marine who has been taking the machinations of war to Vietnam in decrepit ships and knows of disasters that the public is not aware of and another boy with #23 in the lottery this frightens me. We cannot run a war for years without ships. This is a problem that has long been neglected by Washington.

Please give us some hope on Tuesday.

Very truly yours,

R. H. (female)

[Editor's note: Senator Jacob K. Javits (1904–1968) was a New York Republican. Senator John C. Stennis (1901–1995) was a Mississippi Democrat. John G. Tower (1925–1991) was a Texas Republican.]

75. "don't agree with this war"

Gorham, Maine
October 17, 1970

Dear Senator Smith:

I would like pertinent information concerning the present status and future objectives of the Viet Nam war. Please don't refer me to newspapers, articles, or news reports. I want fact, your opinion and hopes—along with any information from the present administration (objective and subjective and labeled as such—without political overtones.)

My brother is leaving for Viet Nam in a few months—he is a Marine. I want to have something to understand about this war. In my present situation I want the truth—as of course many others do, and not propaganda! Is this possible?—or is it so hard to get because of politics, strategy, and numerous other reasons or excuses.

I would appreciate your honesty and forthrightness. I don't agree with this war—this was a decision made before my brother had gotten his orders.

This is a personal letter which I hope will return a personal concern from you—not only for myself but for everyone concerned—all of us.

Thank you for at least listening. I am worried, unhappy, and confused. I am not a member of the SDS, blank panthers, etc.—I am a teacher.
Sincerely,
G. S. (female)
P.S. An answer before November 10, 1970 would be greatly appreciated.

76. *"do what's right not what's Republican or middle American"*

Kennebunkport, Maine
Feb. 7, 1971

Dear Sen. Smith,

I wrote to you concerning the United States action in Cambodia. I received a nice letter in return stating your support for President Nixon.

I would to ask you now, how long are you going to let this ridiculous war continue. Now we attack Laos, where will we be next week or next year. Do we go into Cuba next or how about Santo Domingo, that was a good one wasn't it?

How much longer are you senators going sit back and let this war go on? How many more people have to die before you do something?

Please do what's right not what's Republican or middle American.
Yours,
J. A. (male)

III. PRO-ADMINISTRATION

Senator Smith continued to support the president and maintain other hawkish positions in regards to American troops in Southeast Asia. For example, she stated in late May her intention to vote against the Church-Cooper Amendment that would disallow funding for future military operations in Cambodia and against the McGovern-Hatfield Amendment that would see the end of war funding and removal of all Americans troops from Southeast Asia before the end of 1971. The following letters indicate that her firm position had support. It is interesting that the two authors who disagreed with her were not young antiwar liberals but Nixon supporters who believed Smith failed to give Nixon adequate backing.

77. *"pray Nixon is right"*

West Southport, Maine
June 4, 1970

Dear Margaret Chase Smith,

. . . I'm glad to hear your voice about our troubles. I feel the permissiveness got out of hand. I feel too that Congress could help our President a great deal if it would. I know Cambodia caused a lot of attacks upon him but I feel he thought something drastic was needed. I want the war over too. I don't like having any boys & men killed but I do think we have hindered both Johnson & Nixon by our cries and demonstrations of "Bring the boys home" and such. N. Vietnam is just waiting for that. And now we are trying to tie the President's hands. We didn't tie Truman's. (I had a son over in the undeclared Korean War) We didn't tie Johnson's. I just pray Nixon is right & we can help him "finish" his troubles.

Sincerely,

(Remember me?) V. S. (female)

Doesn't agree w̄ war but doesn't think we should be against the President so much

78. *"Nixon is doing right"*

Searsport, Maine
June 6, 1970

My dear Senator;

I am one of the "silent majority" Who Feels but, too often does not Speak. I am speaking up now to congratulate you upon the recent acclaim given you by the Senate and by the dinner in your honor. I was proud for you and for our State of Maine. You deserve the voice of our appreciation. Your dignity and wisdom is very impressive.

I follow the political news very closely, also the voting. And no wonder for I have six grandsons all doing their patriotic service in training and duty. The oldest who is now . . . on the Cambodian border has recently written me "Nixon is doing right to destroy the sanctuaries". Dissent in our Legislature is encouragement to the opposition even that Church-Cooper amendment, however mild it is. The young and many adults, too, often do not take time to understand and will picture it as dissent. Relying on your helpfulness and with more congratulations,

Sincerely yours

H. A. (female)

79. "His burden is great enough"

Winthrop, Maine
June 1, 1970

Dear Senator:

The Republican Party of the State of Maine has seen fit to return you to the U.S. Senate to represent the citizens of the State of Maine.

It vexes me greatly, as a registered Republican of long standing, to see and hear you on nationally televised news programs, giving aid and comfort to our sworn enemies, both political and international, by attacking our duly elected President. His burden is great enough without the elected members of his own party joining with the aforementioned sworn enemies, to undermine his efforts.

The Press has been less than helpful throughout Mr. Nixon's political career, and people granting interviews to the Press should bear this in mind: that anything they say will be presented in the worst possible construction, as refers to the Administration. It is my opinion that criticism of the Administration, which is after all, your Administration too, should be done within the Administration, and not publicly.

Elected officials of the Republican Party should hearken to the old adage: Papa said, A single stick can be broken; a bundle of sticks, tightly bound, is almost impossible to break. United we stand, Mrs. Smith; Divided we fall.

Cordially yours,

J. M. (male)

✳ Mistake to criticise Nixon as much as he was; should have been done privately

80. "give the President the consideration he needs"

Ogunquit, Maine
June 7, 1970

My dear Senator Smith:

As a member of the Republican party I am some what disappointed in your lack of support to President Nixon. There is no question in my mind and in the minds of the "Silent Majority" that the Cambodian operation is in the best interests of our men in Viet Nam and for the successful operation of our armed forces in the Southeast Asia theater.

Furthermore, President Nixon's Constitutional responsibilities as commander in chief of the armed forces should be upheld by the congress so that he can bring this war to a successful conclusion.

Hoping that you will give the President the consideration he needs I remain

Respectfully yours,

M. K. (male)

81. "standing up for America"

Bethel, Maine
June 2, 1970

My dear Mrs. Smith,

. . . From time to time we [members of the Legion] have been asked to contact our Senators & congressmen, relative to Veterans Affairs.

This time I am writing you on another subject. In this mornings Lewiston Sun an article of yourself of which you will find enclosed. It was nice to hear you come out with some thing good for a change for our country.

Recently I wrote Muskie (I voted for him because he was from Maine) that I was surprised at his speechs on campus riots. I asked him if he wanted an appeasement for America. And asked him to come out more strongly for law & order. But he hasn't. It looks as if he didn't want anything but votes & cared less who he hurt to get them.

He has his sister & a mother residing here in the Rumford Area. And in here in Oxford County are bitterly disappointed in our Sen. Muskie, who will do anything for a (Buck) <u>Money.</u>

I recently sent clippings to Vice Pres. Agnew. He too is standing up for America. This Lewiston Sun good words for him also.

I have been trying to find a muzzle for Sen. Fulbright, but thus far have been unable to find one large enough.

Why tell this whole world what America intends to do? Why not keep the rest of the world guessing. We saved Europe twice? Who is helping us in Europe?

Look what we did for France? And what thanks are we getting. Why not look out for America when this conflict is over. All they want of us is our food, money, & men, and then "go home Yanks."

We are very lucky to be living in a small town. There is less violence.

Allthou we are getting a number of civil righters, at least last year. That means more this year. . . . But it was different last year and we citizens did not like the type sent here. Maybe it is the generation "Gap"?

How ever keep up the good work & stand behind our President. He didn't send our men across Johnson did. But also help the Jews. But for America U.S.A. they would still be wandering on the face of God's earth and no hope in sight. We are very proud of you here back home.

Sincerely,

L. D. (male)

82. *"President Nixon has my support"*

Cape Elizabeth, Maine
June 6, 1970

Dear Senator Smith:

As one of your constituents I wish to register my approval of President Nixon's policy in Southeast Asia. His attempts to try various avenues for resolution of the problems therein are commendable and courageous.

I feel it is strict isolationism to try to force our President to withdraw completely and irrevocably from Southeast Asia and that it would be a betrayal of those who have already sacrificed their lives there.

I have just returned from travelling about Great Britain and Ireland where I met a number of Australians and New Zealanders who claim that "the thinking people and people of good will in our country believe in President Nixon's policy" and they think that he is doing the best he can there.

Further, a number of Englishmen voluntarily said they felt almost ashamed that England wasn't helping out the U.S. in the job in Southeast Asia—considering all that the USA did to help their country previously.

To me, complete withdrawal only means complete overtaking of Southeast Asia by the Communists.

President Nixon has my support, and I hope that he has yours, also.
Sincerely yours,
V. B. (female)

83. *"be loyally supported"*

Cape Elizabeth, Maine
June 6, 1970

Dear Senator Smith:

I believe that America's military presence in Southeast Asia is honouring the solemn commitments made during previous administrations.

I believe that precipitate withdrawal from Southeast Asia—whether from weariness, from disorderly domestic pressures, from the financial demands of the nation's unfortunate, underprivileged and undermotivated, or from just plain political expediency—would dishonor those solemn commitments.

I believe that precipitate withdrawal would throw Southeast Asia into complete chaos, that it would mean more slaughter of innocents by unprincipled aggressors, that thousands of young Americans had given their lives in vain, and that the still small voices of American prisoners of war—now stifled by violations of all humane and accepted rules—would never be heard again.

I believe that for American strategy to be decided by raucous mobs is simply "telegraphing our punches" to Hanoi and that the enemy need fight only hard enough to keep the war unpopular and then just wait.

As a constituent I firmly demand that President Nixon—who is courageous if not popular—be allowed his Constitutional function as commander-in-chief of our armed forces and that his strategy be loyally supported as a hopeful step to an honorable peace.

Very truly yours,

H. B. (male)

P.S. Warm personal regards! Your gracious courtesy to us on our visit to the Capital a few years ago will not soon be forgotten.

* Commitment to honour past Administration decision; and
  * that leaving Nam will cause more deaths of innocent lives

84. *"disagree with this professor-student leisure class"*

Kennebunk, Maine
June 13, 1970

Dear Senator Smith:

My compliments on your recent "Declaration." You have a great talent for phrasing precisely what needs to be said.

I have at hand a letter from a young man who attends a college where I also once spent some time.

Writing calmly and reasonably, with some evidence of thoughtfulness, he shows a sincere concern about the spread of the far Eastern war to Cambodia. He speaks of the faculty allowing—perhaps even encouraging—the students to leave campus before the school year ends in order to participate in the so-called students 'strike" against the war. He mentions "constitutional crisis," and referring to the "social realities of the American system" the need for "tangible pressure upon those persons in positions of real political influence, the members of Congress themselves." He also mentions a "campaign . . . of continuous presence in Washington to lobby for peace. . . ."

He ends with a plea for me to reflect and to write. Hence this letter, and my compliments to the young man and thousands of other students like him who are showing a real concern.

Whether he will like what I write or not, however, is another matter.

Obviously, as it is with all of the young college people with whom I have come in contact, he is deeply influenced by his professors. This is to be expected and since these men represent the fount of knowledge at which students are paying to drink, it should not be otherwise. Sometimes, however, the thought frightens me.

I am not a professor of Government, History, or English. Therefore I cannot play a game of semantics which picks apart the fine distinctions of procedure which make it legal to fight the North Vietnamese on one side of a line and illegal to the extent of being a "grave constitutional crisis" to fight the same enemy on the other side of that line. The fact that the line is the border of Cambodia should be of most importance to Cambodians, and they reportedly did not complain.

Another aspect is explored in the enclosed editorial from the Portland Press Herald. This would seem to indicate that the professors and students may have overlooked the possibility that they, on their campuses, are, perhaps, not as well informed, not in as good a position to make wise decisions as the Chief Executive of the United States.

Often disagreeing with many policies of President Nixon, I still must face the fact that simply by virtue of his position he is vastly better informed than I, and may possibly be basing his decisions on something of which I have no knowledge. Has this simple premise never occurred to our collegians?

When it comes to "watch-dogging" the President, it should seem that Congress itself and the members of the "loyal opposition" would be far better equipped to do that than educators and college students.

Do those who study learn nothing from history? What makes them so certain we are safe and secure on our "little island." We have watched Communist expansion spread throughout the world. Do they really think it will stop if we allow one more takeover in South Vietnam? I wonder if any of today's young people ever heard of Chamberlain.

However, even the war, grave, puzzling, disturbing though it may be, is not my greatest fear. That lies in a thought roused by my young student correspondent. The thought of thousands of educators and greater thousands of students under their influence, actually becoming totally active in exerting "tangible pressure" on members of Congress.

I fear it may happen. I fear that you who are in Congress may find yourselves unduly influenced by students and their guiding professors.

Here we have, arisen in our midst, a whole new leisure class with enormous potential for influence. Each of the two sections of this class, professors and students, supposedly has a job: to teach, and to learn. Each is secure through tenure, scholarship, government loan, or "the old man." Neither apparently takes his job very seriously. Classes are suspended on what appears to be anyone's whim. The "work day" is hardly a long one. Vacations are frequent and lengthy. The responsibility to do one's job—either teaching or learning—doesn't rest very heavily. With time to march, time to demonstrate, time to inundate Congress with letters, time enough apparently to consider "continuous presence in Washington," I sincerely fear this leisure group will make their presence felt in far larger proportion than their actual numbers would warrant.

Unfortunately those of us who may not agree with them are back at the office trying to make a living. Trying to support our families as taxes rise and rise. Some of that very rise is to support the educators who often seem diametrically opposed in their opinions to those of us who pay their salaries. Most of us are paying heavily to send our children to college so they too may learn to demonstrate, lobby, and write to Congress the views taught them by their professors.

So, with all this, listen to them.. Listen closely. They have many valid points. They are, for the most part, dreamers and idealists who are vitally necessary to keep us from complete technocracy. But one could wish they showed more knowledge of the cultural heritage of mankind which they as representatives of "learning" are supposed to uphold. One could wish they had more integrity, more true courage, more sense of responsibility. One could wish they were less concerned with their own self-importance. Nonetheless, listen to them. Congress should hear all sides.

Just remember they are not really as large in numbers as they are loud. Back home, working to support them, are those of us who may just possibly disagree with this professor-student leisure class. Too busy trying to make ends meet under the rising pressures of inflation, we don't very often have the time to organize "protest marches," to demonstrate, to "exert continuous pressure in Washington," or even to write our Senators and Congressmen. All we can do is vote.

Yes, Senator Smith, there IS a "silent majority."
Sincerely,
A. J. (male)

IV. POWS, CHEMICALS, EMOTIONS, AND CHILDREN

As the American military effort was slowly winding down and the antiwar movement was doing likewise, letters sent to Smith in the later months of 1970 and into 1971 covered new issues. No doubt to the relief to a tired Smith, in the twilight of her political life, the days of heavy mail from ordinary small-town Mainers focusing on opposition to the war were gone. And yet there was no end to heart-wrenching issues. For example, the first letters tackle the problem of prisoners of war and the final letter is about life, love, and future generations—the issue of children fathered by American soldiers and other orphans in South Vietnam.

85. "POW"

Falmouth, MA
August 24, 1970

Dear Senator Smith,

After reading a most disturbing editorial today in the Boston Herald Traveler 8/23, I decided to drop everything and write this letter. The article was about our POW's being held in Hanoi. Is there anything we can do?

This is the paragraph that really reached me. "Thousands of young people sincerely fight for an end to suffering, injustice and brutality, yet never has there been a placard raised or a voice heard for this oppressed minority. No campus demonstration has championed the cause of these wretched souls."

Last year there was a surge of public concern and something in the paper everyday. Now it seems no one cares or have lost hope.

My husband is in the Air Force and many of our friends have served in SEA. Several close friends have given their lives and one is believed to be a POW. I feel like I have betrayed these friends if I don't do something.

I have never written to any of my representatives in government before but if it would help I shall write to someone everyday.

Please do all you can to bring this to the public's attention Mrs. Smith.

I was very glad to hear that you are feeling so well after your recent hospitalization.

Maine is my state too.

Very truly yours,
B. G. (female)

86. "prisoners of war"

Houlton, Maine
November 9, 1970

My dear Mrs. Smith,

My concern for the safety, treatment, and welfare of all American prisoners of war being held by the North Vietnamese prompts me to write this letter to you requesting that you please bring to bear all of the influence which you possess regarding this matter on the proper authority to do whatever is necessary to provide better treatment for all American prisoners of war, to obtain the release of all prisoners, or to enter into some sort of exchange program with the Viet Cong. I am happy for you that you have recovered so nicely from your operation. My husband joins me in kindest personal regards.
M. P. (female)

87. "lonely G.I.'s"

North Berwick, Maine
January 18, 1971

Dear Senator Smith:

This letter is in response to a recent newspaper article which appeared in The Portland Press Herald. It stated that the morale in Viet Nam has reached a very low point, and cited several examples. Nowadays, one is forever hearing of U.S.O. addresses at which to address letters to servicemen in Viet Nam, and requests to write to lonely G.I.'s are more numerous than the people who respond. The purpose of all this is, of course, to bolster morale, to make our men know we are thinking of them.

To me, this seems a little strange, for if we are living under a true government of the people, for the people, and by the people, why is there not more done to help this cause? No matter by what name it is called, Viet Nam is a war and men are being killed. It is for their country and for the cause of freedom, which I will not debate, because I am one of the few young people who is of the opinion that there is a purpose for American involvement in Southeast Asia. However, is not morale an important part of any battle, whether it is a highschool basketball game or to prevent Communism? Why does our government allow our morale to sink so low?

My suggestion would be to release all postage costs on all mail to Viet Nam, which would make it possible for more people to write to more servicemen. This cost would be minor compared to the cost of psychiatric care that could result from low morale. Personally, I have the time to write to a dozen servicemen, but lack the funds to do so.

My letter will doubtlessly be lost among all your mail on more important problems, but I do hope it will be given at least a little consideration.

Thank you very much,

Respectfully yours,

P. S. (female)

88. "chemicals"

Eliot, Maine
December 29, 1970

Dear Senator Smith:

We have just watched a news film about the damage done in Vietnam by our defoliation chemicals. It makes us feel ashamed to be United States citizens. Can't officers get their undeserved combat metals without all that? Does anyone know the scope of the ecological chain reaction these chemicals have started? Has Congress exerted any control over these monstrous actions?

We feel that you demonstrate the high morality that this country must have from its leaders if it is to survive; however, we feel that the battle is currently being lost. It is imperative that more money be spent internally on worthwhile humane projects and that the military be more closely controled.
Sincerely,
Mr. & Mrs. W. M.

89. "worries me"

Bethel, Maine
November 21, 1970

Dear Mrs. Smith:

My son . . . took an intensive course in the Vietnamese language. He is in Military Intelligence. He expects to go over sometime after the first of the year.

The problem is that he lost his spleen . . . and we have been told that if he contracts malaria it could well be fatal.

I have talked with boys that were based in or near Saigon and when I asked them if they thought Saigon was malaria controlled, they snorted in derision. So you can see why this worries me.

Would it be possible for you in your busy life to take the time to find out what you can about this situation? I realize it's asking a great deal but I didn't know where else I could possibly find out the truth.

If he dies protecting his country, I could be comforted that it was for a good cause, but if he dies from malaria, I would feel his presence there was for naught.

I would very much appreciate any information you could obtain for me.
Very sincerely,
J. H. (female)

90. "getting my messages through"

Belfast, Maine
April 6, 1971

Honorable:

Thank you for all the wonderful favors you have been doing for me and all the other citizens here in Maine, New England, the other states, and the rest of the world. I also want to thank you for getting my messages through to our President.

You will find an enclosure, a message that I would like to have you read, and if you find it worthy, will you please send it along to President Nixon. This favor will be greatly appreciated.

One other favor I would like to request. When you come to Maine in May, would it be possible for me to get a chance to converse with you for even a short while, because I realize how busy you are and the others who may want to see you too.

Respectfully,

P. M. (male)

Mr. President:

Although this is my sixth message to you, I still find it very difficult to communicate with you. Please don't get the impression that it is you personally, because it would be just as difficult for me to write to any man who holds your office. The reason for this feeling is; even though a person who is an ordinary person on the street, they may feel a little inferior sending their opinion to the Commandor in Chief of the United States Armed Forces, who is also our President of the United States of America.

In the other five messages that I sent to you, you know how concerned and serious I am about, our people, our country, and our existing problems. This message still holds true, to those same feelings. The context of this message may be shared by many people in this country, and many of our friendly countries throughout this world. Being so confident in this last statement that I am willing to send copies of this message to some new's media as an open message, and asking for comments from the readers to let me know how many share this opinion. Then I can let you know what the results are on the number of answers I get, of how many do, and how many who do not agree.

Mr. President, this past week your office has been swamped by a deluge of telegrams caused by the results of Lieutenant William Calley's conviction. In fact, you have seen and heard so much controversy, that you may be screening, and taking only a few out for every one hundred to read for consideration.

Before going to deep in this message; may I elaborate on the results of the Calley case. At first we must admit, that the jury had a very hard decision to make, and regardless of what their decision would be, the results could have been controversial either way. Therefore the people who are protesting the results of this trial, are not questioning the integrity of the officers who were on the jury, it is the matter of principal.

We all know that there are very few people throughout this world who would take another persons life willingly. Because we should respect the rights of others to live, and let live. However there may be times throughout out life time when we may be forced to defend ourself, our country, or help our allies.

If we were to bring out all the conditions similar to the My Lai Massacre, without any doubt that war could stop tomorrow. There have been many known cases throughout this damn Vietnam war where the North Vietnamese have slaughtered many more than were at My Lai, and in many other instances. One such case just happened the other day at Duc Duc.

It is not only Lt. Calley who is being used as the scape goat, it is all of the people who are trying to help the South Vietnamese. But it is the United States who is getting most of the blame.

Mr. President, how many people throughout the world realize why, or how we got sucked into that Vietnam war? Don't you feel safe to assume that the majority of the people who know we are there, do not realize that France granted complete independence to the Boa Dai Government in 1954 just before the French and Nationalist troops were captured, at Dien Bien Phu, as the Geneva Conference was about to open. An armistice was signed in July 1954.

Some of the countries that took part at the Geneva Conference were the United Kingdom, the United States, U.S.S.R., Laos, France, Communist China, the two governments, of Vietnam and Cambodia.

One of the reasons that may be creating so much blame on the United States. That the people do not realize that the United States and the Boa Dai government <u>Did</u> <u>Not Sign</u> the agreements. This <u>Caused</u> <u>Vietnam</u>; to be divided into two parts, at the seventeenth parallel, the northern zone to the Vietminh, and the southern section to the Boa Dai government.

You, and two Presidents before your term of office have tried to prove to the rest of the free nations, and to the communist nations that an armistice may be signed when the North Vietnamese are willing to stay on their side of the seventeenth parallel, and let the South Vietnamese remain free on their side of the same zone.

This sounds easy, but the United States is getting the blame for keeping this war going, while others are unwilling to go back to the seventeenth parallel, and settle for that. However, the United States and some of our allies have been helping to defend South Vietnam for almost ten years. There is no end in sight, as long as Communist Russia and Communist China, are willing to back the North Vietnamese.

If we were to remain there another ten years we have no assurance that the Communist backed Vietnamese will not eventually overthrow the people of South Vietnam on their own side of the seventeenth parallel.

This may seem hypothetical, but, the thought has probably crossed your mind many times, how Karl Marx would be smiling with glee if he could only see the sadness, heartache, and frustration this war in Vietnam caused the French from 1946 until 1954. Then from the later part of 1961 when gourilla warfare had grown out of proportion, that President Kennedy sent U.S. General Maxwell D. Taylor over to see what he could recommend on how this country could help build up the military power of the people of South Vietnam, and we have been there ever since.

If you withdraw all our troops tomorrow it may be a lesson to the rest of the world who is to blame. Because one thing is very obvious, any country that is so one sided, and is too stubborn to talk at a peace conference, it is very obvious they are not willing to negotiate under any circumstances.

It is the enemy of the South Viet's who are putting men like Lt. Calley and many others in these spots trying to create descention on our home front, back there in the United States. Shouldn't we start looking out, and protecting our own interest before it gets out of hand? Let us all get together and pull ourselves together, so we can prove that we care, regardless of what others may think of us, or U.S.

Respectfully,

P. M.

A FRIEND WHO UNDERSTAND'S

[Editor's note: As military representative of President Kennedy, General Taylor went to Vietnam on a fact-finding mission in 1961. He recommended sending combat troops.]

91. "children left in Viet Nam"

South Harpswell, Maine
July 29, 1971

Dear Senator Smith:

In our prayer meeting last night we were discussing an Associated Press article that appeared in the Brunswick-Bath Times Record, July 26, page 5.

The article told about 5,000 children left in Viet Nam that were fathered by our GIs. Also about 25,000 Vietnamese children left in that nation as a result of the War.

We are writing around to organization that specialize in helping children to see what is being done and what help is needed. Could you please tell us if the US government is doing anything about this situation. The article ends "As the French did, Klein suggests the U.S. might liberalize its immigration laws and allow American-fathered Vietnamese to choose in which country they want citizenship." Is any such move underway. Is there any legislation pending to help these children in any way that we can and should lend support to? If so to whom do we write? Can these children be adopted by persons in the United States?

. . . We hear about you all the time via the Harpswell Garden Club, since we are apparently fellow members. This little neck seems so isolated from things, and yet we get most concerned about issues involving our country. What do we do to help? If you have a regular memo that is sent out concerning things that you need opinion or help, or letters on, please put us on the regular mailing list. We particularly are concerned with such areas as drug abuse, conservation, pollution, Viet Nam.

Forgive me if I add a very personal note to this letter. The article mentioned above stated "But black-Vietnamese children are viewed with disdain in Vietnam. Of the 500 American-fathered children in orphanages, . . . 250 are black Vietnamese. . . . " Last year my wife and I adopted a Negro-white boy and are very happy with him. We took him because such children are among the harder to place and we wanted to share our home and love, not replace a family we cannot have. If any of these children in Vietnam are available for adoption we would like to consider taking one. Preferably a boy since we can clothe a baby boy. Do you know if they can be adopted? Would we work through a local agency? (We finalized the legal details for our present child through a Portland agency.) And a final question, if one is available, we could adopt him, and he had to be flown here (of course) could it be arranged through the Brunswick Naval Air Station? We left a very good paying teaching job in Illinois . . . because we felt it was God's will; therefore we could not afford at this point a large transportation fee?

If this latter personal question is too involved to be worth your interest please forgive my presumptiveness.
Sincerely yours,
C. W. (male)

Conclusion

*W*inning reelection in the Senate for the fourth time in 1966, the sixty-eight-year-old Senator Margaret Chase Smith was the "grand old lady" who seemed virtually invincible in Maine. She represented a rare type of politician who did not allow a politically charged environment to sway her from what she believed in her conscience was the correct position to take on an issue. Such individualism was politically risky, but ordinary Maine people praised her courage, integrity, and independent thinking. Both those who supported and opposed America's involvement in the war shared their concerns with Smith and it is the rich and spirited correspondence sent to her office that reveals the contested terrain of foreign policy ideas in Maine small towns and rural areas.

In elite political, media, and activist circles, the ugly Vietnam War experience was a hot and divisive topic that generated countless and vociferous debates throughout the United States. Understandably, histories and other books written on the war's impact at home tend to center on political and activist leaders, but such a focus on elites, albeit valuable, cannot possibly present a full picture of the war.[1] There is a definite need for newer narratives of domestic history that includes the war responses of ordinary Americans.

Untainted by political and legacy concerns, many of the views presented in letters from ordinary people living in small towns and rural areas beyond the periphery of media, political, and urban power suggest a spontaneity that bared raw emotion and honest state of mind. There were passionate responses both to Smith's public statements and to the changing developments of the war. During the Johnson years, Smith received emotional letters detailing the tragic consequences of the government's Vietnam policy. Numerous writers found the lack of progress in Vietnam frustrating; hawkish letters were critical of the "restrained" approach of the American government, opponents

211

wrote of the illegality of weapons and war, and representatives of both groups made reference to the "credibility gap" and the declining trust that Americans had for their leaders. Despite a worsening situation in Vietnam in the second half of 1967 and beyond, Smith maintained traditional Cold War thinking and supported an all-out effort that would defeat the communists rather than bombing pauses that she believed symbolized appeasement and weakness. The devastating results of the Tet Offensive in early 1968 caused greater questioning and more public criticism of American involvement in Southeast Asia.

Like Johnson, President Nixon desired an honorable peace that saw the withdrawal of both American troops and the communists from South Vietnam.[2] He began to outline the plan of increasing South Vietnamese troops and decreasing American troops in South Vietnam, but this Vietnamization took place gradually, too slow for many of those fervently opposed to the war. In early November 1969, he reached out to "the great silent majority," those not voicing antiwar sentiments, and asked for patience as the government dealt with the Vietnam issue. Nixon's televised announcement of the Cambodian incursion, on April 30, 1970, generated an explosion of passionate letters that demanded answers to the government's misguided escalation of military engagements. Although fewer in number, there were also strong letters that supported Nixon's position on Cambodia, arguing that he deserved the support, if not the trust, of the American people. For her part, Smith answered antiwar letters by stating that Nixon had already drawn 115,000 American troops from South Vietnam, a reversal of the trend of the Johnson years.

A renewed polarization of forces was evident in the widespread antiwar demonstrations at colleges throughout the nation in early May 1970. In Maine, college student leaders demanded that Smith and Senator Edmund Muskie (Democrat) return home in order to "give the students of Maine the opportunity to confront you as a person."[3] Muskie set a positive tone with his reply telegram stating that he shared the students' concern for the "deteriorating situation in Southeast Asia."[4] On the steps of Colby College's Millar Library on Saturday, May 9, Smith's defense of Nixon was clearly unpopular with the approximate 2,000 students gathered to hear her speak. A consistent critic, journalist John Cole wrote: "she seemed to have almost no idea of what was happening in the war, and no idea how the students felt about it. It was just a sad performance by an old lady out of touch with reality."[5] When introduced at his meeting with students the following day, Muskie received cheers from a crowd of about 3,500. Reading an eight-page statement, his criticism of Nixon's policies and the "industrial-military complex" was more in tune with the emotions of the striking students.[6]

Small-town Maine wrote to Smith about the Colby espisode, with many offering supportive comments. Nixon supporters, in particular, found her stand "most reassuring" and others congratulated her for the dignified way that she had faced those shouting abuse at her. In the aftermath of this troubling meeting, Smith prepared a second Declaration of Conscience that highlighted the dangers of the "extreme left" and the "exteme right." Influenced by the Colby incident, she declared that "Twenty years ago it was the anti-intellectuals who were most guilty of 'know nothing' attitudes. Today too many of the militant intellectuals are equally as guilty of 'hear nothing' attitudes of refusing to listen while demanding communication." She encouraged "the great center of our people" to demonstrate moral and physical courage rather than capitulating to extimist forces.[7]

The cooling off that Smith was hoping for did occur. In the summer of 1970, there were the distractions of work and leisure, government promises of troop withdrawal, and a decrease in the energy-draining antiwar protests, all of which meant fewer letters sent expressing antiwar sentiments. For many, the war was still morally wrong, self-destructive, and tragic, but an increasing number of Americans were turning their attention elsewhere. In 1970, the so-called silent majority gained greater attention when *Time* magazine named its man and woman of the year "Middle Americans."

The varying degrees and biases of American reaction over the Vietnam War are obvious in the letters sent to Smith in the years 1967 to 1971. Two notable features of the Smith letters were in regards to female responses and the war views of the smallest communities. Of letters stating a position, the women's 67 percent opposition to the war was 10 percent higher than male opposition. Support for the war was 43 percent (males) to 33 percent (females).[8] More striking was the significantly larger percentage of antiwar letters from communities with a population under 1,000. The ratio of opposition to support was a remarkable 72 to 17 percent, an observation that contradicts stereotypes of small-towns as conservative.[9] Rural scholars will hopefully explore this further.

Alongside constant opposition to the war and support for the government were the occasional spikes of letter writing prompted by specific press reports, military operations, or political statements. Overall, for both males and females combined there was greater opposition to the war in the Johnson years with only 23 percent of the letters supportive of the government compared to 64 percent against the war (13 percent were unstated). The Johnson correspondence had more typed letters than the Nixon years, 59 percent to 46 percent. While no precise statement is possible, the 13 percent difference suggests that correspondents of the Johnson years may have had a marginally better education and income.

The total split of handwriting and typing for the 1967–1971 years of 47 percent and 53 percent indicates that many correspondents had at least a high school education and typing lessons.[10] While some letters provided professional identification in the fields of education, medicine, and religion, there were few signs of writers being affluent professionals; likely most of the letters in both the Johnson and Nixon years were from middle-income Maine people, with an average or slightly above average education, living and working ordinary lives in their respective communities.

In the Nixon years, the number of letters opposed and "supportive" of the war was almost equal—40 percent and 42 percent.[11] How does one explain this parity of numbers compared to the uneven percentages for the Johnson years? Compared to the final stage of the Johnson era, the Nixon years apparently witnessed a greater number of people supporting the government because of the perception that Nixon was seeking to end the war. More people were sick of the war during the Nixon years, but many had little confidence in an antiwar movement that often appeared ineffective. Although Nixon's April 30 speech on the Cambodian incursion fanned the passions of millions, the number of troops in Southeast Asia was decreasing whereas troop numbers rose dramatically and remained high during the Johnson administration. There was also the conservative backlash with many Americans repulsed by the journalistic imagery of extreme left activities of antiwar protesters on city streets and college campuses vividly shown in television reports, and later in newspaper texts and photographs. The antiwar movement suffered additionally by the perception that elite antiwar activists looked down on the working class and "ridiculed the symbols and values of patriotic Americans."[12] In small towns and rural areas, those who worked with their hands lived in a world significantly different than the world of most college-educated activists. By 1970, the antiwar movement experienced fragmentation as various leaders bickered over strategy with the result that demonstrations ended in failure. War activists found it difficult to advance a positive image. The situation was forbidding to the point that many of those who viewed the war as a mistake also held activists in contempt: "No matter what they did, activists never escaped the grip of that irony."[13]

Those living in small communities were also passionate about the war issue, but the process of having their voices heard was discreet. The Smith letters represent democracy in action; male and female, young and old, common folk from small-town and rural Maine sought answers and representation on a range of political issues rooted in the Vietnam War experience. In keeping with the tradition of the New England town meeting and the moral obligation to participate in civic life, letter-writers enthusiastically and freely added their voices to the debate over American involvement in Southeast Asia.

The challenge for Smith in the final two years of her Senate term was to sharpen her political instincts in an era that had witnessed major social transformation. Years earlier, in 1966, she had been supportive of American involvement in Southeast Asia and critical of student demonstrations against the war. She made a forceful foreign policy an important component of her reelection campaign in 1966 and she easily defeated a worthy opponent with 59 percent of the vote. Six years later she defeated a wealthy "Massachusetts carpetbagger" in the primary election, but suffered a close but stunning loss in the November 1972 election.[14]

Many issues contributed to her defeat. Christian Potholm claims that Smith's loss hinged on her refusal to embrace modern campaign techniques such as the use of media consultants and powerful thirty-second television commercials.[15] Recent Smith biographers list additional factors: Smith's listless campaign effort, the poor health of her trusted assistant Bill Lewis, the lack of support of Maine feminists, and the desire among many Mainers for change, believing Smith had lost touch with the grassroots. In the end, her advanced age, overconfidence, and her support of the war spoiled her chances for victory.[16] The antiwar movement had shifted its focus to congressional politics rather than urban protest after the Cambodian episode in 1970, but Smith did not waver from her Cold War ideology and thus failed to keep pace with the changes around her including Americans' declining confidence in their leaders.[17]

In the years 1967 to 1971, Senator Margaret Chase Smith was the only female member of the Senate and her reputation of integrity and independent thinking attracted the attention of those seeking to understand the Vietnam War experience. Moreover, a politician with a modest economic background and no college education, she was approachable. Letters sent to Smith from small communities throughout Maine reveal a contested terrain where ordinary people struggled with the effects of the war. Beyond the circle of political and antiwar elites, there were many ordinary letter writers who voiced their concerns with clarity and thoughfulness on a wide range of issues that touched on class, race, gender, foreign policy, patriotism, and dissent. Given the variety and richness of the Vietnam War correspondence, it is inaccurate to characterize small-town responses as conservative and conformist. Although less heard, the Vietnam War voices found in the letters of ordinary small-town Americans provide valuable insight and contribute to a better understanding of the impact of the war on the home front.

216   *Conclusion*

NOTES

1. Even Smith's later statements on the war are a testimony to another potential shortcoming of memoirs and accounts written in post years by politicians, policy-makers, and well-known activists and journalists. Years after America's ignominious retreat from Vietnam, she stated that one reason for American involvement in Vietnam was to prevent the Soviets from gaining additional seaports. This reflection did not have resonance with her published statements of that time and it is also interesting that her biggest criticism was that the government drafted "the boys" to fight jungle warfare with brief training rather than using well-trained reserves. As Smith pointed out, had Johnson ignored the "Kennedy-McNamara influence" and called up the reserves he "would have gone down as a great man in history." See Pamela Neal Warford, ed., *Margaret Chase Smith: In Her Own Words* (Skowhegan, Maine: Northwood University, 2001), 106. Smith's later understanding warns of the fallibility of a leader's memory; for a valuable introduction to the relationship of memory and history see Robert D. Schulzinger, "Memory and Understanding U.S. Foreign Relations" in Michael J. Hogan and Thomas G. Patterson, eds., *Explaining the History of American Foreign Relations*, Second Edition (Cambridge: Cambridge University Press, 2004), 336-352.

2. One aspect of Nixon's strategy, however, differed significantly from Johnson's. He sought to open diplomatic relations with China, drive a wedge between China and the Soviet Union, and then press the Chinese and Soviets to withdraw their support from North Vietnam. The literature on Nixon is immense, but a good starting point is Stephen E. Ambrose, *Nixon: The Triumph of a Politician 1961-1972* (New York: Simon & Schuster, 1989) and Richard Nixon, *The Memoirs of Richard Nixon* (New York: Grosset & Dunlap, 1978). For a recent account on the Vietnam War see Kimball, *Nixon's Vietnam War.*

3. *Waterville Sentinel*, 7 May 1970, 1.

4. Scrapbook, Volume 335, 131, MCSL.

5. Quoted from Patricia Ward Wallace, *Politics of Conscience: A Biography of Margaret Chase Smith* (Westport, Connecticut: Praeger, 1995), 180.

6. *Daily Kennebec Journal*, 11 May 1950, 1; Smith, *Mayflower Hill*, 190.

7. Smith, *Declaration of Conscience*, 433.

8. See Appendix 1.

9. *Ibid.*

10. *Ibid.*

11. *Ibid.*

12. DeBenedetti and Chadfield, *An American Ordeal*, 283.

13. *Ibid*, 280-81, 284.

14. Wallace, *Politics of Conscience*, 183. Born and raised in Massachusetts, Robert Monks, her primary opponent, was a successful businesman with a Harvard Law School degree.

15. Christian P. Potholm, *This Splendid Game: Maine Campaigns and Elections, 1940-2002* (Lanham, Maryland: Lexington Books, 2003), 87. According to Potholm,

"Had she briefly aired even one commercial it is likely she would have defeated Bill Hathaway in 1972."

16. Wallace, *Politics of Conscience*, 187-188; Schmidt, *Margaret Chase Smith*, 319-329; and Sherman, *No Place for a Woman*, 214-218.

17. On the shift to congressional politics and the people's loss of confidence in the government, see DeBenedetti and Chatfield, *An American Ordeal*, 285, 298.

APPENDIX: LETTER DATA

(Percentages rounded to the nearest zero)

	Anti-war	Support	Un-stated	Male	Female	M&F	Hand	Type	Total
Johnson Years	65 (64%)	23 (23%)	13 (13%)	56 (55%)	40 (40%)	5 (5%)	41 (41%)	60 (59%)	101
Nixon Years	36 (40%)	38 (42%)	17 (19%)	38 (42%)	47 (52%)	6 (7%)	49 (54%)	42 (46%)	91
Total	101 (53%)	61 (32%)	30 (16%)	94 (49%)	87 (45%)	11 (6%)	90 (47%)	102 (53%)	192
Small towns (<1000)	26 (72%)	6 (17%)	4 (11%)	21 (58%)	11 (31%)	4 (11%)	20 (56%)	16 (44%)	36
Stated Male Opinion	47 (57%)	35 (43%)							82
Stated Female Opinion	47 (67%)	23 (33%)							70
Stated M &F Opinion	7 (70%)	3 (30%)							10

Select Bibliography

Ambrose, Stephen E. *Nixon: The Triumph of a Politician 1961–1972*. New York: Simon & Schuster, 1989.

Apers, Benjamin L. *Dictators, Democracy, and American Public Culture: Envisioning the Totalitarian Enemy, 1920s–1950s*. Chapel Hill: The University of North Carolina Press, 2003.

Appy, Christian G. *Working-Class War: American Combat Soldiers and Vietnam*. Chapel Hill: The University of North Carolina Press, 1993.

Berman, Larry. *No Peace, No Honor: Nixon, Kissinger, and Betrayal in Vietnam*. New York: The Free Press, 2001.

Borstelmann, *The Cold War and the Color Line: American Race Relations in the Global Arena*. Cambridge: Harvard University Press, 2001.

Calhoun, Charles C. *A Small College in Maine: Two Hundred Years of Bowdoin*. Brunswick: Bowdoin College, 1993.

Chatfield, Charles. "At the Hands of Historians: The Antiwar Movement of the Vietnam Era." *Peace and Change* 29, no. 3 & 4 (2004): 483–526.

Clark, Charles E. *Bates Through the Years: An Illustrated History*. Lewiston: Bates College, 2005.

Condon, Richard H. "Maine Out of the Mainstream, 1945–1965." In *Maine: The Pine Tree State from Prehistory to the Present*. Edited by Richard W. Judd, Edwin A. Churchill, and Joel W. Eastman. Orono: University of Maine, 1995.

Cuordileone, K.A. "'Politics in an Age of Anxiety': Cold War Political Culture and the Crisis of American Masculinity, 1949–1960." *The Journal of American History* 87, no. 2 (2000): 515–545.

Daugherty, Leo. *The Vietnam War: Day by Day*. Miami: Lewis International, 2002.

Davies, Richard O. *Main Street Blues: The Decline of Small-Town America*. Columbus: Ohio State University Press, 1998.

Dean, Robert D. "Masculinity as Ideology: John F. Kennedy and the Domestic Politics of Foreign Policy." *Diplomatic History* 22, no. 1 (1998): 29–62.

DeBenedetti, Charles and Charles Chatfield (assisting author). *An American Ordeal: The Antiwar Movement of the Vietnam War.* Syracuse: Syracuse University Press, 1990.

DeGroot, Gerald J. *A Noble Cause? America and the Vietnam War.* Essex: Longman, 2000.

Edelman, Bernard, ed. *Dear America: Letters Home From Vietnam.* New York: Pocket Books, 1986.

Ellsberg, Daniel. *Secrets: A Memoir of Vietnam and the Pentagon Papers.* New York: Viking, 2002.

Foley, Michael S. *Confronting the War Machine: Draft Resistance During the Vietnam War.* Chapel Hill: The University of North Carolina Press, 2003.

———, ed. *Dear Dr. Spock: Letters about the Vietnam War to America's Favorite Baby Doctor.* New York: New York University Press, 2005.

Garfinkle, Adam. *Telltale Hearts: The Origins and Impact of the Vietnam Antiwar Movements.* New York: St. Martin's Press, 1995.

Granastein, J. L. and Norman Hillmer. *For Better or For Worse: Canada and the United States to the 1990s.* Toronto: Copp Clark Pitman Ltd., 1991.

Greenberg, Amy D. "Babbit Who? The Decline of Small-Town America." *Reviews in American History,* 27, no. 2 (1999): 267–274.

Halberstam, David. *The Best and the Brightest.* Fawcett Crest: New York, 1972.

Hall, Mitchell K. *Because of Their Faith: CALCAV and Religious Opposition to the Vietnam War.* New York: Columbia University Press, 1990.

Heale, M. J. *American Anticommunism: Combating the Enemy Within, 1830–1970.* Baltimore: The John Hopkins University Press, 1990.

Heineman, Kenneth J. *Campus Wars: The Peace Movement at American State Universities in the Vietnam Era.* New York: New York University Press, 1993.

Herring, George C. *America's Longest War: The United States and Vietnam, 1950–1975.* 2nd Ed. New York: Alfred A. Knopf, 1986.

Hess, Gary R. *Presidential Decisions for War: Korea, Vietnam, and the Persian Gulf.* Baltimore: The John Hopkins University Press, 2001.

Hogan, Michael J. and Thomas G. Paterson, eds. *Explaining History of American Foreign Relations.* 2nd Ed. Cambridge: Cambridge University Press, 2004.

Jeffreys-Jones, Rhodri. *Changing Differences: Women and the Shaping of American Foreign Policy, 1917–1994.* New Brunswick, New Jersey: Rutgers University Press, 1997.

Kaiser, David. *American Tragedy: Kennedy, Johnson, and the Origins of the Vietnam War.* Cambridge: Harvard University Press, 2000.

Kimball, Jeffrey. *Nixon's Vietnam War.* Lawrence: University Press of Kansas, 1998.

Kovel, Joel. *Red Hunting in the Promised Land: Anticommunism and the Making of America.* London: Cassell, 1997.

Landers, James. *The Weekly War: Newsmagazines and Vietnam.* Columbia: University of Missouri Press, 2004.

Levy, David W. *The Debate Over Vietnam.* 2nd Ed. Baltimore: The John Hopkins University Press, 1995.

Lewis, Sinclair. *Main Street.* New York: First Caroll & Graf Publishers, 1996.

Liebs, Chester H. *Main Street to Miracle Mile: American Roadside Architecture*. Boston: Little Brown, 1985.

Logevall, Frederik. *Choosing War: The Lost Chance for Peace and the Escalation of War in Vietnam*. Berkeley: University of California Press, 1999.

Lorence, James J. *Screening America: United States Through Film Since 1900*. New York: Pearson, 2006.

Mann, Robert. *A Grand Delusion: America's Descent into Vietnam*. New York: Basic Books, 2001.

McAuliffe, Mary S. "Liberals and the Communist Control Act of 1954." *The Journal of American History* 63, no. 2 (1976): 351–367.

McNamara, Robert S. *In Retrospect: The Tragedy and Lessons of Vietnam*. New York: Vintage Books, 1995.

Moen, Matthew C., Kenneth T. Palmer, and Richard J. Powell. *Changing Members: The Maine Legislature in the Era of Term Limits*. Lanham, Massachusetts: Lexington Books, 2005.

Morgan, Ted. *Reds: McCarthyism in Twentieth-Century America*. New York: Random House, 2003.

Nixon, Richard. *The Memoirs of Richard Nixon*. New York: Grosset & Dunlap, 1978.

Potholm, Christian P. *This Splendid Game: Maine Campaign and Elections, 1940–2002*. Lanham, Massachusetts: Lexington Books, 2003.

Powers, Richard Gid. *Not Without Honor: The History of American Anticommunism*. New York: The Free Press, 1995.

Russo, David J. *American Towns: An Interpretive History*. Chicago: Ivan R. Dee, 2001.

Schmidt, Patricia L. Schmidt. *Margaret Chase Smith: Beyond Convention*. Orono, Maine: University of Maine Press, 1996.

Settje, David. "'Sinister' Communists and Vietnam Quarrels: The *Christian Century* and *Christianity Today* Respond to the Cold and Vietnam Wars." *Fides et Historia* XXXII, no. 1 (2000): 81–97

Sherman, Janann. *No Place for a Woman: A Life of Senator Margaret Chase Smith*. New Brunswick, New Jersey: Rutgers University Press, 2001.

Small, Melvin. *Antiwarriors: The Vietnam War and the Battle for America's Hearts and Minds*. Wilmington, Delaware: SR Books, 2002.

———. *Covering Dissent: The Media and the Anti-Vietnam War Movement*. New Brunswick, New Jersey: Rutgers University Press, 1994.

———. *Johnson, Nixon, and the Doves*. New Brunswick, New Jersey: Rutgers University Press, 1988.

———. "Public Opinion." In *Explaining the History of American Foreign Relations*. Edited by Michael J. Hogan and Thomas Patterson. Cambridge: Cambridge University Press 1991.

Smith, David C. *The First Century: A History of the University of Maine, 1865–1965*. Orono: The University of Maine Press, 1979.

Smith, Earl H. *Mayflower Hill: A History of Colby College*. Hanover: University Press of New England, 2006.

Smith, Margaret Chase. *Declaration of Conscience*. Edited by William C. Lewis, Jr. Garden City, New York: Doubleday & Company, Inc., 1972.

Sobel, Richard. *The Impact of Public Opinion on U.S. Foreign Policy Since Vietnam: Constraining the Colossus.* New York: Oxford University Press, 2001.

Taylor, Mark. *The Vietnam War in History, Literature and Film.* Tuscaloosa: The University of Alabama Press, 2003.

Tucker, Spencer C., ed. *Encyclopedia of the Vietnam War: A Political, Social, and Military History.* Oxford: Oxford University Press, 1998.

U.S. Bureau of the Census, Census of Population: 1970, Vol. 1, Characteristics of the Population, U.S. Government Printing Office, Washington, D.C., 1973.

Wallace, Patricia Ward. *Politics of Conscience: A Biography of Margaret Chase Smith.* Westport, CT: Praeger Publishers, 1995.

Warford, Pameal Neal, ed. *Margaret Chase Smith: In Her Own Words.* Skowhegan, Maine: Northwood University, 2001.

Wells, Tom. *The War Within: America's Battle over Vietnam.* Berkeley: University of California Press, 1994.

Woods, Randall B., ed. *Vietnam and the American Political Tradition: The Politics of Dissent.* Cambridge: Cambridge University Press, 2003.

Index

United States troops, 17, 88, 101, 112,
117, 132, 140, 168-69, 195, 208; and
antiwar protest, 113; in Cambodia,
11-161; casualties, 21, 28, 30, 40, 52,
75, 87, 102, 118, 123, 196; deprived
of mail, 46-47; escalation, 18-19, 31,
151, 173; equipment shortages, 41,
75-76, 98, 149; financial drain, 86;
immediate withdrawal, 86, 139;
liquor, 47-48; poor morale, 204;
prisoners of war, 42, 202-3; public
support, 58, 77, 162-65, 167;
mistakes by leaders, 37, 42, 64, 74,
87; secret operations, 178; tortured
by Vietcong, 65; Vietnamese victims,
39, 55, 84, 95, 122, 193, 204
University of Maine, 126, 129-130, 137,
164, 171, 178
University of New Brunswick (Canada),
38
University of Wisconsin, 174, 183-89
US News & World Report, 11, 80
USS *Maddox*, 17-18
USS *C. Turner Joy*, 18
U Thant, 24. 30, 114

Vietcong, 18, 29, 33, 75, 99-100, 104-
106, 118, 203; in Cambodia, 35, 125,

176; civil war, 24, 50; flags in antiwar
parades, 189; released from P.O.W.
camps, 42; Tet Offensive, 19, 110,
116; torture of U.S. soldiers, 65; U.S.
killing of, 25, 94, 130
Vietnam. *See* North Vietnam, South
Vietnam

Wallace, George, 182-83
Warsaw, 62
Washington, D.C., 17, 20-21, 27, 44,
54, 62, 72, 104, 106; antiwar
demonstrations in, 17, 21, 83, 90, 92,
135, 139, 161, 200-202
Waterville Sentinel, 30
Westmoreland, William, 19, 60, 77, 80,
97, 99, 110, 114, 173
Wheeler, Earle G., 110
"The Wisconsin plan," 104-5
Woodstock (music), 188
working class. *See* the United States.
World War I, 37, 40, 69, 74, 80, 100, 107
World War II, 39-40, 44, 56, 64, 74, 80,
85, 91, 100, 107, 141, 161, 179

Young Americans for Freedom, 138

Zinoviev, Grigory, 73

About the Editor

Eric R. Crouse is associate professor of history at Tyndale University College, Toronto, where he teaches courses on U.S. foreign policy since 1945, the United States and the Middle East, and American history and film. His earlier publications include a book and articles on social and religious history. Crouse's main research focus is on the relationship between U.S. foreign policy and Main Street opinion in the late 1940s to the early 1970s.